# FULFILL YOUR COVENANT IN ME, LORD

365 Scripture passages and prayers to draw you closer
to our precious Lord and Savior Jesus Christ

Linda Kay

Exulon
ELITE

Dear Friend, Joint Heir with Christ,

Years ago, a friend of mine asked me to write some encouraging cards to a friend of hers with cancer and to her niece. My first thought was that she should write cards herself, but the Lord pricked me and told me that He had prepared this opportunity for me. What a blessing! The time that I spent digging in the Word for passages to share was far more inspiring and valuable than I could ever have imagined. The Holy Spirit spoke to my heart continually as I copied from the Bible beautiful promise after precious promise. As I claimed the promises in prayer, I knew that God had been waiting all my life for me to stop resisting Him. I needed to let go of my selfishness, pride, and unbelief, and let Him work His work in me. Only a complete surrender can demolish the wall of resistance.

It has been a tremendous privilege, treasure, blessing, and joy for me to meditate on scripture passages and write prayers to claim the promises therein. I have been drawn so much closer to our beautiful Husband, Jesus Christ. It is my sincere hope and prayer that as you read these short devotionals, you will spend long hours contemplating the truths in them. Our Savior wants to free us from sin so we can commune with Him face to face. He will not come again until He can first accomplish this in us. We are not waiting on Jesus, my friend, He is waiting on us. Let us hasten His return by emptying our selfish hearts and letting Him fill us with His magnificent character of agape love.

May God richly bless you and fulfill His covenant in you as you spend this year contemplating the matchless gift He has given you.

Joint Heir with Christ,

Linda Kay

# JANUARY 1

Dear Friend, Loved from Everlasting,

In the beginning God created the heavens and the earth. The earth was without form, and void; and darkness *was* on the face of the deep. And the Spirit of God was hovering over the face of the waters. Then God said, "Let there be light," and there was light. And God saw the light, that *it was* good; and God divided the light from the darkness. God called the light Day, and the darkness He called Night. So the evening and the morning were the first day.

Genesis 1:1–5

Lord,

Before You created this earth You knew me, and You had a plan to redeem me. You could have refrained from creating me, but You did not. You could not, and cannot, help but love Your creatures, no matter what. Jesus, You are the Word that created this world for which You have given Your life. You are the Word that said, "Let there be light." Jesus, You, too, are the Light. When You speak, it is done. Your word accomplishes what You say; as You say it, so it is. You alone are God. You are the Light, the Day. Your adversary, the devil, is darkness, the night. I was without form, and void. I was in darkness but Your Spirit hovered over me and filled me with Your Light. You have brought me from darkness to Light. Thank You, Jesus, for Your creative and re-creative power. Thank You for dividing the Light from the darkness. You are a God of love and a God of order. Please order my life according to Your will, Your covenant with me. Amen.

# JANUARY 2

Dear Friend, Wooed by the Spirit,

Then God said, "Let there be a firmament in the midst of the waters, and let it divide the waters from the waters." Thus God made the firmament, and divided the waters which *were* under the firmament from the waters which *were* above the firmament; and it was so. And God called the firmament Heaven. So the evening and the morning were the second day.

Genesis 1:6–8

Lord,

Thank You for Your orderly care. You created light first. Then You surrounded earth with a protective canopy of water. You have surrounded us with a beautiful lesson of the atmosphere of Your love and grace. Jesus, You are the Water of Life. You are in me, and surrounding me, just as water is in and surrounds the earth. Just as our bodies are mostly water, fill my spirit with the Water of Life. Forgive me for dehydrating my body, mind, and spirit. I eat and drink things that bring my body down. I think thoughts and listen to things that dry out my spirit and separate me from You. Forgive me for polluting the water. Forgive me for polluting the Water of Life that others may drink. Renew me and refresh me. Fill me with Your holy love and with Your holy character that I may be an atmosphere of Your grace to those that are around me. I love You. Amen.

# JANUARY 3

Dear Friend, Fed by the Almighty,

Then God said, "Let the waters under the heavens be gathered together into one place, and let the dry *land* appear;" and it was so. And God called the dry *land* Earth, and the gathering together of the waters called the Seas. And God saw that *it was* good. Then God said, "Let the earth bring forth grass, the herb that yields seed, *and* the fruit tree *that* yields fruit according to its kind, whose seed *is* in itself, on the earth;" and it was so. And the earth brought forth grass, and the herb *that* yields seed according to its kind, and the tree *that* yields fruit, whose seed *is* in itself, according to its kind. And God saw that *it* was good. So the evening and the morning were the third day.

Genesis 1:9–13

Lord,
You are a wise God, who understands all and does nothing without a view of eternal consequences. You provided for us before You created us. You have created the fruits, herbs, nuts, and grasses or grains, for us to eat. Jesus, please forgive me for thinking that I can improve on what You created to heal and sustain my body. Lord, man's processes and refinement of the foods You created are an insult to You. So, too, processed and refined spiritual food does not satisfy or sustain. Please help me, Lord, to eat natural foods in their natural state; just as You created them. Help me not to add or subtract anything from You, the Bread of Life. Fill my heart fully with the Bread of Life, unaltered and unrefined. Fill me with the fruit of the Spirit, whose Seed is in itself. May my life bear fruit for Your honor and glory. Let Your character shine through me that others may be fed. Thank You, my almighty Provider. Amen.

# January 4

Dear Friend, Loved by the Son,

Then God said, "Let there be lights in the firmament of the heavens to divide the day from the night; and let them be for signs and for seasons, and for days and for years; and let them be for lights in the firmament of the heavens to give light on the earth;" and it was so. Then God made two great lights: the greater light to rule the day, and the lesser light to rule the night. *He made* the stars also. God set them in the firmament of the heavens to give light on the earth, and to rule over the day and over the night, and to divide the light from the darkness. And God saw that *it was* good. So the evening and the morning were the fourth day.

Genesis 1:14–19

Lord,
You command the sun, the moon, and the stars. You speak, and the elements obey You. You, Jesus, are the true Light of the world. You rule the day. Your word is a light unto my path. Satan is darkness; ruler of the night—he is lesser, but You, Lord, are the greater. And the devil himself does not have breath except by your grace. There is no darkness the devil can try to surround me with that You cannot dispel with Your perfect Light of love. Jesus, please rule my heart; rule my days and my nights; rule my life. I want to be like the moon, a reflector of You, the Son. Remind me that I have no light or warmth of my own. You are my Light and my warmth is Your perfect love. Let me always have my face and my heart turned toward You so that Your Light always reflects on me. When You speak, let it be so in my heart. Let me be like You. Oh, how I love Your ways. Amen.

# JANUARY 5

Dear Friend, Loved by the Creator,

Then God said, "Let the waters abound with an abundance of living creatures, and let birds fly above the earth across the face of the firmament of heavens." So God created great sea creatures and every living thing that moves, with which the waters abounded, according to their kind, and every winged bird according to its kind. And God saw that *it was* good. And God blessed them, saying, "Be fruitful and multiply, and fill the waters in the seas, and let birds multiply on the earth." So the evening and the morning were the fifth day.

Genesis 1:20–23

Lord,

You are so thoughtful. You created the grass, flowers, food, sunshine, and birds and fish for us to enjoy. You created all these things before You created us. The earth was ready. You blessed the earth with many things, but we have wastefully lived for ourselves and for today and not taken care of the earth. We have not eaten what You provided for us to eat. We have eaten what You did not provide as food. We have shot at and poisoned and abused Your creatures. Forgive us, Lord. We have slighted You and Your gifts, yet You ever provide for our needs. Thank You for the wake-up song the birds sang to me this morning—the song of birds that do not worry because they know their Creator cares for their needs. Thank you for all the beautiful and fascinating creatures you have created for me to enjoy and learn from. Amen.

# January 6

Dear Friend, Loved of God,

Then God said, "Let the earth bring forth the living creature according to its kind: cattle and creeping thing and beast of the earth, *each* according to its kind;" and it was so. And God made the beast of the earth according to its kind, cattle according to its kind, and everything that creeps on the earth according to its kind. And God saw that *it was* good.

Genesis 1:24–25

Lord,
How marvelous are the ways that You care for Your creatures! You have clothed the lily so beautifully. You care about the fallen sparrows. Lord, please help us to care for Your creatures as You do. Thank You for the beautiful variety of living things that You have placed on this earth. You have created each according to its kind. Forgive us for ignoring Your Sovereign Majesty. In our ignorance of You we try to improve on the kinds that You created. Thank You for the amazing lessons I learn from observing the creatures that You have made. How sad that animals often take better care of their own than we do. Forgive me for not taking care of my fellow humans as you intend for me to do. Help me to care for all of Your creatures as You do. You are indeed a creative God. How marvelous are the ways that You care for Your creatures! Amen.

## JANUARY 7

Dear Friend, Created in His Image,

Then God said, "Let Us make man in Our image, according Our like-ness; let them have dominion over the fish of the sea, over the birds of the air, and over the cattle, over all the earth, and over every creeping thing that creeps on the earth." So God created man in His *own* image; in the image of God He created him; male and female He created them. Then God blessed them, and God said to them, "Be fruitful and multiply; fill the earth and subdue it; have dominion over . . . every living thing . . ." And God said, "See, I have given You every herb *that* yields seed which *is* on the face of all the earth, and every tree whose fruit yields seed; to you it shall be for food. Also, to every beast . . . I *have given* every green herb for food;" and it was so. And God saw everything that He had made, and indeed *it was* very good. So the evening and the morning were the sixth day.

Genesis 1:26–31

Lord,

Created in Your image—what an incredible privilege! How amazing, that You have loved us so very much. We are indeed Your children, created by Your hand and bought with Your precious blood. You created us in Your image and then Jesus came to this earth and identified with us forever. We are closer to You than the angels. You have given man the privilege of revealing Your character of redeeming love to all the universe. How marvelous to be Your chosen child! Father, please cleanse my heart, my mind, my body. Please restore me to Your perfect image. Jesus, You have made every effort to redeem me from my pitiful, sinful state. I want to be like You. When others look at me, may they see You permeating through my life. You have given us dominion over the earth. Help me to care for the earth and *all* its inhabitants as You care. Amen.

# JANUARY 8

Dear Friend, Loved of God,

Thus the heavens and the earth, and all the host of them, were finished. And on the seventh day God ended His work which He had done, and He rested on the seventh day from all His work which He had done. Then God blessed the seventh day and sanctified it, because in it He rested from all His work which God had created and made.

Genesis 2:1–3

Lord,
You never let a moment go by that You are not fully attuned to our needs and caring for our infirmities. Yet You knew the desperate need we would have for rest—physical, emotional, and spiritual rest. You lovingly set apart the seventh day of the week for a special rest. You blessed, sanctified, and rested on the seventh day. Father, may I, through the whole week, and especially when I come to the end of my week and my work, wholly rest in You. Help me to cast *all* my cares on You and experience a complete trusting rest in You in my heart. Help me to truly put everything else in my mind aside and spent the Sabbath focused on nothing but You. I need the *full* recharge—not just a partial charge. Thank You for Your rest—a rest that reminds me that it is not I who changes my heart, but You, my Creator and Redeemer. Fulfill Your covenant in me, Lord. Create in me a clean heart and fill me with the faith that rests wholly on You. Amen.

# JANUARY 9

Dear Friend, Redeemed by the Lamb,

So the Lord God said unto the serpent: "Because you have done this, you *are* cursed more than all cattle, and more than every beast of the field; on your belly you shall go, and you shall eat dust all the days of your life. And I will put enmity between you and the woman, and between your seed and her Seed; He shall bruise your head, and you shall bruise His heel."

Genesis 3:14–15

Lord,

Before the foundation of the world, You knew that the serpent would deceive Eve; that Adam would sin. But the victory was already Yours, Adam's, and mine. You had a beautiful plan. Though we are born with a sinful nature inherited from the first Adam, You have put an enmity for evil in us. Jesus, You crushed the head of Satan when You surrendered up Your Life for us on the cross. No more can anyone say that You do not love this fallen race with an infinite love. You became sin and died the death that disobedience requires. You have given of Yourself for eternity to prove Your love. O how that warms and woos my heart. Jesus, may Your precious sacrifice for me not be in vain. I desperately want that perfect selfless love with which You love me. Cause me to fully detest sin and what it does not only to me, but to You. I hate this separation between us, Lord. Bring me back to You. Amen.

# JANUARY 10

Dear Friend, Called of God,

Now the Lord said unto Abram: "Get out of your country, from your family and from your father's house, to a land that I will show you. I will make you a great nation; I will bless you and make your name great; and you shall be a blessing. I will bless those who bless you, and I will curse him who curses you; and in you all families of the earth shall be blessed." So Abram departed as the LORD had spoken to him, and Lot went with him. And Abram *was* seventy-five years old when he departed from Haran.

Genesis 12:1–4

Lord,
Give me the ears to hear Your calling and the faith to follow. You called Abram to follow You to a place that he did not know. Yet Abram packed up and left because You said, "I will show you." You promised to make a great nation of a seventy-five year old man with no children. Lord, *nothing* is impossible for You. Please help me to believe that what You say is exactly as You say it is. I accept and believe Your holy Word, O God. Fill my heart with it. Fill me with Your faith that compels me to do whatever You ask, whether it makes sense to me or not. In Jesus' Name, Amen.

# JANUARY 11

Dear Friend, Loved by the Promise Keeper,

After these things the word of the Lord came to Abram in a vision, saying, "Do not be afraid, Abram, I am your shield, your exceedingly great reward." But Abram said, "Lord God, what will You give me seeing I go childless, and the heir of my house is Eliezer of Damascus?" Then Abram said, "Look, You have given me no offspring: indeed one born in my house is my heir!" And behold the word of the Lord *came* to him, saying, "This one shall not be your heir, but one who will come from your own body will be your heir." Then He brought him outside and said, "Look now toward heaven, and count the stars if you are able to number them." And He said to him, "So shall your descendants be." And he believed in the Lord, and He accounted it to him for righteousness.

Genesis 15:1–6

Lord,

Thank You for being my Creator God. You protect me though I treat You with disrespect and disdain. You are my great Reward though I deserve only death. Please forgive me for doubting Your promises. I struggle, as Abram did, to believe that You will accomplish of Your own power and strength what You say. You do not need my pitiful efforts. You promised to make a great nation of Abram. This is the beautiful promise of the gospel. You were promising Yourself—not through a servant, but through Abram and Sarai. The true spiritual descendants of Abraham are *Your* children; those who acknowledge that their salvation is in You. I am Your child! I am a spiritual descendant of faithful Abraham! Help me to ever believe in You, my Inheritance! Amen.

# JANUARY 12

Dear Friend, Purchased and Freed,

Now Sarai, Abram's wife, had borne him no children. And she had an Egyptian maidservant whose name was Hagar. So Sarai said to Abram, "See now, the Lord has restrained me from bearing children. Please, go into my maid; perhaps I shall obtain children by her." And Abram heeded the voice of Sarai. Then Sarai, Abram's wife, took Hagar her maid, the Egyptian, and gave her to her husband Abram to be his wife, after Abram had dwelt ten years in the land of Canaan. So he went in to Hagar, and she conceived. And when she saw that she had conceived, her mistress became despised in her eyes. Then Sarai said to Abram, "My wrong be upon you! I gave my maid into your embrace; and when she saw that she had conceived, I became despised in her eyes. The Lord judge between me and you."

Genesis 16:1–5

Lord,
Please help me to believe Your Word; to trust You completely, no matter what. Like Sarai, I try to fulfill Your promises for You. Your promise is not for us to be slaves or descendants of slaves, but to be free; free from the slavery of sin. Sarai offered a bondwoman to fulfill Your promise. Forgive me for offering my slavery to selfishness and my pride in what I think I can accomplish as a way to fulfill Your covenant in me. Like Abram, I go along with things that I know are not Your way because I cannot see You working—I cannot see how You are fulfilling Your promise. Please forgive me for my unbelief. Give me spiritual eyes that see Your sovereign majesty. Heal my heart. Fulfill Your covenant in me. Amen.

# JANUARY 13

Dear Friend, Receiver of God's Gift,

When Abram was ninety-nine years old, the Lord appeared to Abram and said unto him, "I am Almighty God; walk before Me and be blameless. And I will make My covenant between Me and you, and will multiply you exceedingly." Then Abram fell on his face, and God talked with him, saying: "As for Me, behold My covenant is with you, and you shall be a father of many nations."

Genesis 17:1–4

Lord,

You made a beautiful covenant between Yourself and Abraham, but it was not just for Abraham. It is for me, also. You promised that You would make Abraham a father of many nations. All who believe on You are descendants of Abraham, just as Jesus became a descendant of Abraham and took each one of us into Himself. When Christ comes again, the spiritual children of Abraham will be gathered from every kindred, tribe, and nation. I am honored beyond what words can express to be Your child! Holy Spirit, cleanse my heart that I may walk blameless before You. Amen.

# JANUARY 14

Dear Friend, Cherished by God,

No longer shall your name be called Abram, but your name shall be Abraham; for I have made you a father of many nations. I will make you exceedingly fruitful; and I will make nations of you, and kings shall come from you. And I will establish My covenant between Me and you and your descendants after you in their generations, for an everlasting covenant, to be God to you and your descendants after you.

Genesis 17:5–7

Lord,
Over and over, Jesus, You have established Your covenant. You have, from the moment Adam sinned, been desperately trying to show us how much You love us no matter what; that You foresaw our predicament and have from eternity past paved a beautiful way for us. You have never asked anyone to do anything but believe. This is so unlike the covenants that humans usually make. I am used to "I'll do this, *if* you do that." It is a knock in my pride to receive something for free. I feel I should at least receive the thing because I am good, "worthy," or because I have accomplished a task. Lord, please correct my devilish thinking. I am never worthy. I am nothing. *You are Everything*. Take away the pride in my heart that wants part kingship with You. Fulfill Your covenant in me. Amen.

# JANUARY 15

Dear Friend, Redeemed by the Lamb,

Then they came to the place of which God had told him. And Abraham built an altar there and placed the wood in order; and he bound Isaac his son and laid him on the altar, upon the wood. And Abraham stretched out his hand and took the knife to slay his son. But the angel of the LORD called to him from heaven and said, "Abraham, Abraham!" So he said, "Here I am." And He said, "Do not lay your hand on the lad, or do anything to him; for now I know that you fear God, since you have not withheld your son, your only *son* from Me."

Genesis 22:9–12

Lord,

I am amazed by the love You had for Abraham and Isaac; the love Abraham and Isaac had for You; the faith You had in Abraham and Isaac, and the faith Abraham and Isaac had in You. O how I long for such an intimate relationship with You. As Abraham discovered, Father, You experienced the excruciating pain of allowing Your Son to suffer and die. You did not withhold Your Son, Your only Son, from a cruel death on the cross, because Your immeasurable love for the likes of me could not let You do otherwise. Jesus, I want to be completely surrendered as Isaac was, as You are. May I love You so fully that no one and *nothing* can come between us. You are my Savior. Hallelujah! Amen.

# JANUARY 16

Dear Friend, Loved of I AM,

And God said to Moses, "I AM WHO I AM." And He said, "Thus you shall say to the children of Israel, 'I AM has sent me to you.'"

Exodus 3:14

Lord,
You are the great and holy I AM. You are the everlasting, eternal God who was and is and is to come. You are the Alpha and the Omega, the Beginning and the End. You are all-knowing. You knew me before the foundation of the world. You were already wooing me with Your loving plan to redeem me from the dreadful clutches of sin. You have sent Your prophets with messages from Your mouth. Father, please help me to listen and understand Your holy words. Thank You for being my God. Fulfill Your covenant in me and send me to others that they may know You, the great I AM. May my life always reflect You, and only You. Amen.

# January 17

Dear Friend, Nourished by the Creator,

And when the layer of dew lifted, there, on the surface of the wilderness, was a small round substance, as fine as frost on the ground. So when the children of Israel saw it, they said to one another, "What is it? [manna]" For they did not know what it was. And Moses said to them, "This is the bread which the Lord has given You to eat. This is the thing which the Lord has commanded: 'Let every man gather it according to each one's need, one omer for each person, according to the number of persons . . .'" Then the children of Israel did so and gathered, some more, some less. So when they measured it . . . he who gathered much had nothing left over, and he who gathered little had no lack. Every man had gathered according to each one's need. And Moses said, "Let no one leave any of it till morning."

Exodus 16:14–19

Lord,
You have promised to supply my every need: body, mind, and spirit. The Israelites were slaves in Egypt for so long, they did not know how to trust You. Lord, I have been a slave to sin for so long that I don't know how to trust You. Just as You supplied fresh manna every morning for the Israelites, so You will supply fresh Manna for my soul every morning, for You are the Bread of Life. Like manna, Your mercies are new every morning. Help me to share every blessing I have each day, physical and spiritual, rejoicing in the promise that You will fill me again tomorrow. Amen.

# JANUARY 18

Dear Friend, Saved by Christ,

And God spake all these words, saying, "I *am* the LORD thy God, which hath brought thee out of the land of Egypt, out of the house of bondage. Thou shalt have no other gods before me."

Exodus 20 :1–3 KJV

Lord,
You are my God. You have indeed brought me out of bondage. Your life, Jesus, is victory over the bondage of sin. Help me to ever remember that You have done this for me. Please keep Your covenant in me. Spare me from putting anything in my heart before You. I desperately need Your help for I am surrounded by selfishness and pride, lust, and greed. Society cries out "it's all about me," but my heart cries out, "I'm drowning Jesus, save me!" May you be first in my life, first in my heart, first in my thoughts, first in my day. May You be my *All* and my *Only*. You are my God. You, and *You alone*. Hallelujah! Amen.

# JANUARY 19

Dear Friend, Child of the Living God,

Thou shalt not make unto thee any graven image, or any likeness *of any thing* that *is* in heaven above, or that *is* in the earth beneath, or that *is* in the water under the earth: Thou shalt not bow down thyself to them, nor serve them: for I the LORD thy God *am* a jealous God, visiting the iniquity of the fathers upon the children unto the third and fourth *generation* of them that hate me; And shewing mercy unto thousands of them that love me, and keep my commandments.

Exodus 20:4–6 KJV

Lord,

We have made images of just about everything under the sun. Our homes are full of them—covering our mantles, bookshelves, dressers, desks, and more. But, Lord, I wouldn't think of bowing to them, would I? O forgive me, Father. I bow to my resources and my time, shopping for and dusting things that are but a cheap imitation of what You have created, and I have destroyed and ignored Your creations. I bow to my job and my culture, trying to serve You as it fits into my lifestyle. My children, and my children's children suffer the consequences and repeat the pattern. Jesus, show mercy unto me. Fulfill Your covenant in me. Give me Your grace to let go of *everything* that does *not* draw me closer to You. Amen.

# JANUARY 20

Dear Friend, Bride of Christ,

Thou shalt not take the name of the LORD thy God in vain; for the LORD will not hold him guiltless that taketh his name in vain.

Exodus 20:7 KJV

Lord,

Please forgive me for saying I am a Christian and then acting like anyone but Christ. When I say I am Yours and I do as I see fit, I take Your name in vain. I hate to be misrepresented, yet I misrepresent You day in and day out without a thought of how You feel about it. I assume that since You gave me a brain, that anything I decide or think up is from You; as if it is indeed what You want for me. I have falsely believed that You will help me once I am doing everything I can do by myself. I can of myself do nothing. My very breath is a gracious gift from You. Jesus, please be the Ruler of my brain and my heart. Fulfill Your covenant in me. Remove my guilt and my selfishness, and make me a true reflector of Your holy Name. Cleanse me now. Amen.

# JANUARY 21

Dear Friend, Created by God,

Remember the Sabbath day, to keep it holy. Six days shalt thou labour and do all thy work: But the seventh day *is* the sabbath of the LORD *thy* God: *in it* thou shalt not do any work, thou, nor thy son, nor thy daughter, thy manservant, nor thy maidservant, nor thy cattle, nor thy stranger that *is* within thy gates. For *in* six days the LORD made heaven and earth, the sea, and all that in them *is*, and rested the seventh day: wherefore the LORD blessed the sabbath day and hallowed it.

Exodus 20:8–11 KJV

Lord,

Forgive me for forgetting to keep the Sabbath holy. Forgive me for forgetting that it is the Sabbath of the LORD my God—not my Sabbath for the traditions that I choose. You have known from eternity past that I would work myself to an eternal grave without You. You created the earth in six days and rested on the seventh. You blessed the seventh day and made it holy. It is a beautiful memorial of Your creative and redemptive power. Fulfill Your covenant in me. Father, help me to fully rest in You. Forgive me for my "form of godliness," for stopping my physical labor and attending church but still laboring in my heart and mind. Help me to rest my body, mind, and spirit in You. Let me surrender *everything* in my life to You. Let me dwell on Your holy character with no distractions. May all that are in my house, or pass my way, find rest in You. Your grace saves. Amen.

# JANUARY 22

Dear Friend, Child of God,

Honor thy father and thy mother: that thy days may be long upon the land which the LORD thy God giveth thee.

Exodus 20:12 KJV

Lord,

You are my Father. You are my Brother. You are my Husband. Help me to always honor You, in thought, in word, and in deed. Help me to remember that the land that You have given me is a land that is "fairer than day," a land that is yet to come. This world is not my home. Fulfill Your covenant in me. Place Your honor in me. Help me to honor You by completely surrendering my selfish will and pride to Your eternal wisdom and grace. I want to emulate You, Jesus. Please forgive me for not honoring my earthly parents, a gift from You. Help me to honor them by allowing You to live in and through me. I love You, Father. Thank You for making me Your child. Amen.

# JANUARY 23

Dear Friend, Saved by Grace,

Thou shalt not kill.

Exodus 20:13 KJV

Lord,
O how I would love to say I could never be guilty of this one. Killing sounds so despicable to me, and yet—here I am, a hopeless, helpless serial killer. Forgive me for killing Your precious children with my thoughtless words, actions, looks, and attitudes. You did not just mean "do not kill the body" (though You do mean this also). Jesus, You said that saying we hate our brother is murder. Unkind and hateful things too often fly out of my mouth without check. Father, forgive me for selfishly crushing the spirit of others with my proud and self-focused ways. How many times have I given an ugly picture of You to those around me, and walked away oblivious? I need more than forgiveness, Father, I need Your cleansing and grace to change my heart. Jesus, forgive me for trying to kill myself by resisting and failing to heed Your Holy Spirit's leading. Fulfill Your covenant in me. Lord, help me to value life as You do. Help me to value You so I can truly value others. You are my Life. Amen.

# JANUARY 24

Dear Friend, Bride of Christ,

Thou shalt not commit adultery.

Exodus 20:14 KJV

Lord,

Forgive me for my horrible, wandering, adulterous heart. O how I wander after so many things—following people, following trends and traditions, and following my own ideas. How often I do my own thing under the disguise that I am doing it for You. I am not. Yes, I can rationalize my actions very creatively, but it does not change the truth that my heart is wavering and wandering. My love for You so often is but a love for myself that I need You to help me fulfill. You are an incredibly patient, loving, and forgiving Husband. Jesus, I do not want to be an adulterous wife. Please forgive me for disgracing You so. I do not deserve Your love for me at all, but that never changes Your eternal love for me. I really don't want to be separated from You. I love You. Fulfill Your covenant in me. Cleanse my heart. Make me pure and wholly Thine. Empty my selfish heart and pour in Your Spirit that unites us. I want to be Your bride. Fill me now. I love You. Amen.

# JANUARY 25

Dear Friend, Purchased of God,

Thou shalt not steal.

Exodus 20:15 KJV

Lord,

Forgive me for stealing from You, my Creator and Savior, my God, from whom *all* blessings flow. I have stolen the time and resources You have given me and used them for myself. I have stolen Your love for me and the love for others that You intended to give them through me—I have kept it for myself. I have stolen the very breath I breathe. You have provided it for me with Your blood because of Your tremendous love for me that I may draw others to You, but I live for myself and show others contempt when they interfere with my plans. Forgive me, Father, for stealing Your grace, mercy, forgiveness, and all the things that You have given me to use to bless others. Jesus, fulfill Your covenant in me. Help me to use every moment, every thought, word, and breath for *Your* honor and glory. My life belongs to You. Take me now. I give myself back to You. Take *all* of me. Amen.

# JANUARY 26

Dear Friend, Daughter/Son of God,

Thou shalt not bear false witness against thy neighbor.

Exodus 20:16 KJV

Lord,

Please forgive me for bearing false witness against my neighbor and against You. I so often judge and assume wrongly, and when it is not even my place to judge anyway. Forgive me for the damage I do with my expressions and my tongue, my attitudes, and my complacency. Jesus, I bear false witness against You daily, saying things so unlike You in one breath and claiming to be Yours in the next. What do people think of You because of me? O, I am so sorry for the disgrace I bring to You, even as You love me so deeply and bless me so abundantly. Fulfill Your covenant in me. I surrender my thoughts and my heart to You. Take over. Consume me. Live out Your life within me. Fill me with Your love. Amen.

# JANUARY 27

Dear Friend, Child of God,

Thou shalt not covet thy neighbor's house, thou shalt not covet thy neighbor's wife, nor his manservant, nor his maidservant, nor his ox, nor his ass, nor any thing that is thy neighbor's.

Exodus 20:17 KJV

Lord,

You know my heart is full of covetousness. I have long suffered from "grass is greener on the other side" syndrome. Please forgive my constant longing for something else. There is absolutely nothing I can take past this life but my character. I need a selfless character that can abide with You. All the money and stuff in this world is eternally useless. And You provide everything I need as I need it. Lord, forgive me for coveting Your power. I know all too well that I would not use it as You do, with such love and grace and mercy. I would use it for self-gratification. I would use it to give myself life and health to do my own thing. You have blessed me every day of my life. Fulfill Your covenant in me. How can I possibly want anything else when I have You? Jesus, please help me realize that obedience is a gift from You; a result of total surrender and belief in *Your Word*. Cleanse me of unbelief. I am nothing. *You are Everything*. Thank You for making me Your child. Amen.

# JANUARY 28

Dear Friend, Lifted by His Mercy,

And the cherubim shall stretch out *their* wings above, covering the mercy seat with their wings, and they shall face one another, the faces of the cherubim *shall be* toward the mercy seat. You shall put the mercy seat on top of the ark, and in the ark you shall put the Testimony that I shall give you. And there I will meet with you, and I will speak with you from above the mercy seat, from between the two cherubim which *are* on the ark of the Testimony, about everything which I will give you in commandment to the children of Israel.

Exodus 25:20–22

Lord,

You gave the ark of the testimony to show Your great love for all mankind throughout the ages. Your holy law was placed inside. Place Your holy law inside me, Lord. Write it on my stony heart. On the top were placed angels facing a mercy seat. Lord, Your mercy is the crowning beauty of Your law, which is Your character. Thank You for Your mercy that caused You to surrender Yourself for the likes of me. Thank You for the angels You send to continually bestow Your mercy upon me. The ark was wood overlaid with gold. This reminds me, Jesus, that You made salvation possible by surrendering Yourself to a wooden cross, a wooden cross covered with the golden character of God. How beautiful! Cover me with Your life. Amen.

# JANUARY 29

Dear Friend, Fed by the Bread of Life,

You shall also make a table of acacia wood; two cubits *shall be* its length, a cubit its width, and a cubit and a half its height. And you shall overlay it with pure gold, and make a molding of gold all around. You shall make for it a frame of a handbreadth all around, and you shall make a gold molding for the frame all around . . . You shall make its dishes, its pans, its pitchers, and its bowls for pouring. You shall make them of pure gold. And you shall set the showbread on the table before Me always.

Exodus 25:23–25, 29–30

Lord,

Thank You for reminding me that You are the Bread of Life. It is not possible for me to partake of You except through the cross—that wooden object that was covered by Your golden character. Please forgive me for not coming to You for fresh Bread every day. I allow myself to spiritually starve for long periods of time when You are ever before me, patiently wooing me and longing for me to partake of You. Feed my starved soul, Father. Send Your Spirit to fill me to overflowing with the Bread of Life. I want no other food. Make me one of Your golden dishes that I may serve others and feed them Your perfect love. Refine me like gold tried in the fire. Amen.

# JANUARY 30

Dear Friend, Bride of the Selfless Husband,

Now it came to pass on the next day that Moses said to the people, "You have committed a great sin. So now I will go up to the Lord; perhaps I can make atonement for your sin." Then Moses returned to the Lord and said, "Oh, these people have committed a great sin, and have made for themselves a god of gold! Yet now, if You will forgive their sin—but if not, I pray, blot me out of Your book which You have written." And the Lord said to Moses, "Whoever has sinned against Me, I will blot him out of My book. Now therefore, go, lead the people to *the place* of which I have spoken to you. Behold, My Angel shall go before you. Nevertheless, in the day when I visit for punishment, I will visit punishment upon them for their sin."

Exodus 32:30–34

Lord,

How beautiful! Moses experienced the selfless love You have for Your wayward bride. Though he had not lived a perfect life, he had grown deeper and deeper in love with You, spending much time in communion with You, and therefore seeing things more and more through Your eyes. He knew that You are a loving, forgiving, and patient God. He also knew that the Israelites had been rejecting You in their actions, though their words claimed to love You. Moses reached a point of selflessness that caused him to be truly willing to give up his own eternal life for the sake of those who stubbornly rebelled. Jesus, this is what You did for me. I want to return that kind of love to You. Fulfill Your covenant in me. Help me to love You more than life itself. May I be willing to surrender even eternal life if it will bring honor to You. Amen.

# JANUARY 31

Dear Friend, Drawn by His Patience,

Then the Lord said to Moses, "Depart *and* go up from here, you and the people whom you have brought out of the land of Egypt, to the land of which I swore to Abraham, Isaac, and Jacob, saying, 'To your descendants will I give it.' And I will send *My* Angel before you, and I will drive out the Canaanite and the Amorite and the Hittite and the Perizzite and the Hivite and the Jebusite. *Go up* to a land flowing with milk and honey; for I will not go up in your midst, lest I consume you on the way, for you *are* a stiff-necked people." And when the people heard this bad news, they mourned, and no one put on his ornaments.

Exodus 33:1–4

Lord,

Your spirit of forgiveness and tender longsuffering leave me in a sweet awe. The Israelites claimed to serve You, then almost immediately set up an idol to worship. This is what I do. I claim that I will serve and obey You forever and then immediately continue trying to solve everything and serve in my own strength. This is no different than bowing down to an idol made of my material possessions. You are a holy and righteous God. You do not want me to be consumed by Your presence but transformed by Your love that I may dwell in Your presence forever. Thank You for Your willingness to rewrite Your law in my heart after I have broken and trampled on it. I want to cherish Your law as You cherish me. Amen.

# FEBRUARY 1

Dear Friend, Loved by the True Friend,

Moses took his tent and pitched it outside the camp, and called it the tabernacle of meeting. And it came to pass *that* everyone who sought the Lord went out to the tabernacle of meeting which *was* outside the camp. So it was, whenever Moses went out to the tabernacle, *that* all the people rose, and each man stood at his tent door and watched Moses until he had gone into the tabernacle. And it came to pass, when Moses entered the tabernacle, that the pillar of cloud descended and stood *at* the door of the tabernacle, and *the* Lord talked with Moses. All the people saw the pillar of cloud standing *at* the tabernacle door, and all the people rose and worshipped, each man *in* his tent door. So the Lord spoke to Moses face to face, as a man speaks to his friend. And he would return to the camp, but his servant Joshua the son of Nun, a young man, did not depart from the tabernacle.

Exodus 33:7–11

Lord,
You call each of us apart from the world to commune one on one with You. You call away not just our bodies but our hearts. Please help me to remember that it is not a church building that is holy, or that makes me holy, but it is a submitted heart in Your presence that is truly worship. I know that You long to communicate with me as a Friend, just as You did with Moses and Joshua. Make me the kind of friend for You that freely speaks to You face to face in loving adoration. Thank You for meeting with me just now, and always. Amen.

## FEBRUARY 2

Dear Friend, Led by His Presence,

Then Moses said to the Lord, "See, You say to me, 'Bring up this people.' But You have not let me know whom You will send with me. Yet You have said, 'I know you by name, and you have also found grace in My sight.' Now therefore, I pray, if I have found grace in Your sight, show me now Your way, that I may find grace in Your sight. And consider that this nation *is* Your people." And He said, "My Presence will go *with you,* and I will give you rest."

Exodus 33:12–14

Lord,
Thank You for the assurance of Your Presence. Like Moses, I long to know Your ways and see clearly what You have planned for me, but I need Your faith to help me trust You when the way is unclear to me. Thank You for faithful promises to take with me, to lead me, and to take me where You know that it is best for me to go. I am Yours. Increase my faith. Fill me with Your faith, a faith that rests completely in the Father's almighty love. I long for that rest in my heart which only You can give. Amen.

# FEBRUARY 3

Dear Friend, Overwhelmed by His Goodness,

Then he said to Him, "If Your Presence does not go *with us*, do not bring us up from here. For how then will it be known that Your people and have found grace in Your sight, except You go with us? So we shall be separate, Your people and I, from all the people who *are* upon the face of the earth." So the Lord said to Moses, "I will also do this thing that you have spoken; for you have found grace in My sight, and I know you by name." And he said, "Please, show me Your glory." Then He said, "I will make all My goodness pass before you, and I will proclaim the name of the Lord before you. I will be gracious to whom I will be gracious, and I will have compassion on whom I have compassion."

Exodus 33:15–19

Lord,
You have separated those who put their trust in You. It is not just a separation of location, but a separation of heart. You have set apart Your people for a distinct, holy purpose. You have been gracious to me, Father. I have found favor in Your sight through the blood of Jesus. Your glory is Your precious, merciful character of love. Your goodness is all around me, Lord. Please forgive me for ignoring it and focusing on the evil that abounds instead of Your grace which much more abounds. Your compassion and Your graciousness sustain my every breath. If it were not for Your mercies, I would be consumed. I know that Your goodness will follow me all the days of my life. Hallelujah! Thank You, Jesus! Amen.

## FEBRUARY 4

Dear Friend, Illuminated by His Glory,

Then He said, "I will make all My goodness pass before you, and I will proclaim the name of the Lord before you. I will be gracious to whom I will be gracious, and I will have compassion on whom I have compassion." But He said, "You cannot see My face; for no man shall see Me, and live." And the Lord said, "Here is a place by Me, and you shall stand on the rock. So it shall be, while My glory passes by, that I will put you in the cleft of the rock, and will cover you with My hand while I pass by. Then I will take away My hand, and you shall see My back; but My face shall not be seen."

Exodus 33:19–23

Lord,

How desperately You must long to commune with me face to face. But I am wicked, not just by nature but I have a character that is focused on my own selfish desires. If You appeared to me right now, I would indeed be consumed. My character is the opposite of Yours. I would melt from within as Your love burned through my wickedness. O Jesus, I want to be like You. I want You to purge me of my selfish sin. I want to be transformed into Your character of selfless love. You have promised to do this for me. You have made a covenant with me. You will write Your law of love on my heart and in my mind. I surrender to You. Fulfill Your covenant in me. I want to live with You face to face. Amen.

# FEBRUARY 5

Dear Friend, Honored by the Lord,

Now the Lord descended in the cloud and stood with him there, and proclaimed the name of the Lord. And the Lord passed before him and proclaimed, "The Lord, the Lord God, merciful and gracious, longsuffering, and abounding in goodness and truth, keeping mercy for thousands, forgiving iniquity and transgression and sin, by no means clearing *the guilty,* visiting the iniquity of the fathers upon the children and the children's children to the third and fourth generation."

Exodus 34:5–7

Lord,
You have created me with a free will. You have given me the power to choose my own destiny, even though You have in Your love destined me to be with You forever. How painful it must be for You to watch me choose death, to watch me choose an evil pattern of living that will affect my children and their children and grandchildren. I have seen firsthand how the pattern of iniquity carries on from generation to generation. Reverse this pattern in me, O Lord. Keep me in Your mercy and forgiveness. Sin cannot exist in Your presence. There is no more excuse for it. I choose You. Fill me with Your mercy, graciousness, longsuffering, and truth. Cleanse me from all iniquity. Amen.

# FEBRUARY 6

Dear Friend, Chosen of God,

Nadab and Abihu, the sons of Aaron, each took his censer and put fire in it, put incense, and offered profane fire before the Lord, which He had not commanded them. So fire went out from the Lord and devoured them, and they died before the Lord. And Moses said to Aaron, "This is what the Lord spoke, saying: 'By those who come near Me I must be regarded as holy; and before all the people I must be glorified.'" So Aaron held his peace.

Leviticus 10:1–3

Lord,

Forgive me for being like Nadab and Abihu—for coming to Your sanctuary with my own "fire." I come before Your presence in private prayer and in church with my own agenda, my own expectations and demands, my own opinions, and my own works. This is not acceptable to You, Almighty God. As Nadab and Abihu have shown with their choice and results, my foolish efforts to rule Your kingdom will result in sure death; eternal death. O forgive me, Jesus. Please be the Ruler of the kingdom of my heart forever and always. Fulfill Your covenant in me. I long for Your cleansing. Lord, be glorified in my life. Amen.

# FEBRUARY 7

Dear Friend, Daughter/Son of God,

And the Lord spoke to Moses, saying, "Take outside the camp him who has cursed; then let all who heard *him* lay their hands on his head, and let the congregation stone him. Then you shall speak to the children of Israel, saying: 'Whoever curses his God shall bear his sin. And whoever blasphemes the name *of the Lord* shall surely be put to death. All the congregation shall stone him, the stranger as well as him who is born in the land. When he blasphemes the name of the Lord, he shall be put to death.'"

Leviticus 24:13–16

Lord,

Taking Your name in vain is deserving of death. I am amazed that You have taken upon Yourself the punishment I deserve for cursing You; for esteeming myself as god above You and Your Holy Word. You are indeed God. I am nothing. You are *everything*. Your chosen leaders tried to stone You for blasphemy—for saying that You are God. This they could not accomplish, for You are not a blasphemer but a holy and righteous God. Yet You did take my death that I might live. Thank You, Jesus, for bearing my sin and shame. Make me more like You. I am Yours. Cleanse me so that I will speak only truth when I say I am a Christian. Amen.

## FEBRUARY 8

Dear Friend, Blessed by God,

If one of your brethren becomes poor, and falls into poverty among you, then you shall help him, like a stranger or sojourner, that he may live with you. Take no usury or interest from him; but fear your God, that your brother may live with you. You shall not lend him your money for usury, nor lend him your food for a profit. I *am* the Lord your God, who brought you out of the land of Egypt, to give you the land of Canaan and to be your God.

Leviticus 25:35–38

Lord,

I am such a selfish person. I feel like I have worked hard for everything I get, and so should everybody else. I forget that my every breath is a precious gift from You. I forget that I was in such debt from sin that I could never repay; I deserve only death. But You purchased my life with *Your own life*; never asking me to pay back any part of it, only pleading with me to never reject Your absolutely free gift. Please help me to see others as You see them, the same as You see me. Everything is Yours, and You have promised me all eternal blessings. May I be like You. Amen.

# FEBRUARY 9

Dear Friend, Blessed by the Father,

The Lord bless you and keep you; the Lord make His face shine upon you, and be gracious to you; the Lord lift up His countenance upon you, and give you peace.

Numbers 6:24–26

Lord,

How You have blessed me! You have shined Your face upon me and given me peace by the gift of Yourself as the plan of salvation. Thank You for the blessings of life, of breath, of sight, smell, hearing, taste, and touch. Thank You for family and friends, a home, flowers, and sunshine and rain. Thank You for food, for warmth when it is cold, and cool breezes when it is hot; for Your grace and peace when I am hot-tempered, and for the warmth of Your love when my heart is cold. Thank You, Father, for being God! Thank You, Spirit, for being God! Thank You, Jesus, for being God! I love You, I love You, I love You! Amen.

# FEBRUARY 10

Dear Friend, Blessed by God,

And he took up his oracle and said: "Balak the king of Moab has brought me from Aram, from the mountains of the east. 'Come, curse Jacob for me, and come, denounce Israel!' How shall I curse whom God has not cursed? And how shall I denounce *whom* the Lord has not denounced? For from the top of the rocks I see him, and from the hills I behold him; there! A people dwelling alone, not reckoning itself among the nations. Who can count the dust of Jacob, or number one-fourth of Israel? Let me die the death of the righteous, and let my end be like his!"

Numbers 23:7–10

Lord,

Balaam realized that cursing You and Your people was not worth it. He had wanted material gain instead of eternal riches. You lovingly put Your words in His mouth. He understood that it is unwise to try to curse those whom You have blessed because You keep Your promises of blessings and protection for Your children. Father, please help me to remember this when I feel like cursing or speaking ill of my neighbor. You have chosen *all* to be Your children. Let me never be the cause for anyone to reject their chosen position in You. I want to be as the dust of Jacob—one of Your precious children—one who believes in You. Please help me to act like You. Let my words bless others, and never curse. Thank You, in Jesus' name. Amen.

# FEBRUARY 11

Dear Friend, Blessed by the Father,

God is not a man, that He should lie, nor a son of man, that He should repent. Has He said, and will He not do? Or has He spoken, and will He not make it good? Behold, I have received a command to bless; He has blessed, and I cannot reverse it.

Numbers 23:19–20

Lord,

When You bless, we are blessed indeed. When You promise, it is a sure thing as You say it. Your Word is truth. Your Word accomplishes itself. Balaam, for all he was worth, could not curse where You intended there to be blessings. He could speak only the words You provided. Jesus, I want to be so consecrated to You that nothing can come out of my mouth save Your blessings. Cleanse me completely, please. Father, thank You so much for the many blessings You lavish on me each day. Thank You for the promise of an eternal relationship with You. Fill me to overflowing with the blessings You want to bestow on others. Amen.

# FEBRUARY 12

Dear Friend, Redeemed by His Blood,

He has not observed iniquity in Jacob, nor has He seen wickedness in Israel. The Lord his God *is* with him, and the shout of a King *is* among them. God brings them out of Egypt; He has strength like a wild ox. For *there is* no sorcery against Jacob, nor any divination against Israel. It now must be said of Jacob and of Israel, "Oh, what God has done!" Look, a people rises like a lioness, and lifts itself up like a lion; it shall not lie down until it devours the prey, and drinks the blood of the slain.

Numbers 23:21–24

Lord,

How beautiful! You have sacrificed Yourself for me. You have become me and have taken my death sentence. And now You see the perfect life and sacrifice of the blood of Jesus when You look at me. I can never be worthy of this but, Lord, I want to be fully surrendered to Your will. Bring me out of a life of sinfulness. Give me a complete victory. You are my King. You are the one and only true King. No one can stand against You. I want to be counted among Your people. May others say, 'O what God has done!' when they look at the transformation You are bringing to my life. Do not stop until You have fulfilled Your covenant in me. May the devil's words never have sway in my life. Make me a blessing to Yourself. Amen.

# FEBRUARY 13

Dear Friend, Child of God,

Hear, O Israel: the LORD our God *is* one LORD: And thou shalt love the LORD thy God with all thine heart, with all thy soul, and with all thy might. And these words, which I command thee this day, shall be in thine heart. And thou shalt teach them diligently unto thy children, and shalt talk of them when thou sittest in thine house, and when thou walkest by the way, and when thou liest down, and when thou risest up. And thou shalt bind them for a sign upon thine hand, and they shall be as frontlets between thine eyes. And thou shalt write them upon the posts of thy house, and on thy gates.

Deuteronomy 6:4–9 KJV

Lord,

Thank You for being a God that changes not. Thank You for being a God who loves us so intimately. Lord, I want to love You with *all* my heart, *all* my soul, and *all* my strength. Please put Your words in my heart. May Your words be ever upon my lips, whether I am at home or away, walking or lying in my bed. May all my actions reflect You. May all my thoughts reflect You. When people enter into my gates, may they feel and know Your presence. Give me grace to diligently teach Your precepts to the children You have placed in my path, for we are all Your children. You word is the pillar that holds up the house of my heart, Your holy temple. Amen.

# February 14

Dear Friend, Wooed by the Almighty,

"The Lord your God will raise up for you a Prophet like me from your midst, from your brethren. Him you shall hear, according to all you desired of the Lord your God in Horeb in the day of the assembly, saying, 'Let me not hear again the voice of the Lord my God, nor let me see this great fire anymore, lest I die.' And the Lord said to me: 'What they have spoken is good. I will raise up for them a Prophet like you from among their brethren, and will put My words in his mouth, and He shall speak to them all that I command Him. And it shall be *that* whoever will not hear My words, which He speaks in My name, I will require *it* of him.'"

Deuteronomy 18:15–19

Lord,

Moses loved You so much that he became very much like You. You even compared Jesus to him. Your children were afraid to listen to You or to speak to You face to face. They brought with them from Egypt a false concept of a God who needs to be appeased. But You love us deeply, no matter what we think of You. You gave Moses a prophecy of Yourself. You reminded him of Your promise to come as a Man and dwell among us and to share the love of the Father with us in our midst. Lord, help me to listen to Your words, to believe what You say, and to believe that You love me infinitely. I want to be like You. I want Your words in my mouth, and Your thoughts in my heart. Thank You for speaking to me, and calling me Your child. Amen.

# FEBRUARY 15

Dear Friend, Redeemed by the Lamb,

If a man has committed a sin deserving of death, and you hang him on a tree, his body shall not remain overnight on the tree, but you shall surely bury him that day, so that you do not defile the land which the Lord your God is giving you as an inheritance; for he who is hanged is accursed of God.

Deuteronomy 21:22–23

Lord,

When You told Moses that anyone who is hung on a tree is accursed of God, You knew full well that Jesus, an innocent Man, would be hanged on a tree. Jesus, how precious to my heart that You, an innocent God, became an innocent Man. You became accursed of God because You became the guilty me who truly deserves to be accursed of God. Jesus, You did not remain on a tree overnight. You did not defile the land or the inheritance. You are the Inheritance. You have purchased a new and beautiful, eternal land. You have purchased a new and beautiful eternal life. Please remove this cursed sin from my heart. Thank You, Jesus. Amen.

# FEBRUARY 16

Dear Friend, Witness for Jesus,

And before they were laid down, she [Rahab] came up unto them on the roof, and she said unto the men, "I know that the Lord hath given you the land, that your terror is fallen upon us, and that all the inhabitants of the land faint because of you. For we have heard how the LORD dried up the water of the Red Sea for you, when ye came out of Egypt; and what ye did unto the two kings of the Amorites, that *were* on the other side of the Jordan, Sihon and Og, whom ye utterly destroyed. And as soon as we heard *these things,* our hearts did melt, neither did there remain any more courage in any man because of you: for the LORD your God, he *is* God in heaven above, and in earth beneath."

Joshua 2:8–11 KJV

Lord,

Often I don't feel like witnessing because I don't think anyone wants to hear it or will even listen. I forget that while I live and breathe, I am a witness, either for good or for evil. The children of Israel had not been openly sharing Your love and a knowledge of Your redemptive plan for humanity with other nations as You had wanted them to. They thought they were keeping You to themselves, but You are a big God. No one can keep You to themselves. Rahab, and the other inhabitants of Jericho were well aware of Your power. Use me as a witness of Your love and grace. Let my life, my thoughts and actions, my expressions and gestures, always reflect You. Amen.

# FEBRUARY 17

Dear Friend, Covered with Kindness,

"Now therefore, I beg you, swear to me by the Lord, since I have shown you kindness, that you also will show kindness to my father's house, and give me a true token, and spare my father, my mother, my brothers, my sisters, and all that they have, and deliver our lives from death." So the men answered her, "Our lives for yours, if none of you tell this business of ours. And it shall be, when the Lord has given us the land, that we will deal kindly and truly with you." Then she let them down by a rope through the window, for her house *was* on the city wall; she dwelt on the wall.

Joshua 2:12–15

Lord,
Rahab had seen and heard of Your great care for those who trust in You. She did not trust the thick, manmade walls of Jericho. She knew that man could do nothing to resist Your power. She also knew that, though she was not an Israelite, You would not reject her trust in You. Indeed, Lord, You honor those who honor You. You have given the most beautiful token of Your love—Jesus Christ! And how beautiful that Rahab found an honorable place in Your earthly genealogy. You are no respecter of persons. Those who believe in You, who surrender their lives completely to You, are Your true children, regardless of race or class or possessions. What a beautiful God You are! Thank You! Amen.

# FEBRUARY 18

Dear Friend, Blessed by His Covenant,

Behold, the ark of the covenant of the Lord of all the earth is crossing over before you into the Jordan. Now therefore, take for yourselves twelve men from the tribes of Israel, one man from every tribe. And it shall come to pass, as soon as the soles of the feet of the priests who bear the ark of the Lord, the Lord of all the earth, shall rest in the waters of the Jordan, *that* the waters of the Jordan shall be cut off, the waters that come down from upstream, and they shall stand as a heap.

Joshua 3:11–13

Lord,

The ark of the covenant symbolized God's promise of a Savior who would conquer sin in the flesh and who would conquer death itself. Lord Jesus Christ, You crossed over the Jordan before me. You came and lived a sinless life, and died my eternal death that I might live and not die. You have accomplished everything. You will hold back the waters that I might walk on dry land to the promised land; the inheritance of a new earth and eternal life with You. Teach me to trust in You without doubt or question. Give me Your faith that gives the peace and assurance to step into the waters, to go forward into what seems like sure doom, trusting that You will pave the way. Father, if You can pile up the waters of a flooded river so that millions can cross on dry land, then You can protect me through any crisis I may face. Thank You for Your everlasting covenant with me. Amen.

# FEBRUARY 19

Dear Friend, Held by His Love,

So it was, when the people set out from their camp to cross over the Jordan, with the priest bearing the ark of the covenant before the people, and as those who bore the ark came to the Jordan, and the feet of the priests who bore the ark dipped in the edge of the water (for the Jordan overflows all its banks during the whole time of harvest), that the waters which came down from upstream stood *still*, and rose in a heap very far away at Adam, the city that is beside Zaretan. So that the waters that went down into the Sea of the Arabah, the Salt Sea, failed, *and* were cut off; and the people crossed over opposite Jericho. Then the priests who bore the ark of the covenant of the Lord stood firm on dry ground in the midst of the Jordan; and all Israel crossed over on dry ground, until all the people had crossed completely over the Jordan.

Joshua 3:14–17

Lord,
What can I say? You are an incredibly, awesome, and eternally capable God. The smile cannot come off my face when I think about the simple and extravagant ways You use to take care of Your children. You will stop at nothing. How easy for You to stop up a flooded river with a word. All of nature is at Your command. Father, You must be chomping at the bit to hold back flooded rivers of trouble and road blocks for me. Please forgive me for my unbelief. Fill me with the faith to step right out in whatever direction You lead, fully believing that *You will* part the waters. Your everlasting covenant stands steadfast and unquenchable. Hallelujah! Amen.

# FEBRUARY 20

Dear Friend, Servant of the Lord,

Now therefore, fear the Lord, serve him in sincerity and truth, and put away the gods which your fathers served on the other side of the River in Egypt. Serve the Lord! And if it seems evil to you to serve the Lord, choose for yourselves this day whom you will serve, whether the gods which your fathers served on the other side of the River, or the gods of the Amorites, in whose land you dwell. But as for me and my house, we will serve the Lord.

Joshua 24:14–15

Lord,

May I ever serve You in sincerity and truth. Please forgive me for serving other gods—the god of my checkbook, the god of fashion, the god of time and pleasure, the god of my own creative ideas, the food god, and so on. Service to any and all of these gods truly, Lord, I admit, is service to myself. I have put my own will and whims before You. I rationalize for You and bask in the knowledge that You are a loving and understanding God. I think You realize that I just "have to do what I have to do" sometimes. In other words, I totally insult Your character of true agape love and Your promises of grace and faith, while doing my own thing. I confess. I repent. I surrender. I want to serve *You and You only*. I commit my life to You. Fulfill Your everlasting covenant in me. I claim Your promises. As for me and my house, we will serve the Lord. In Jesus' Name, Amen.

# FEBRUARY 21

Dear Friend, Carried in His Hand,

Then Jerubbaal (that *is* Gideon) and all the people who *were* with him rose early and encamped beside the well of Harod, so that the camp of the Midianites was on the north side of them by the hill of Moreh in the valley. And the Lord said to Gideon, "The people who *are* with you *are* too many for Me to give the Midianites into their hands, lest Israel claim glory for itself against Me, saying, 'My own hand has saved me.' Now therefore, proclaim in the hearing of the people, saying, 'Whoever *is* fearful and afraid, let him turn and depart at once from Mount Gilead.'" And twenty-two thousand of the people returned, and ten thousand remained.

Judges 7:1–3

Lord,

You well understand the pitfalls of sinful human nature. Jesus, You have experienced the temptation to take credit for Yourself. So often I fall into the trap of thinking that it is by something I am doing, some Bible study or church work, that is accomplishing my salvation for me. You take care of my needs and solve problems for me continually. I can clearly see that it is You and not me who is accomplishing all this. Yet, I still seem to take credit for things by rationalizing that it is because I have worked hard that You are able to do these things for me. Please forgive me, Lord. You and I both know that the truth is, I am fearful and afraid and would truly depart were it not for Your patience and drawing love and grace. Fill me with Your faith. In Jesus' name. Amen.

## FEBRUARY 22

Dear Friend, Sustained by the Living Water,

But the Lord said to Gideon, "The people *are* still *too* many; bring them down to the water, and I will test them for you there. Then it will be, *that* of whom I say to you, 'This one shall go with you,' the same shall go with you; and of whomever I say to you, 'This one shall not go with you,' the same shall not go." So he brought the people down to the water. And the Lord said to Gideon, "Everyone who laps from the water with his tongue, as a dog laps, you shall set apart by himself; likewise everyone who gets down on his knees to drink." And the number of those who lapped, *putting* their hand to their mouth, was three hundred men; but all the rest of the people got down on their knees to drink water. Then the Lord said to Gideon, "By the three hundred men who lapped I will save you, and deliver the Midianites into your hand. Let all the *other* people go, every man to his place."

Judges 7:4–7

Lord,
Please help me to remember that there is a serious battle going on. Although You have already won the victory, Satan is walking about as a roaring lion, seeking whom he may devour. As I drink spiritual water from you, let me remain alert for the temptations that come upon me unaware. Help me to watch and pray as You have instructed. Let me put my full trust in You and ever be ready for an opportunity to serve You, to stand up and proclaim Your sovereign majesty and eternal love. Cause me to think more of Your needs than my own. May my focus always be on You, never on myself. This is my plea, Father. Amen.

# FEBRUARY 23

Dear Friend, Protected by the Lord's Might,

So the people took provisions and their trumpets in their hands. And he sent away all *the rest of* Israel, every man to his tent, and retained those three hundred men. Now the camp of Midian was below him in the valley. It happened on the same night that the Lord said to him, "Arise, go down against the camp, for I have delivered it into your hand. But if you are afraid to go down, go down to the camp with Purah your servant, and you shall hear what they say; and afterward your hands shall be strengthened to go down against the camp." Then he went down with Purah his servant to the outpost of the armed men who *were* in the camp. Now the Midianites and the Amalekites, all the people of the East, were lying in the valley as numerous as locusts; and their camels *were* without number, as the sand by the seashore without multitude.

Judges 7:8–12

Lord,
Please give me faith that causes me to believe what You say; to take You at Your word without question, whether what You say seems possible to me or not. You have *never* failed in one of Your promises. And You do not leave me without encouragement. You had already honored Gideon's fleece experiment, and You used him anyway, knowing that he was still afraid. You do marvelous things for those who trust in You, for those who allow You to do marvelous things in their lives. May I trust You when temptation surrounds me like a vast multitude of armed men. Fill me with the faith of Jesus. Amen.

# FEBRUARY 24

Dear Friend, Encouraged by His Love,

And when Gideon had come, there was a man telling his dream to his companion. He said, "I have had a dream: To *my* surprise, a loaf of barley bread tumbled into the camp of Midian; it came to a tent and struck it so that it fell and overturned, and the tent collapsed." His companion answered and said, "This *is* nothing else but the sword of Gideon the son of Joash, a man of Israel! Into his hand God has delivered Midian and the whole camp." And so it was, when Gideon heard the telling of the dream and its interpretation, that he worshipped. He returned to the camp of Israel, and said, "Arise, for the Lord has delivered the camp of Midian into your hand."

Judges 7:13–15

Lord,

What a beautiful thing You did for Gideon when You sent him to hear the Midianite's dream. You were not just telling him that he would win on the morrow, but You were sharing with him the everlasting gospel of Jesus Christ. Just like the loaf of bread that came into the enemy camp and destroyed it, You, Jesus, the Bread of Life, have come into the enemy's camp and destroyed the enemy. You have overturned sin and its deadly clutches with Your perfect and holy life. Give me the complete victory that You revealed to Gideon. Overturn sin in my life. When I am discouraged and faithless, remind me that the barley loaf victory is in reality the true victory of the Bread of Life. Amen.

# FEBRUARY 25

Dear Friend, Carried by Faith,

Then he divided the three hundred men *into* three companies, and he put a trumpet into every man's hand, with empty pitchers, and torches inside the pitchers. And he said to them, "Look at me and do likewise; watch, and when I come to the edge of the camp you shall do as I do: When I blow the trumpet, I and all who *are* with me, then you also blow the trumpets on every side of the whole camp, and say, '*The sword of the* Lord and of Gideon!'"

Judges 7:16–18

Lord,
I am thrilled at the faith of Gideon and his three hundred companions. Having not yet seen Your day in reality, they, by faith, proclaimed the message of Your victory. They sounded the trumpet of victory, by faith proclaiming the victory in Your name. They broke the pitchers, the shrouds of doubt that held back the light, and let Your light shine forth in the darkness. The light of Your love and Your victory of sin and darkness surrounded the enemy, and the enemy could only tremble in fright. Jesus, I want to proclaim Your victory to the darkness in my life. Thank You for reminding me that the battle is Yours; the honor of proclaiming the victory is mine. Thank You for winning the battle of selfishness, pride, and unbelief in my heart. Help me to remember that You are the Accomplisher. Let me never hinder You from accomplishing Your work in me. Amen.

# FEBRUARY 26

Dear Friend, Witness for the Lord,

So Gideon and the hundred men who *were* with him came to the outpost of the camp at the beginning of the middle watch, just as they had posted watch; and they blew the trumpets and broke the pitchers that *were* in their hands. Then the three companies blew the trumpets and broke the pitchers—they held the torches in their left hands and the trumpets in their right hands for blowing—and they cried, "The sword of the Lord and of Gideon!" And every man stood in his place all around the camp; and the whole army ran and cried out and fled. When the three hundred blew the trumpets, the Lord set every man's sword against his company throughout the whole camp; and the army fled to Beth Acacia, toward Zererah, as far as the border of Abel Meholah, by Tabbath.

Judges 7:19–22

Lord,
What a lesson this story gives! Let me never be sleeping in the enemy's camp. Though they may be the most numerous, the victory is with You. Those who hold onto darkness, who refused to allow You to lead them, will perish by self-destruction just as surely as the Midianites perished by their own swords. This is a revelation of what will happen when You return, Jesus. Those who reject You will be destroyed as those who are with You sing Your praises. I want to be Yours. Snatch me from the enemy for Your holy purposes. Remove the sin of doubt from my heart. Fulfill Your covenant in me, Lord. Amen.

# FEBRUARY 27

Dear Friend, Chosen by God,

Then Samson called to the Lord, saying, "O Lord God, remember me, I pray! Strengthen me, I pray, just this once, O God, that I may with one *blow* take vengeance on the Philistines for my two eyes!" And Samson took hold of the two middle pillars which supported the temple, and he braced himself against them, one on his right and the other on his left. Then Samson said, "Let me die with the Philistines!" And he pushed with all *his* might, and the temple fell on all the lords and all the people who *were* in it. So the dead that he killed at his death were more than he had killed in his life.

Judges 16:28–30

Lord,

Samson was chosen by You for a holy purpose—to declare Your perfect character among the nations. It was never by his own strength that he was able to do this. When he surrendered his complete trust in You to please himself, it served him only ruin. His eyes were put out that he might see *only* You. Your forgiveness is overwhelmingly awesome. You completely healed Samson's heart. Father, please help me to always remember that I have no strength whatsoever of myself. *You* are my strength. Let me die to self. Let all my enemies, my sins, die with me that I may be wholly Yours. Jesus, I want to be like You. I want to be Yours. I want to reflect You fully. I want everyone to know You as You truly are. I love You. Amen.

# February 28

Dear Friend, Daughter/Son of God,

But Ruth said: "Entreat me not to leave you, or to turn back from following after you: for wherever you go, I will go; and wherever you lodge, I will lodge; your people shall be my people, and your God, my God. Where you die, I will die, and there will I be buried. The Lord do so to me, and more also, if anything but death parts you and me." And when she [Naomi] saw that she [Ruth] was determined to go with her, she stopped speaking to her.

Ruth 1:16–18

Lord,

What did Ruth see in Naomi that caused her to cling to her so? She left family, friends, and country to follow it. She *must* have seen a beautiful picture of *You* in Naomi. People don't normally vow to follow their mother-in-laws until death. O that people would see *You* when they look at me; that *nothing* would cause them to turn back from You! I want to follow You, Lord. Where You go, I will go. Help me to take up my cross as You did. I want to lodge where You lodge. May I.dwell in the secret place of the Most High. I want Your people to be my people. Help me to remember that every person is Your child. You are my God. Jesus, help me to die as You did; a totally surrendered death to self. Bury me as You were buried—in the Father's love. Cleanse me. Use me. Let me be a beacon of Your precious light in a sea of sinful darkness. Amen.

# MARCH 1

Dear Friend, Redeemed by the Lamb,

Then he said to the close relative, "Naomi, who has come back from the country of Moab, sold the piece of land which *belonged* to our brother Elimelech. And I thought to inform you, saying, 'Buy *it* back in the presence of the inhabitance and the elders of my people. If you will redeem *it*, redeem *it*; but if you will not redeem *it, then* tell me, that I may know; for *there is* no one but you to redeem *it*, and I *am* next after you.'" And he said, "I will redeem *it*." Then Boaz said, "On the day you buy the field from the hand of Naomi, you must also buy *it* from Ruth the Moabitess, the wife of the dead, to perpetuate the name of the dead through his inheritance." And the close relative said, "I cannot redeem *it* for myself, lest I ruin my own inheritance. You redeem my right of redemption for yourself, for I cannot redeem *it*."

Ruth 4:3–6

Lord,
You are my Kinsman Redeemer. Unlike the man who was willing to redeem the land for himself, but not for Naomi and Ruth, You are willing to redeem not only the earth, but all of its inhabitants. You have purchased this earth back from the evil prince. You have purchased it not for Yourself but for Your bride. You have gone to eternal lengths to give Your bride an inheritance. What a beautiful example Boaz gave of Your love. He, like You, was willing to take a foreigner under his wing as his bride to perpetuate the name of the dead. Though I am dead in sin, You have loved me, a Gentile, and called me Your bride. You have redeemed me. Thank You, my precious Redeemer and Husband. Amen.

# MARCH 2

Dear Friend, Blessed of God,

But the Lord said to Samuel; "Do not look at his appearance or his physical stature, because I have refused him. For the Lord *does* not *see* as man sees; for man looks at the outward appearance, but the Lord looks at the heart."

I Samuel 16:7

Lord,

Please help me to take my focus off the external. Like Samuel when he visited the home of Jesse, I judge people by first impressions and outward appearance. We focus so much on the outward appearance in this world. Lord, this is not Your way. You look at our hearts. O horrors, the things You see when You look in my heart. Yet, when You look at me, You see a beautiful child, covered by the blood of Jesus Christ. Forgive me for my critical and judgmental view of my brothers and sisters. Help me to see them through *Your* eyes. Help me to listen with *Your* ears. Father, forgive me for making judgments about *You* based on things I have heard second-hand, or things that have been done supposedly in Your Name. Help me to look at *Your* heart; to know You as You *truly* are. May I meditate on Your Word, Jesus. He *is* the revelation of Your heart. Focus my eyes on Your heart, Lord. Focus my eyes on Your heart alone. Amen.

# MARCH 3

Dear Friend, Cherished by God,

Then Jonathan and David made a covenant, because he loved him as his own soul. And Jonathan took off the robe that was on him and gave it to David, with his armor, even to his sword and his bow on his belt.

I Samuel 18:3–4

Lord,
You have made a beautiful covenant with us. You have loved us *more* than Your own soul. You have laid down Your robe, Your throne, Your very position as God, for us. You surrendered *everything* to show us the Father's love for us. You have given us Your robe of righteousness. You have given us Your armor that we may resist the devil. You've given us the waistband of truth, the breastplate of righteousness, the shoes of the gospel of peace, the shield of faith, the helmet of salvation, and the sword of the spirit—the word of God. Jesus, there is nothing for me to bring to Your beautiful covenant, but my surrendered, believing heart. Fulfill Your covenant in me. O how I want to be like You. Accomplish this in me. Please help me to love my fellow man as You love them. Help me to love You as You love me. Thank You for being such an incredible Friend. Amen.

## MARCH 4

Dear Friend, Chastened by the Father's Love,

And David's heart condemned him after he had numbered the people. So David said to the Lord, "I have sinned greatly in what I have done; but now, I pray, O Lord, take away the iniquity of Your servant, for I have done very foolishly." Now when David arose in the morning, the word of the Lord came to the prophet Gad, David's seer, saying, "Go and tell David, Thus says the Lord, 'I offer you three *things;* choose one of them for yourself, that I may do *it* to you.'" So Gad came to David and told him . . . Shall seven years of famine come to you in your land? Or shall you flee three months before your enemies, while they pursue you? Or shall there be three days' plague in your land? Now consider and see what answer I take back to Him who sent me." And David said to Gad, "I am in great distress. Please let us fall into the hand of the Lord, for His mercies *are* great; but do not let me fall into the hand of man."

II Samuel 24:10–14

Lord,

Thank You Holy Spirit for convicting me of my sin. Thank You for not only lovingly showing me my horrible condition, but for providing a way of escape from it. Thank You for allowing me to fall into Your merciful hand. You have promised to be responsible for my salvation; You have been faithful. Please forgive me for looking at numbers. Forgive me for comparing the wisdom and power of man with Your matchless power and love, and for basing Your goodness and mercy on the dollar, plans, or decisions of man. Help me to look to You as the Author and Finisher of my faith. I love Your Word. Amen.

# MARCH 5

Dear Friend, Led by His Wisdom,

At Gibeon the Lord appeared to Solomon in a dream by night; and God said, "Ask! What shall I give you?" And Solomon said: "You have shown great mercy to Your servant David my father, because he walked before You in truth, in righteousness, and in uprightness of heart with You; You have continued this great kindness for him, and You have given him a son to sit on his throne, as it *is* this day. Now, O Lord my God, You have made Your servant king instead of my father David, but I *am* a little child; I do not know *how* to go out or come in. And Your servant *is* in the midst of Your people whom You have chosen, a great people, too numerous to be numbered or counted. Therefore give to Your servant an understanding heart to judge Your people, that I may discern between good and evil. For who is able to judge this great people of Yours?"

I Kings 3:5–9

Lord,
You have continued to keep Your promises, from the beginning of time. You honor those who honor You. Solomon was king of Israel and knew that he was but a child in need of Your wisdom and guidance. Lord, I too, am but a little child. I need an understanding heart and the ability to discern between good and evil. Truly, I do not know when or how to go out or to come in. I need You to direct every aspect of my life. Please hold me close to Your heart. I want to be a witness for You. I want to reflect Your wisdom and love to all those I come in contact with. Amen.

# MARCH 6

Dear Friend, Unique Child of God,

Now two women who *were* harlots came to the king, and stood before him. And one woman said, "O my lord, this woman and I dwell in the same house; and I gave birth while she *was* in the house. Then it happened, the third day after I had given birth, that this woman also gave birth. And we *were* together; no one was with us in the house, except the two of us in the house. And this woman's son died in the night, because she lay on him. So she arose in the middle of the night and took my son from my side, while your maidservant slept, and laid him in her bosom, and laid her dead child in my bosom. And when I rose in the morning to nurse my son, there he was, dead. But when I had examined him in the morning, indeed, he was not my son whom I had borne."

I Kings 3:16–21

Lord,

Two women were arguing over two sons. Each was claiming that the live child was theirs and the dead belonged to the other. Father, thank You that You are never confused nor fooled. You have known me clearly, distinctly, and intimately since before the foundation of the world. You have loved me while I am crushed to death in the tight grips of sin. You have made me alive, alive in Jesus Christ. Save me from my spiritual amnesia, Lord. Let me always know of a surety that I am Your precious, unique child. Amen.

# MARCH 7

Dear Friend, Loved by the True Father,

Then the other woman said, "No! But the living one *is* my son, and the dead one *is* your son." And the first woman said, "No! But the dead one *is* your son, and the living one *is* my son." Thus they spoke before the king. And the king said, "The one says, 'This *is* my son, who lives, and your son *is* the dead one'; and the other says, 'No! But your son *is* the dead one, and my son *is* the living one.'" Then the king said, "Bring me a sword." So they brought a sword before the king. And the king said, "Divide the living child in two, and give half to one, and half to the other." Then the woman whose son *was* living spoke to the king, for she yearned with compassion for her son; and she said, "O my lord, give her the living child, and by no means kill him!" But the other said, "Let him be neither mine nor yours, *but* divide *him*." So the king answered and said, "Give the first woman the living child, and by no means kill him; she *is* his mother."

I Kings 3:22–27

Lord,
The message is clear. These two women represent two governments: the government of Satan and Your holy government. Satan claims that we living children, alive by Your creative and redemptive power, are his. You know that we are Yours and that the children of Satan are dead. Satan does not want to see any child live. You do not want any to die. You have gone beyond this story and proven that You would rather die than see any of Your children perish. Holy and wise Father, You have given the living to Jesus Christ, and to Yourself, the True Father. Thank You. Amen.

# MARCH 8

Dear Friend, Loved of the Sovereign Lord God,

And it came to pass, *at the time of* the offering of the *evening* sacrifice, that Elijah the prophet came near and said, "Lord God of Abraham, Isaac, and Israel, let it be known this day that You *are* God in Israel and I *am* Your servant, and *that* I have done all these things at Your word. "Hear me, O Lord, hear me, that this people may know that You *are* the Lord God, and *that* You have turned their hearts back *to You* again." Then the fire of the Lord fell and consumed the burnt sacrifice, and the wood, and the stones, and the dust, and it licked up the water that *was* in the trench. Now when the people saw *it*, they fell on their faces; and they said, "The Lord, He *is* God! The Lord, He *is* God!"

I Kings 18:36–39

Lord,
Elijah knew that he did not need to fear the prophets of Baal. He knew that it was You who was being rejected and You who was being tested. I ask You now to increase my faith in You. I want to serve You, stand for You, trust in You, and uphold Your gospel of peace, even when everyone else is against me. I know that You are able to see me through anything. You have promised this. You surely reward those that seek You and put their trust in You. You not only honored the sacrifice, You consumed the wood, the stones, the dust, and the water. Surely You are a mighty and able God! Fulfill Your covenant in me. Magnify Your holy Name in my life. Praise be to You! The Lord, He is God! The Lord, He is God! The Lord, He is God! Amen.

# MARCH 9

Dear Friend, Precious Child of God,

And there he went into a cave, and spent the night in that place; and behold, the word of the Lord *came* to him, and He said to him, "What are you doing here, Elijah?" So he said, "I have been very zealous for the Lord God of hosts; for the children of Israel have forsaken Your covenant, torn down Your alters, and killed Your prophets with the sword. I alone am left; and they seek to take my life." Then He said, "Go out, and stand on the mountain before the Lord." And behold, the Lord passed by, and a great and strong wind tore into the mountains and broke the rocks in pieces before the Lord, *but* the Lord *was* not in the wind; and after the wind an earthquake, *but* the Lord *was* not in the earthquake; and after the earthquake a fire, *but* the Lord *was* not in the fire; and after the fire a still small voice.

I Kings 19:9–12

Lord,
There are times that I feel that no one seems to care about You. It seems that everyone around me has abandoned You for the cares of this world. I feel like I am alone in my love and zeal for You. Thank You for making Yourself known to me. You are not in the wind that is here for a moment and then gone like passing trends and fancies. You are not in the earthquake; the things that try to shatter me. You are not in the fire; a life that consumes me with its fuel of duty. You control all things, Lord, but You speak to me in a still, small voice. Lord, sharpen the ears of my heart. Let me listen to You more closely. I need You. Amen.

# MARCH 10

Dear Friend, Fed by the Lord,

Then a man came from Baal Shalisha, and brought the man of God bread of the firstfruits, twenty loaves of barley bread, and newly ripened grain in his knapsack. And he [Elisha] said, "Give *it* to the people, that they may eat." But his servant said, "What? Shall I set this before one hundred men?" He said again, "Give it to the people, that they may eat; for thus says the Lord: 'They shall eat and have *some* left over.'" So he set *it* before them; and they ate and had *some* left over, according to the word of the Lord.

II Kings 4:42–44

Lord,
Forgive me for continually focusing on man's feeble perspective of things. You are Almighty God. You are the Creator and Sustainer of Life. You are the one who provides everything I have, even when I think the things I have are a product of my own hard labor. You have stretched food and supplies, time and money, and more for me. I have seen it with my own eyes. Father, please help me to believe that You will keep Your promises to care for me. Help me to remember that when You bless, there is enough and more left over. There is no end to the blessings You can provide. Thank You for feeding me body, mind, and spirit. Amen.

# MARCH 11

Dear Friend, Washed by the Blood of the Lamb,

Then Naaman . . . stood at the door of Elisha's house. And Elisha sent a messenger to him, saying, "Go and wash in the Jordan seven times, and your flesh shall be restored to you, and you shall be clean." But Naaman became furious and went away and said, "Indeed I said to myself, he will surely come out *to me*, and stand and call on the name of the Lord his God, and wave his hand over the place, and heal the leprosy. "*Are* not . . . the rivers of Damascus better than all the waters of Israel? Could I not wash in them and be clean?" So he turned and went away in a rage. And his servants came near . . . and said, "My father, *if* the prophet had told you *to do* something great, would you not have done *it?* How much more then, when he says to you, 'Wash, and be clean?'" So he went down and dipped seven times in the Jordan, according to the saying of the man of God; and his flesh was restored like the flesh of a little child, and he was clean.

II Kings 5:9–14

Lord,
My pride wants to do some great and mighty thing for You, and my selfish, unbelieving heart does not have the faith to do even a small thing. Jesus, You have been to the muddy river Jordan. One complete immersion was all it took for You to be baptized. You humbly confessed the sins of the world as though they were Your own. No place was, or is, too low for You to stoop to save Your precious, fallen humans. Please forgive me. Wash away the leprosy of sin. Restore me. I am in eternal awe of Your loving gift of salvation. Immerse me completely in You. Bury my sin-sick, unbelieving heart, my sinful flesh, and create in me a clean heart, O God. I am Your little child. Wash me and make me clean. Amen.

# MARCH 12

Dear Friend, Loved by the Savior,

Then *the* Rabshakeh said to them, "Say now to Hezekiah, 'Thus says the great king, the king of Assyria: 'What confidence is this in which you trust? You speak of *having* plans for war; but *they are* mere words. And in whom do you trust, that you rebel against me? Now look! You are trusting in the staff of this broken reed, Egypt, on which if a man leans, it will go into his hand and pierce it. So *is* Pharoah king of Egypt to all who trust in him.'"

II Kings 18:19–21

Lord,

Please forgive me for drastically misrepresenting You. I call myself a follower of Christ, and yet live wholly for myself in unbelief and fear. I am rebuked, just as Assyria rebuked Hezekiah. I plan to thwart the enemy, sin, but I rely on the power of bondage to do so. I trust "Egypt," the bondage to selfish, sinful thinking and living. I trust my own will-power to accomplish that which is far greater than myself. The very thing I think will save me (my own works) is piercing me. My hands are useless. I have met face to face once again with the real enemy, and it is me. Only You can save me from myself. You see through the pious nonsense of my words, and You love me ever more deeply. You have the way of escape for me. O my Savior, lift me out of my hopeless bed of pride, selfishness, and unbelief. Fulfill Your covenant in me. Renew my heart with Your Spirit. Amen.

# MARCH 13

Dear Friend, Wooed by the Spirit,

But if you say to me, "We trust in the Lord our God," *is* it not He whose high places and whose altars Hezekiah has taken away, and said to Judah and Jerusalem, "You shall worship before this altar in Jerusalem?" Now therefore, I urge you, give a pledge to my master king of Assyria, and I will give you two thousand horses—if you are able on your part to put riders on them!' How then will you repel one captain of the least of my master's servants, and put your trust in Egypt for chariots and horsemen?

II Kings 18:22–24

Lord,

I am embarrassed and ashamed. I have brought shame to Your holy name and Your faithful promises. I am assailed by the enemy and so I say, "I trust in the Lord," though I display faithlessness. I tear down the altars of sacrifice in my heart, and build altars of compromise and excuse, bitterness, and despair. I worship dogma and tradition. Jesus, how horrible this is for You. The world clearly sees my contradictory life and mocks. They invite me to give up my hopeless foolishness and join them. They think to offer me gain. Satan holds out his lure of deception and challenge for my ego. O how I have made a mockery of Your holy Name. Forgive and restore me. Fill me and use me. Proclaim You righteous name before all men through me. I surrender all. Amen.

# MARCH 14

Dear Friend, Chastened with Love,

"Have I now come up without the Lord against this place to destroy it? The Lord said to me, 'Go up against this land and destroy it.'" Then Eliakim the son of Hilkiah, Shebna, and Joah said to *the* Rabshakeh, "Please speak to your servant in Aramaic, for we understand *it;* and do not speak to us in Hebrew in the hearing of the people who *are* on the wall." But *the* Rabshakeh said to them, "Has my master sent me to your master and to you to speak these words, and not to the men who sit on the wall, who will eat and drink their own waste with you?"

II Kings 18:25–27

Lord,

When I refuse to trust wholly in You for protection, I am really saying that You are my enemy. Though You love me so very deeply, You will not cross my will without my permission, though You long to intervene in my behalf. I realize now how much incredible pain it causes You to allow me to be defeated. Your enemy delights in attacking Your unbelieving children. Even those who do not worship You recognize a compromising, contradictory Christian. Like Eliakim, Shebna, and Joah, I do not want the little ones to hear the stark reality of what happens to those who do not rely on the Lord, though they think they do. Father, forgive me for giving lip service instead of heart surrender. The world is dying in desperate need to know Your true character of agape. I have failed You as a representative. Forgive me. Heal me. Let not Your name be mocked forever. Fulfill Your covenant in me. Amen.

# MARCH 15

Dear Friend, Protected by the Almighty,

Then *the* Rabshakeh stood and called out with a loud voice in Hebrew, and spoke, saying, "Hear the word of the great king, the king of Assyria! Thus says the king: 'Do not let Hezekiah deceive you, for he shall not be able to deliver you from his hand; nor let Hezekiah make you trust in the Lord, saying, 'The Lord will surely deliver us; this city shall not be given into the hand of the king of Assyria.'"

II Kings 18:28–30

Lord,

There are those around me who claim to be led by You, who speak many things that sound like You, but are really using Your words for their own benefit, or in hopes that if they proclaim it long enough, their words will become the truth. As the Rabshakeh spoke in Hebrew, so those who proclaim a tainted gospel, use the language of the Bible. They are telling me to not let my God-appointed leaders fool me. Father, I know that the leaders You have set up do not always put their trust in You. It is because they suffer with the same proud, selfish, unbelieving nature that I suffer with. So I lift up to You now the leaders of this church, of this nation, of every home. Renew their hearts toward You, just as You did for Hezekiah. Let not my trust in You ever be a false hope. Let me never pull away from You and into the hands of Assyria. Holy Spirit, be my one and only Teacher of righteousness. Amen.

# MARCH 16

Dear Friend, Led by the Spirit,

Do not listen to Hezekiah; for thus says the king of Assyria: "Make peace with me by a present and come out to me; and every one of you eat from his own vine and every one from his own fig tree, and every one of you drink the waters of his own cistern; until I come and take you away to a land like your own land, a land of grain and new wine, a land of bread and vineyards, a land of olive groves and honey, that you may live and not die. But do not listen to Hezekiah, lest he persuade you, saying, 'The Lord will deliver us.'"

II Kings 18:31–32

Lord,

I need to be ever connected to Your Holy Spirit for discernment of spiritual things. The Rabshakeh spoke in the Hebrew language and offered Judah the same things that You had already given them. He bid Judah to come to the king of Assyria for peace; inferring that he would give them vines, fig trees, their own cisterns, grain, groves, and more—even a land like their own. O Lord, this world is full of false promises. This world is full of those who deny Your almighty power and propose to be a savior for peace and wealth. They promote what they believe to be an easier way: one does not have to deny self to live. Jesus, forgive me. Please forgive me for even listening to these false gospels. *You, and You alone*, can fulfill such promises—and You have. You have already given me peace and a new land. You are the spring of Living Water that never shall run dry. I cling to You, Father. Holy Spirit, be my guide into *all* spiritual truth. Amen.

# MARCH 17

Dear Friend, Led by the True Vine,

"'Has any of the gods of the nations at all delivered its land from the king of Assyria? Where *are* the gods of Hamath and Arpad? Where *are* the gods of Sepharvaim and Hena and Ivah? Indeed, have they delivered Samaria from my hand? Who among all the gods of the lands have delivered their countries from my hand, that the Lord should deliver Jerusalem from my hand?'" But the people held their peace and answered him not a word; for the king's commandment was, "Do not answer him." Then Eliakim the son of Hilkiah, who *was* over the household, Shebna the scribe, and Joah the son of Asaph, the recorder, came to Hezekiah with *their* clothes torn, and told him the words of *the* Rabshakeh.

II Kings 18:33–37

Lord,
There are those in high places who blaspheme Your holy Name. They think to put You on par with worldly idols, and to esteem themselves as god, calling me to follow them instead of, or as, You. Jesus, give me Your faith and Your Spirit to hold my peace when under attack for loyalty to You, just as You did before Your accusers. You had already won the battle for Hezekiah. He needed only to trust You and to wait and watch. Jesus, You have already won the battle for me, too. Help me to trust You, to watch Your mercy and blessings surround me, and to wait on You for Your holy teachings and direction for my life. Give me Your perfect faith and love that casts out all fear. Amen.

# MARCH 18

Dear Friend, Child of God,

So the servants of King Hezekiah came to Isaiah. And Isaiah said to them, "Thus you shall say to your master, Thus says the Lord: 'Do not be afraid of the words which you have heard, with which the servants of the king of Assyria have blasphemed Me. Surely I will send a spirit upon him, and he shall hear a rumor and return to his own land; and I will cause him to fall by the sword in his own land.'"

II Kings 19:5–7

Lord,

Thank You for making me Your child. Thank You for Your loving protection. Father, help me to remember that when others are insulting me, it is really You they are insulting. I am nothing. You are Everything. You are the Giver and Sustainer of life. Forgive me for ignoring Your pain when Your name is blasphemed and for having a pity party for myself instead. Jesus, I am so sorry that Your name is taken in vain so often. Help me to remember how deeply You love those who hate You. Help me to know what pain it causes You to feel their rejection of Your great love. Help me to represent You more accurately so I am not a stumbling block for those who do not know You. Help me to remember that those who reject You will come to their own ruin—I do not need to be the judge or the executor, You have this covered. I trust in You. Thank You for making me Your child. Amen.

# MARCH 19

Dear Friend, Loved by the Father,

Then Hezekiah prayed before the Lord, and said: "O Lord God of Israel, *the One* who dwells *between* the cherubim, You are God, You alone, of all the kingdoms of the earth. You have made heaven and earth. Incline Your ear, O Lord, and hear; open Your eyes, O Lord, and see; and hear the words of Sennacherib, which he has sent to reproach the living God. Truly, Lord, the kings of Assyria have laid waste the nations and their lands, and have cast their gods into the fire; for they *were* not gods, but the work of men's hands—wood and stone. Therefore they destroyed them. Now therefore, O Lord our God, I pray, save us from his hand, that all the kingdoms of the earth may know that You *are* the Lord God, You alone."

II Kings 19:15–19

Lord,
You are the Almighty, the Sovereign, the One and only God. You are the Creator, Sustainer, Redeemer, Father, Brother, Husband, Savior, and Righteousness. I am nothing. You are everything. Please listen to my humble cry. Please see my hopeless plight. I have put my stock in the gods of the nations; in buildings and institutions, in material possessions and bank accounts, in education, technology, and the wisdom of man. All these things have failed to save me—they destroy me. All these things become useless or disappear in their turn without warning or hope of return. I cannot save myself. I cannot rid myself of sin and selfishness. Save me from the hand of the destroyer. You are the Lord God, You alone. Amen.

# MARCH 20

Dear Friend, Blessed by God,

Oh, give thanks to the Lord! Call upon His name; make known His deeds among the peoples! Sing to Him, sing psalms to Him; talk of all His wondrous works! Glory in His holy name; let the hearts of those rejoice who seek the Lord! Seek the Lord and His strength; seek His face evermore! Remember His marvelous works which He has done, His wonders, and the judgments of His mouth, O seed of Israel His servant, You children of Jacob, His chosen ones!

I Chronicles 16:8–13

Lord,

Thank You for Your sustaining love and power. Thank You for the beauty of nature that surrounds us and is ever changing. How I rejoice in the multitude of blessings You bestow upon me each day! You are the sole source of my strength. You are my life. Gladly I take the advice of Your servant David, and seek Your face continually. May Your face be all I ever see. Help me to ever have Your mighty Name on my lips. You have truly carried me through each and every day of my life. You have cared for my every need and problem, no matter how great or small. I am nothing. *You* are Everything. How I praise You for that! Amen.

# MARCH 21

Dear Friend, Blessed by the Lord,

Therefore David blessed the Lord before all the assembly; and David said: "Blessed are You, Lord God of Israel, our Father, forever and ever. Yours, O Lord, *is* the greatness, the power and the glory, the victory and the majesty; for all *that is* in heaven and earth *is Yours;* Yours is the kingdom, O Lord, and You are exalted as head over all. Both riches and honor *come* from You, and You reign over all. In Your hand *is* power and might; in Your hand *it is* to make great and to give strength to all."

I Chronicles 29:10–12

Lord,

Praise be to You forever and ever! Everything I have, everything I am, is a gift from You. My every breath is a gift of Your mercy. Forgive me for my constant return to my stubborn selfish ways. How ridiculous that I think I can use my "good sense" to get by and accomplish things. You alone have wisdom. This is why You are exalted over all. Thank You, Lord, for Your greatness, Your power, Your glory, Your victory, and Your majesty. Thank You for Your kingdom and Your exalted leadership. Thank You for being my Almighty Lord God. Hallelujah! Amen.

# MARCH 22

Dear Friend, Child of God,

Now therefore, our God, we thank You and praise Your glorious name. But who *am* I, and who *are* my people, that we should be able to offer so willingly as this? For all things *come* from You, and of Your own we have given You. For we *are* aliens and pilgrims before You, as *were* all our fathers; our days on earth *are* as a shadow and without hope.

I Chronicles 29:13–15

Lord,

Thank You very much for the way that You provide everything I need and much, much more. Everything I have, and what small portions I return to You are all already Yours. I am nothing. *You are Everything.* Help me to remember this. You are my life and my Reward. I would have nothing, yes, I would be nothing without You. Thank You for giving me the opportunity to return my humble gratitude to You for what You have done for me. You have given me life eternal and a beautiful hope. You have made me Your precious child, purchased with Your own blood. I love You, Lord. Praise be to You for ever and ever. Amen.

# MARCH 23

Dear Friend, Child of God,

If my people, which are called by my name, shall humble themselves, and pray, and seek my face, and turn from their wicked ways; then will I hear from heaven, and will forgive their sin, and heal their land.

II Chronicles 7:14 KJV

Lord,

Humble me. O how I need Your forgiveness. Lord, I am in a desperate need of Your humility and grace. Fulfill Your covenant in me. Cause me to seek Your face continually. I cannot turn from my wicked ways, You alone can turn me. Forgive me, heal me, and turn me ever toward You. How wonderful to be called by Your Name, Lord Jesus. Christ, please forgive me for disgracing Your holy Name with my wicked ways. I am Your bride; I use Your Name so all will know that I am Yours. Yet I do not act like You. I do not honor my Husband. Thank You for drawing me to Yourself. Jesus, You have drawn me with You patient power. O what love! What wooing. Turn me ever closer to You. Let me forever serve You. Make me Your servant and use me to proclaim Your holy majesty. This I plead in Jesus' Name. Amen.

# MARCH 24

Dear Friend, Protected by God,

And he said, "Listen, all you of Judah and you inhabitants of Jerusalem, and you, King Jehoshaphat! Thus says the Lord to you: 'Do not be afraid or dismayed because of this great multitude, for the battle is not yours, but God's. Tomorrow go down against them. They will surely come up by the Ascent of Ziz, and you will find them at the end of the brook before the Wilderness of Jeruel. You will not *need* to fight in this *battle*. Position yourselves, stand still and see the salvation of the Lord, who is with you O Judah and Jerusalem!' Do not fear or be dismayed; tomorrow go out against them, for the Lord is with you."

II Chronicles 20:15–17

Lord,

You have promised to be with all those who will put their trust in You. As King Jehoshaphat saw that his enemies were too great for him and that only You are mighty and able to save, so, I too, know that only You can save me from multitudes of sin. Let me not fear, but let me put my *complete* trust in You and stand still and see the salvation of the Lord. Fulfill Your covenant in me. Only You can stop me from yielding to the temptations of the devil. Help me to always surrender my self-focused will and leave the battle to You. Please increase my faith, almighty Father in heaven. Help me to remember who I am. I am nothing. Help me to remember who You are. You are everything. Amen.

# MARCH 25

Dear Friend, Redeemed by the Lamb,

And I said, O my God, I am ashamed and blush to lift up my face to thee, my God: for our iniquities are increased over *our* head, and our trespass is grown up unto the heavens. Since the days of our fathers *have* we *been* in a great trespass unto this day; and for our iniquities we, our kings, *and* our priests, have been delivered into the hand of the kings of the lands, to the sword, to captivity, to a spoil, and to confusion of face, as *it is* this day. And now for a little space grace hath been *shewed* from the LORD our God, to leave us a remnant to escape, and to give us a nail in his holy place, that our God may lighten our eyes, and give us a little reviving in our bondage.

Ezra 9:6–8 KJV

Lord,

I also feel too utterly ashamed and humiliated to lift up my face to You. My iniquities have piled up so high around me, that I cannot see the light of day. I am helplessly reaping the results of my own sins. I have succumbed to the traditions and education of the lands, to physical destruction, to the captivity of my selfish heart, to the plunder of my emotions that is the result of a proud, self-focused life, and to the humiliation that I am not what I proclaim to be. Forgive me; forgive us for disregarding You and Your loving, leading hand as we would discard an old, worn cloth. Thank You, Father, for Your marvelous grace, for Jesus, and for victory over the bondage of sin. Fulfill Your covenant in me. Thank You for a beautiful inheritance. You are a holy God. Amen.

# MARCH 26

Dear Friend, Bride of Christ,

For we *were* bondmen; yet our God hath not forsaken us in our bondage, but hath extended mercy unto us in the sight of the kings of Persia, to give us a reviving, to set up the house of our God, to repair the desolations thereof, and to give us a wall in Judah and in Jerusalem. And now, O our God, what shall we say after this? for we have forsaken thy commandments, which thou hast commanded by thy servants the prophets, saying, The land, unto which ye go to possess it, is an unclean land with the filthiness of the people of the land, with their abominations, which have filled it from one end to another with their uncleanness.

Ezra 9:9–11 KJV

Lord,
You have not forsaken me in my deep bondage to sin. You have had mercy on me, revived me, repairing my body, mind, and spirit—Your temple—that You may dwell in me and give me the promised inheritance of the earth made new. Forgive me for forsaking Your beautiful commandments, the promises that You long to fulfill in me. Forgive me for my blatant adultery, for preferring the wicked ways of this world above You. In Your mercy, You hold back many of the deadly consequences of my sin. Draw me to Yourself. Keep my face ever turned toward You. I do not want to continue to wallow helplessly in my iniquity. I humbly bow before Your mercy. Amen.

# MARCH 27

Dear Friend, Loved without Measure,

And after all that has come upon us for our evil deeds and for our great guilt, since You our God have punished us less than our iniquities *deserve,* and have given us such deliverance as this, should we again break Your commandments, and join in marriage with the people *committing* these abominations? Would You not be angry with us until You had consumed *us,* so that *there would be* no remnant or survivor? O Lord God of Israel, You *are* righteous, for we are left as a remnant, as *it is* this day. Here we *are* before You, in our guilt, though no one can stand before You because of this!

Ezra 9:13–15

Lord,

I often forget that sin and death are the same. Please forgive me for carelessly taking Your sacrifice for me in vain and for continuing on in my track of evil doing. You have saved me. I do not need to continue to wallow in sin. You can remove it from my life. Forgive me for needlessly yoking myself with the bondage of pride, selfishness, and unbelief. I know that sin cannot exist in Your presence. This is why the devil had to be cast from heaven, lest he be consumed. Though he will ultimately be consumed with fire, this is not want You want for me. I cannot stand before You, but I humbly bow, in gratitude and surrender. Thank You for Your righteousness. Amen.

# MARCH 28

Dear Friend, Child of God,

Stand up *and* bless the Lord your God forever and ever! Blessed be Your glorious name, which is exalted above all blessing and praise! You alone *are* the Lord; You have made heaven, the heaven of heavens, with all their host, the earth and everything on it, the seas and all that is in them, and You preserve them all. The host of heaven worships You. You *are* the Lord God, who chose Abram, and brought him out of Ur of the Chaldeans, and gave him the name Abraham; You found his heart faithful before You, and made a covenant with him to give the land of the Canaanites, the Hittites, the Amorites, the Perizzites, the Jebusites, and the Girgashites— to give *it* to his descendants. You have performed Your words, for You *are* righteous.

Nehemiah 9:5–8

Lord,

I am nothing. You are everything. I praise Your name for being such a wonderful and holy God. You alone have the power to create beauty out of nothing. Your love is the sustainer of my every breath. When You chose Abraham, You chose me; You chose every one of Your children to inherit a beautiful land. You led Abraham to Canaan and gave the land to his descendants to show me that You lead Your children even today. You have given the True Inheritance—Yourself. Jesus, You performed Your words with Your very life. You made a covenant with Your children to give them the earth made new; the earth conquered and retrieved from the enemy. Perform Your words in my heart, Lord. You are righteous. Amen.

# MARCH 29

Dear Friend, Rescued from Peril,

You saw the affliction of our fathers in Egypt, and heard their cry by the Red Sea. You showed signs and wonders against Pharaoh, against all his servants, and against all the people of his land. For You knew that they acted proudly against them. So You made a name for Yourself, as *it is* this day. You divided the sea before them, so that they went through the midst of the sea on dry land; and their persecutors You threw into the deep, as a stone into the mighty waters. Moreover You led them by day with a cloudy pillar, and by night with a pillar of fire, to give them light on the road which they should travel.

Nehemiah 9:9–12

Lord,

You are a God who sees the affliction and hears the cries of Your children. You are a mighty God who stretches forth Your mighty and loving hand to rescue Your children from bondage. You are a God who is not satisfied merely with rescue from physical slavery, but who rescues from the slavery of sin. You are a God who is undaunted by what seems helplessly overwhelming to me. You are a God who can stop mighty waves in midair and hold them there as easily as if You were brushing aside a bit of dust. You are a God who can destroy any enemy by removing Your sustaining hand, just as the entire Egyptian army was destroyed when You removed Your hand that held back the sea. You are a God who lights the way when the road seems dark. May Your light go before me and make my path plain and clear. Amen.

# MARCH 30

Dear Friend, Sustained by the Almighty,

You came down also on Mount Sinai, and spoke with them from heaven, and gave them just ordinances, and true laws, good statutes and commandments. You made known to them Your holy Sabbaths, and commanded them precepts, statutes and laws, by the hand of Moses Your servant. You gave them bread from heaven for their hunger, and brought them water out of the rock for their thirst, and told them to go in to possess the land which You had sworn to give them.

Nehemiah 9:13–15

Lord,

How awesome it must have been when You came down to Mount Sinai to speak words of love and promises of Your covenant to them. I tremble with excitement and humble awe at the thought of hearing Your voice. Please forgive me for misunderstanding Your loving purpose as You shared Your holy law. You want to write Your ways in my heart. I repent of my foolish thoughts of accomplishing Your purpose in my own way (with "Your help" of course). Fulfill Your commandments in me. Thank You for being the Bread of life from heaven that alone satisfies my true hunger, the hunger for You in my heart. Thank You for being the Water of life that revives and refreshes my soul. Thank You for being the Rock that I can cling to and drink from. Let me fall on You, Jesus, the Rock of my salvation. I am Yours. Amen.

# MARCH 31

Dear Friend, Child of God,

When Mordecai learned all that had happened, He tore his clothes and put on sackcloth and ashes, and went out into the midst of the city. He cried out with a loud and bitter cry. He went as far as the front of the king's gate, for no one *might* enter the king's gate with sackcloth. And in every province where the king's command and decree arrived, *there was* great mourning among the Jews, with fasting weeping and wailing; and many lay in sackcloth and ashes. So Esther's maids and eunuchs came and told her, and the queen was deeply distressed. Then she sent garments to clothe Mordecai and take away his sackcloth away from him, but he would not accept *them.*

Esther 4:1–4

Lord,
The Jews had had an opportunity to return to their homeland. Many did, but many did not. You have given us an opportunity to return to our homeland—to You. Some have turned to You; some have not. Father, I, like Mordecai, find myself wandering in a land that is not my destination or inheritance. Let me mourn as Mordecai mourned. I am being sold to destruction. The enemy has long tried to get me to bow to him on a regular basis. He succeeded in causing Adam to bow. All humanity has bowed, and he would have destroyed us long before this, had it not been for You who purchased my freedom by becoming me, and taking my death. Let me grieve because of the evil that faces me. Let me weep for those that defy Your sovereignty and for those who do not put their trust fully in You. I will serve You forever. Amen.

# APRIL 1

Dear Friend, Cared for by the Father,

Then she sent garments to clothe Mordecai and take his sackcloth away from him, but he would not accept *them*. Then Esther called Hathach, *one* of the king's eunuchs . . . and she gave him a command concerning Mordecai, to learn what and why this *was*. So Hathach went out to Mordecai in the city square that *was* in front of the king's gate. And Mordecai told him all that had happened to him, and the sum of money that Haman had promised to pay into the king's treasuries to destroy the Jews.

Esther 4:4–7

Lord,
The leaders of Your people were willing to pay money to be able to kill You. Judas, Your close companion, betrayed You for thirty pieces of silver. Forgive me, Lord, for I am equally as guilty. I have chosen jobs, money, an easier road, less hassle—essentially my own wishes—over You. I am Haman, and I am Mordecai. Let me be deeply distressed for my condition. I have let my heart take up residency in a foreign land. I have tried to blend in, and it has only caused hate. If I am to be hated, let me be hated for Jesus' sake. Fulfill Your covenant in me, Lord. Bring me home to You. Cleanse me within. Fill me with an attitude of supplication for every person around me. I need You. I need You. I need You. Amen.

# APRIL 2

Dear Friend, Chosen of God,

He also gave him a copy of the written decree for their destruction, which was given at Shushan, that he might show it to Esther and explain it to her, and that he might command her to go in to the king to make supplication to him and plead before him for her people. So Hathach returned and told Esther the words of Mordecai. Then Esther spoke to Hathach, and gave him a command for Mordecai: "All the king's servants and the people of the king's provinces know that any man or woman that goes into the inner court to the king, who has not been called, *he has* but one law: put *all* to death, except the one to whom the king holds out the golden scepter, that he may live. Yet I myself have not been called to go in to the king these thirty days."

Esther 4:8–11

Lord,

Satan has decreed that all Your creatures must die. He especially hates those who have fully surrendered to You. Father, help me to never fear man's decrees but to always trust Your unchangeable promises. You have promised to place us before princes and rulers to declare Your perfect loving character of agape. You have promised to give us the words to say every time we open our mouths to declare You before men. Thank You for the privilege and the promise of being Your chosen child. Amen.

# April 3

Dear Friend, Protected by God,

So they told Mordecai Esther's words. And Mordecai told *them* to answer Esther: "Do not think in your heart that You will escape in the king's palace any more than all the other Jews. For if You remain completely silent at this time, relief and deliverance will arise for the Jews from another place, but you and your father's house will perish. Yet who knows whether you have come to the kingdom for *such* a time as this?" Then Esther told *them* to reply to Mordecai: "Go gather all the Jews who are present in Shushan, and fast for me; neither eat nor drink for three days, night or day. My maids and I will fast likewise. And so I will go to the king, which *is* against the law; and if I perish, I perish!" So Mordecai went his way and did according to all that Esther commanded him.

Esther 4:12–17

Lord,

There is no way that I can escape Satan's clutches except I trust completely in You. Give me the power and grace to stand up against evil. Please forgive me for an attitude that thinks that if people would listen to me, they would be better off. I am nothing. You are everything. You have given me the privilege to spread the gospel and rescue my fellow men from the clutches of sin. What a great privilege You have bestowed upon me, to be Your ambassador of love. Father, let me fast and pray to empty my heart of its selfish desire to cling to this life. Let me die to self, that I may live for You. Amen.

# APRIL 4

Dear Friend, Called to Witness,

Now there was a day when the sons of God came to present themselves before the LORD, and Satan also came among them. And the LORD said unto Satan, Whence comest thou? Then Satan answered the LORD, and said, From going to and fro on the earth, and from walking up and down in it. And the LORD said unto Satan, Hast thou considered my servant Job, that *there is* none like him in the earth, a perfect and upright man, one that feareth God, and escheweth evil?

Job 1:6–8 KJV

Lord,
Satan claimed to be the representative of this world. He was right that Adam had given his authority to him. However, He was not considering Your plan of redemption. He was not considering the fact that You have redeemed this world from the clutches of Satan. From the time Adam sinned, You revealed Your plan of salvation to man. Job believed Your word. He trusted You. Lord, I want to trust You with my life. I want to stand before Satan and the universe as a witness of Your great love and creative power. I am Yours. Use me for Your honor and glory. Amen.

# April 5

Dear Friend, Blessed by the Faithful One,

Then Satan answered the LORD, and said, Doth Job fear God for naught? Hast not thou made an hedge about him, about his house, and about all that he hath on every side? thou hast blessed the work of his hands, and his substance is increased in the land. But put forth thine hand now, and touch all that he hath, and he will curse thee to thine face. And the LORD said unto Satan, Behold, all that he hath *is* in thy power; only upon himself put not forth thine hand. So Satan went forth from the presence of the LORD.

Job 1:9–12 KJV

Lord,

Satan has long accused You of forcing Your created beings to serve You out of fear. He has put his own selfish and evil characteristics on You, making You out to look like the harsh, vindictive ogre that he is. You love to protect me from the evil things Satan would do to me if You let him. Help me to remember that I wrestle not with flesh and blood but with principalities and powers of darkness. Satan is desperately trying to convince as many as he possibly can to hate You and follow him. He wants to prove that I only serve You because You protect me. Jesus, give me the faith to trust and obey You when Satan attacks me from every side. I want to be a witness for You. I know Your love for me is eternal. Let it never be true that I serve You only to serve myself. Amen.

# APRIL 6

Dear Friend, Sustained by His Love,

Then Job arose, and rent his mantle, and shaved his head, and fell down upon the ground and worshipped, And said, "Naked came I out of my mother's womb, and naked shall I return thither: the LORD gave, and the LORD hath taken away; blessed be the name of the LORD. In all this Job sinned not, nor charge God foolishly."

Job 1:20–22 KJV

Lord,

Job had just lost all his children and all his possessions. It must have been so painful to hear that his three daughters and seven sons had all just perished. But Job understood that he had been made from dust and would return to dust. He understood that every gift—children and possessions—had come from God. It is amazing to me that though Job actually thought that You had caused all the trouble, he did not curse or sin against You! I know that You do not pour evil on me, Lord, and yet I still blame You for things that the devil has done to me. Please forgive me. Thank You for being patient with me; for accepting blame that is not Yours, just as You did with Job. Make me a beacon of faithfulness of Your love. Amen.

# APRIL 7

Dear Friend, Covered by God Almighty,

Again there was a day when the sons of God came to present themselves before the LORD, and Satan came also among them to present himself before the LORD. And the LORD said unto Satan, From whence comest thou? And Satan answered the LORD, and said, From going to and fro in the earth, and from walking up and down in it. And the LORD said unto Satan, Hast thou considered my servant Job, that *there is* none like him in the earth, a perfect and upright man, one that feareth God, and escheweth evil? and still he holdeth fast his integrity, although thou movedst me against him, to destroy him without cause.

Job 2:1–3 KJV

Lord,

I am eternally grateful to You for purchasing the rights to this world back from Satan. Actually, it has never really been his because from before the foundation of the world, You have sacrificed Yourself for me. Satan is at war with You. He hates Your undying love for me, and therefore hates me, the recipient of Your agape love. By Your grace, Jesus, I can be proof to the devil himself that it is Your love that compels me to serve You, never force or bribery. Father, You took the blame for the evil that Satan did to Job, and You take the blame for things that Satan does to me. Please forgive me for blaming You for Satan's hatred. Help me to show the devil and all his angels, the world, and the inhabitants of the universe that Your love draws me to Yourself. Use me for Your honor and glory to proclaim Your holy and righteous character. Amen.

## APRIL 8

Dear Friend, Preserved by His Blood,

And Satan answered the LORD, and said, Skin for skin, yea, all that a man hath will he give for his life. But put forth thine hand now, and touch his bone and his flesh, and he will curse thee to thy face. And the LORD said unto Satan, Behold, he *is* in thine hand; but save his life. So went Satan forth from the presence of the LORD, and smote Job with sore boils from the sole of his foot unto his crown.

Job 2:4–7 KJV

Lord,

There are many things said about You in this world that are definitely not true—they are true about Your accuser. How heart-wrenching it must be for You to watch and listen to all the things that are said "in Your name." It must be extremely painful to allow Satan to bring calamity on Your children. I know You allow this to show that there are those of us who serve You faithfully because You have drawn us to Your heart with Your selfless love. Father, forgive me for serving You out of fear of hell. Forgive me for serving You to gain an eternal reward for myself. I do not want to count my life as anything but a witness for Your compassionate and merciful majesty. Fulfill Your covenant in me, Lord. Amen.

# APRIL 9

Dear Friend, Filled with His Righteousness,

And he [Job] took him a potsherd to scrape himself withal; and he sat down among the ashes. Then said his wife unto him, Dost thou still retain thine integrity? curse God, and die. But he said unto her, Thou speakest as one of the foolish women speaketh. What? shall we receive good at the hand of God, and shall we not receive evil? In all this did not Job sin with his lips.

Job 2:8–10 KJV

Lord,
Please forgive me for thinking evil of You and wallowing in pity for myself when I am in a crisis. Forgive me for speaking foolishly to others who are down and pushing them to even deeper depths. Help me to remember that You want nothing but good for me. Help me to remember that though Satan desires to crush me, You are always at my side to hold me up through good and through bad. Job lost nearly all his possessions, and all his children. He was left only with a doubting spouse. Yet, he believed that You are Almighty, You know all things, and You are worthy to be praised no matter what. Fill me with the faith that trusts You no matter what. Fulfill Your covenant in me. May I never sin against You. Make me pure as gold. I believe in Your love. Amen.

## APRIL 10

Dear Friend, Redeemed by the Lamb,

For I know *that* my Redeemer lives, and He shall stand at last on the earth; and after my skin is destroyed, this *I know,* that in my flesh I shall see God, Whom I shall see for myself, and my eyes shall behold, and not another. How my heart yearns within me!

Job 19:25–27

Lord,
You are my Redeemer. O how I love You! How marvelous that you have conquered sin and death! Neither could hold *You* in its ugly grips. Jesus, You hold the key to release all of Your children from Satan's power. Fulfill Your covenant in me. I want the victory over sin that You give. Thank You for conquering death for me. Like Job, I know, that though this body may return to the ground from whence it came, You have promised a new and glorified body upon Your return. I will behold You when You come again! Because You, my Redeemer, live, You will raise me up from this wicked earth or from the grave that pretends to keep me from You. O how my heart does yearn for You. I see You in the beauty of Your holiness and Your love for me. What a wonderful thing to behold You face to face! Come quickly, Lord Jesus. Amen.

# April 11

Dear Friend, Blessed of God,

Blessed is the man that walketh not in the counsel of the ungodly, nor standeth in the way of sinners, nor sitteth in the seat of the scornful; But his delight *is* in the law of the Lord; and in his law doth he meditate day and night. And he shall be like a tree planted by the rivers of water, that bringeth forth his fruit in his season; his leaf also shall not wither; and whatsoever he doeth shall prosper.

Psalm 1:1–3 KJV

Lord,

Please forgive me for taking counsel that is not of You. Forgive my scornful attitudes. Cleanse me, Father, and be my resistance to temptation. Fulfill Your covenant in me. Help me to meditate on Your law day and night, instead of meditating on my own needs and plans and then continually failing to keep Your law. Show me Your uprightness, goodness, and love. Plant Your ways in every fiber of my being. Let me be a tree, rooted and grounded in You, the River of Life. Lord; make me a fruitful tree. May the fruit of Your Spirit come forth from me. Prosper Your cause through me. I love You, Lord. Amen.

## APRIL 12

Dear Friend, Led by God,

Give ear to my words, O Lord, consider my meditation. Hearken unto to the voice of my cry, my King, and my God; for unto Thee will I pray. My voice shalt thou hear in the morning, O Lord; in the morning I will direct *my prayer* unto thee, and will look up . . . But as for me, I will come *into* thy house in the multitude of thy mercy: *and* in thy fear will worship toward thy holy temple. Lead me, O Lord, in thy righteousness because of mine enemies; make thy way straight before my face.

Psalm 5:1–3, 7–8 KJV

Lord,

I desperately need You to hear me. No one else understands or cares as You do. You are my God, my Savior, my Healer, Guide, and Comforter. My strength and my courage come from You. Father, help me to take *all* my directions from You. My selfish pride, my enemy, seeks to destroy me continually. O how I need Your multitude of mercies. Forgive my sins, O Lord. Let me worship You in Your holy temple. Lead me in *Your* righteousness. Keep me on Your straight path of truth. Thank You for being my God. I love You. Amen.

# APRIL 13

Dear Friend, Precious Child of God,

O Lord our Lord, how excellent *is* thy name in all the earth! who hast set thy glory above the heavens. Out of the mouth of babes and sucklings hast thou ordained strength because of thine enemies, that thou mightest still the enemy and the avenger. When I consider thy heavens, the work of thy fingers, the moon and the stars, which thou hast ordained; What is man, that thou art mindful of him? and the son of man, that thou visitest him? . . . O Lord our Lord, how excellent *is* thy name in all the earth!

Psalm 8:1–4, 9 KJV

Lord,

How excellent is Your Name! The mere mention of it causes devils to flee and tremble. Fulfill Your covenant in me. Make me like a helpless babe that trusts completely in You, Father, that I may be a witness for You. I am in awe of You. Humble me. Remind me that I am but dust into which You have breathed the breath of life and then redeemed with Your own life blood. You have ordained strength in the mouth of babes and nursing infants because they cannot but rely on You. As we grow older, we depend more on ourselves and our strength disappears because *all* strength comes from You. Lord, I want to be fully dependent on You. I am so sorry for insisting on my own cheap way. I want to be a nursing infant, gaining all of my nourishment from You. How excellent is the Name of Jesus! Amen.

# APRIL 14

Dear Friend, Loved by the Rock,

I will love thee, O Lord, my strength. The Lord is my rock, and my fortress, and my deliverer; my God, my strength, in whom I will trust; my buckler, and the horn of my salvation, *and* my high tower. I will call upon the Lord, *who is worthy* to be praised: so shall I be saved from mine enemies.

Psalm 18:1–3 KJV

Lord,
I love You so much. I feel so feeble and lost so much of the time. How I need You to be my stable and secure Rock. You are indeed my Fortress; may I always hide in You. Please deliver me from sin. Fulfill Your covenant in me—not just forgiveness for sin, Lord, but deliverance *from* sin. Only You can do this in me. Thank You for being my God; my Strength. Help me to trust You as my Shield from the temptations of the evil one. Grab me with Your merciful hand when I think to go it alone. You are my Savior. Who can I call on but You? I am nothing. You are everything. I love You so much. Amen.

# April 15

Dear Friend, Purchased of God,

The heavens declare the glory of God; and the firmament showeth his handiwork. Day unto day uttereth speech, and night unto night sheweth knowledge. *There is* no speech nor language, *where* their voice is not heard. Their line is gone out through all the earth, and their words to the end of the world. In them hath he set a tabernacle for the sun.

Psalm 19:1–4 KJV

Lord,

Nature declares Your love and Your creative power. You bring the earth back from the dead each spring. New life bursts into color everywhere. Each bud declares the promise of new life in You. Father, bring spring into my heart. Let me praise You for Your awesome deeds. Praise be to You for the language of nature. How marvelous that You have surrounded the earth with Your love. Jesus, are the rocks tired of waiting on me? Are they ready to burst forth with songs of praise for their Creator? O forgive me for being slow to declare Your majesty. Fulfill Your covenant in me, Lord. Make me an everlasting fountain of praise for You, refreshing souls with Your goodness wherever I go. Thank You for the beautiful sunrises and sunsets; for the numberless, endless, magnificent blessing You lavish on me. You do supply my every need. Hallelujah! Amen.

# APRIL 16

Dear Friend, Loved of God,

The law of the Lord *is* perfect, converting the soul: the testimony of the Lord *is* sure, making wise the simple. The statutes of the Lord *are* right, rejoicing the heart: the commandment of the Lord *is* pure, enlightening the eyes. The fear of the Lord *is* clean, enduring forever: the judgments of the Lord *are* true *and* righteous altogether. More to be desired *are they* than gold, yea, than much fine gold: sweeter also than honey and the honeycomb. . . . Let the words of my mouth, and the meditation of my heart, be acceptable in thy sight, O Lord, my strength, and my redeemer.

Psalm 19:7–10, 14 KJV

Lord,

Your law is perfect because it is a reflection of You. Your perfect character of love converts the soul. The testimony of Jesus is truth. Studying You brings wisdom to the simple. More than anything in this world, Lord, let me desire You. Cause me to despise myself and cling to You alone. Fulfill Your covenant in me. You established Your everlasting covenant, and You, and You alone, will be the keeper of it. O how I long to be filled with Your Spirit. All my efforts are dung. The taste of Your precious love is sweeter than honey. Work Your marvelous works through my life, Jesus. May I be a beacon of Your perfect law. Amen.

# APRIL 17

Dear Friend, Loved by the Father,

My God, my God, why hast thou forsaken me? *why art thou so* far from helping me, and *from* the words of my roaring? O my God, I cry in the daytime, but thou hearest not; and in the night season, and am not silent. But thou *art* holy, O thou that inhabitest the praises of Israel. Our fathers trusted in thee: they trusted, and thou didst deliver them. They cried unto thee, and were delivered: they trusted in thee, and were not confounded.

Psalm 22:1–5 KJV

Lord,
How agonizing for You in every way! My Father, how could You watch Your Son feel that You had forsaken Him and not intervene—crying out, "I am right here!" Holy Spirit, how You must have longed to bring comfort. My Jesus, such horror to be separated from the Father and Spirit with whom You had been One from eternity past. Help me to set my crushing feelings aside as You did and cling by faith to the Father's love. May I trust in You even when I cannot see You working or hear You speaking to me. Give me the faith of Jesus. Faith is the victory that overcomes this world of sin; that cleanses my heart. I will trust in You alone, O my God. Amen.

## APRIL 18

Dear Friend, Rescued from the Enemy,

But I *am* a worm, and no man; a reproach of men, and despised by the people. All they that see me laugh me to scorn: they shoot out the lip, they shake the head, *saying*, he trusted on the Lord *that* he would deliver him: let him deliver him, seeing he delighted in him. But thou *art* he that took me out of the womb: thou didst make me hope *when I was* upon my mother's breasts. I was cast upon thee from the womb: thou *art* my God from my mother's belly. Be not far from me; for trouble *is* near; for *there is* none to help. Many bulls have compassed me: strong *bulls* of Bashan have beset me round. They gape at Me *with* their mouths, *like* a raging and roaring lion.

Psalm 22:6–13 KJV

Lord,
You experienced in Gethsemane and on the cross a far greater distress than anyone can ever imagine. You were despised and rejected, and we esteemed You not. Forgive me, Jesus, for despising You. When I want my own selfish way, I ridicule You. I mock the way You choose to rescue me because it is so opposite of what I know and beyond my understanding. Please forgive me for disdaining Your holy covenant—Your rescue from sin. Jesus, Satan assailed You with doubts and grievous torment like never before as You submitted Yourself to the dregs of Calvary. You clung to Your Father and His love, though He seemed to have forsaken You. I need Your faith; I want to trust You even when I feel forsaken. Jesus. Please fill me now. Amen.

## APRIL 19

Dear Friend, Redeemed by the Lamb,

I am poured out like water, and all my bones are out of joint: my heart is like wax; it is melted in the midst of my bowel. My strength is dried up like a potsherd, and my tongue cleaveth to my jaws; and thou hast brought me into the dust of death. For dogs have compassed me: the assembly of the wicked has enclosed me: they pierced my hands and my feet. I may tell all my bones: they look *and* stare at me. They part my garments among them, and cast lots upon my vesture. But be thou not far from me, O Lord: O my strength, haste thee to help me. Deliver my soul from the sword; my darling from the power of the dog. Save me from the lion's mouth: for thou hast heard me from the horns of the unicorns.

Psalm 22:14–21 KJV

Lord,

Tears flow like rivers down my face as I realize the shear torture of body, mind, and spirit You endured for the likes of me. Your spirit was tormented far beyond what Your body endured. Jesus, please, please forgive my petty, nauseating complaints about the trivial things that come my way. I do not know suffering as You know it. Help me to take up my cross continually and follow You. Give me the grace and true heart conversion and repentance to endure the agony of sincere self-denial and surrender. Let me endure the reviling of others for Your sake. I want to be like Jesus. I want to be like Jesus. I want to be like Jesus. O to be like You! Amen.

# APRIL 20

Dear Friend, Guided by the Father,

The Lord *is* my shepherd; I shall not want. He maketh me to lie down in green pastures: he leadeth me beside the still waters. He restoreth my soul: He leadeth me in the paths of righteousness for his name's sake. Yea, though I walk through the valley of the shadow of death, I will fear no evil: for thou *art* with me; thy rod and thy staff they comfort me. Thou preparest a table before me in the presence of mine enemies: thou anointest my head with oil; my cup runneth over. Surely goodness and mercy shall follow me all the days of my life: and I will dwell in the house of the Lord forever.

Psalm 23 KJV

Lord,
You are my Shepherd. When I let You lead, I do not want for anything. I do not want any other shepherd. You, Father, were Christ's Shepherd as He walked this earth. You led, restored, comforted, and anointed Him. Christ dwells with You forever. Lord, I rest in Your Word. Help me to be still and drink in the Water of Life. Restore my weary soul, and lead me in Your paths. Though I wander like a dumb sheep, Father, Your correction and Your love bring me back to where I belong. You rescue me from fear. You bless me in the midst of trial and adversity. Your goodness and mercy follow me continually. May I dwell with You, forever. Thank You for being my Shepherd. Amen.

# APRIL 21

Dear Friend, Student of the Master,

Unto thee, O Lord, I lift up my soul. O my God, I trust in thee: let me not be ashamed; let not mine enemies triumph over me. Yea, let none that wait on thee be ashamed: let them be ashamed which transgress without cause. Shew me thy ways, O Lord; teach me thy paths. Lead me in thy truth, and teach me: for thou *art* the God of my salvation; on thee do I wait all the day.

Psalm 25:1–5 KJV

Lord,

I lift up my broken soul to You. I trust You to take care of my every need. I will wait on You. O Lord, help me to surrender my will, and to truly wait on You. Empty me of my selfishness and teach me Your unselfish ways. I cannot save myself, Lord, though I do try. Forgive me for trying to be my own salvation. *You* are God. Give me eyes to see and ears to hear as You show me Your holy ways of love. Take this proud heart from me and give me a teachable one. Teach me the beautiful and mysterious ways of Your salvation. Let me learn everything from You. I am full and sick with the wisdom of man. Purge me, and let me start afresh at Your feet. I am nothing. You are everything. To You, I lift up my broken soul. Amen.

## APRIL 22

Dear Friend, Bride of Christ,

*I had fainted,* unless I had believed to see the goodness of the Lord in the land of the living. Wait on the Lord: be of good courage, and he shall strengthen thine heart; wait, I say, on the Lord!

Psalm 27:13–14 KJV

Lord,

I do not live in a society that waits. I am living in a *"Me, right now!"* world. Please take my mind off this world that will exist only for a mere blink in time. A thousand years are as a day to You, Lord. You live in eternity. Help me to realize that this is what You want for me—to live in eternity. Fulfill Your covenant in me. Strengthen my faith in You. Correct my view, Lord. I often think this life is about me. Forgive me, Father. It's *not* about me. It's *all about You.* Give me the grace and the faith to rest wholly in Your eternal knowledge and plan. Lord, You are the One who is being misunderstood and mistreated. Thank You for the courage You give to my feeble, wavering heart. I love You, Lord. Let me ever wait for You. Amen.

## APRIL 23

Dear Friend, Created by the Word,

By the word of the Lord the heavens were made; and all the host of them by the breath of his mouth. He gathereth the waters of the sea together as an heap: he layeth up the depth in storehouses. Let all the earth fear the Lord: let all the inhabitants of the world stand in awe of him. For He spake, and it was *done;* He commanded, and it stood fast.

Psalm 33:6–9 KJV

Lord,

Your word is power. It creates worlds, and moves mountains and seas as though they were a speck of dust or a drop of water. I am in awe of You. You, Jesus, *are* the Word. When You speak, it is just as You say it is, and just as You say it. When You say You love me, let me believe You; for it is sure. When You say You have redeemed me, let me believe You; for it is done. When You say You have provided a way of escape for the temptations I face, let me believe You, for it is accomplished. You *have* accomplished salvation for all. I believe it. Fulfill Your covenant in me. Re-create my heart. O Jesus, heal me body, mind and spirit. Cleanse me from every evil with Your Word. Thank You for being my Creator and Redeemer. Amen.

# APRIL 24

Dear Friend, Blessed by God,

The angel of the Lord encampeth round about them that fear him, and delivereth them. O taste and see that the Lord *is* good: blessed *is* the man *that* trusteth in him. O fear the Lord, ye his saints: for *there is* no want to those that fear him. The young lions do lack, and suffer hunger: but they that seek the Lord shall not want any good *thing*.

Psalm 34:7–10 KJV

Lord,
You have promised to protect Your children. Please forgive me for feebly trying to protect myself. May I ever have a holy fear for You, and rely completely on Your bountiful mercies. I have tasted; I have seen; Lord, You are marvelous beyond description. You have supplied all my needs beyond what I could ever ask for or think of. You know what *good things* truly are. Please help me to remember to look to You for guidance as I make choices every day. May I always choose You. Thank You for Your eternal love and protecting power. You protect me body, mind, and spirit. I am Yours, Lord: body, mind, and spirit. Amen.

# APRIL 25

Dear Friend, Blessed of God,

I waited patiently for the Lord; and he inclined unto me, and heard my cry. He brought me up also out of an horrible pit, out of the miry clay, and *set* my feet upon a rock, *and* established my goings. And he hath put a new song in my mouth, *even* praise unto our God: many will see *it,* and fear, and shall trust in the Lord. Blessed *is* that man that maketh the Lord his trust, and respecteth not the proud, nor such as turn aside to lies.

Psalm 40:1–4 KJV

Lord,

How diligent and patient You have been with me. I continually rush on, guessing and assuming, acting and doing, as if You would miss an opportunity if I did not "catch it for You." I do not see the whole picture as You do. I forget that You are all-knowing and that eternity belongs to You. Please help me to always wait patiently for Your timely instruction. You have indeed pulled me out of the horrible pit of eternal destruction. Jesus, You trusted Your Father to bring You up from the depths of our sins that You took upon Yourself to accomplish my salvation. Who else can I trust but You? You have put a new song in my mouth: the song of redemption. I will trust in You and praise You for evermore. Amen.

# APRIL 26

Dear Friend, Daughter/Son of God,

As the hart panteth after the water brooks, so panteth my soul after thee, O God. My soul thirsteth for God, for the living God: when shall I come and appear before God? My tears have been my meat day and night, while they continually say unto me, Where *is* thy God? When I remember these *things,* I pour out my soul within me: for I had gone with the multitude, I went with them to the house of God, with the voice of joy and praise, with a multitude that kept holyday. Why art thou cast down, O my soul? and *why* art thou disquieted in me? Hope thou in God: for I shall yet praise Him *for* the help of His countenance.

Psalm 42:1–5 KJV

Lord,

How my soul longs after You, the Living God. I want so desperately to be with You, Lord. You are my strength. How I cry in my heart for You. I know You are with me though I cannot see You. Sometimes I wonder if I can really hear Your voice, or if You hear me, or if my words are at all acceptable to You. I will ever trust in You. Fulfill Your covenant in me. Please help me to depend on You and Your strength. Lift my soul up to You. I hope in You. The very thought of You is strength and grace to my soul. I praise You for Your longsuffering and faithfulness and for Your wisdom and patience. How my soul longs for You, my Savior and my Friend. Amen.

# APRIL 27

Dear Friend, Protected by God,

God is our refuge and strength, a very present help in trouble. Therefore will not we fear, though the earth be removed, and though the mountains be carried away into the midst of the sea; *Though* the waters thereof roar *and* be troubled, *though* the mountains shake with the swelling thereof.

Psalm 46:1–3 KJV

Lord,

Please help me to remember that You are my refuge. You are my physical refuge, my mental refuge, my spiritual refuge, my financial refuge, and my stress refuge. The earth being removed and the mountains jumping into the sea is not too much for You to handle. O that I would trust You with the little things. Help me to turn to You for decisions about every aspect of my life. Help me to trust You with the little things. Forgive me for thinking that I have all those things under control. Father, every thought, word, and action needs to come directly from You. O that I would remember this. Jesus, be ever on my mind. Jesus, let Your mind be in me that I might not sin against You. I am nothing. You are everything. You are a beautiful Refuge. "Rock of ages, cleft for me, let me hide myself in Thee." Amen.

## April 28

Dear Friend, Loved by the Father,

Create in me a clean heart, O God; and renew a right spirit within me. Cast me not away from thy presence; and take not thy holy spirit from me. Restore unto me the joy of thy salvation; and uphold me *with thy* free spirit. *Then* will I teach transgressors thy ways; and sinners shall be converted unto thee.

Psalm 51:10–13 KJV

Lord,
Please don't ever cast me away from Your presence. How desperately I do indeed need You to purge me of my wicked and selfish mentality. You have blessed me with Your love and Your presence. Please don't ever leave me. Forgive me for shunning and ignoring Your still, small voice of love. Restore me, Lord, to what You have always intended for me. Fill me with Your joy and Your Spirit. O Lord, I want to be a *true* witness for You. Only You can represent Yourself in me. Use me, Father. I love You. Fulfill Your covenant in me. Create in me a clean heart, O God. Amen.

# APRIL 29

Dear Friend, Precious Treasure,

Hear my cry, O God; attend unto my prayer. From the end of the earth will I cry unto thee, when my heart is overwhelmed: lead me to the rock *that* is higher than I. For thou hast been a shelter for me, *and* a strong tower from the enemy. I will abide in thy tabernacle forever: I will trust in the covert of thy wings.

Psalm 61:1–4 KJV

Lord,

Who can I cry to but You? My heart is so encouraged that You would and do listen to me in my distress. You are the solid Rock of ages. Jesus, You lowered Yourself to the level of sinful humanity, and yet You are the highest in the universe. My heart is full of wonder as I contemplate Your matchless love. You are my Strength. Help me, Lord, to fully trust in You. Where else can I find such a complete shelter? I can even hide from myself when I hide in You. You are a Tower to help me see the needs around me. Help me to never waste time fretting. Let me always remain sheltered under Your wing. Thank You for Your faithfulness. Amen.

# APRIL 30

Dear Friend, Protected by God,

My soul, wait thou only upon God; for my expectation *is* from him. He only *is* my rock and my salvation: *he is* my defense; I shall not be moved. In God *is* my salvation and my glory: the rock of my strength, *and* my refuge, *is* in God. Trust in him at all times, ye people, pour out your heart before him: God *is* a refuge for us.

Psalm 62:5–8 KJV

Lord,
My expectations come from Your promises. What You say, You will do. Fulfill Your covenant in me. Let me place all my hope and my trust in You. Silently, I will stand in awe with my eyes fixed on You. How wonderful that You are my Rock, my hope, and my all. Victory over the grips of faithlessness and pride are in You. Thank You for being my defense when I am defenseless. Let me always trust You. Forgive me for depending on my own strength. I pour out my heart to You. I am nothing. You are everything. What peace, to hide in You. Amen.

# MAY 1

Dear Friend, Child of God,

O God, thou *art* my God; early will I seek thee: my soul thirsteth for theee, my flesh longeth for thee in a dry and thirsty land, where no water is; To see thy power and thy glory, so *as* I have seen thee in the sanctuary. Because thy lovingkindness *is* better than life, my lips shall praise thee. Thus will I bless thee while I live: I will lift my hands in thy name. My soul shall be satisfied as *with* marrow and fatness; and my mouth shall praise *thee* with joyful lips.

Psalm 63:1–5 KJV

Lord,
Help me to seek You early: early in the morning, early before I bumble into my day headlong and headstrong. I feel lost without You. Fulfill Your covenant in me. Draw me into Your sanctuary. Cleanse me. Fill me with Your holy presence. How I thirst for You! Just as nothing quenches thirst like water, You are the Water of Life! Your power and glory redeem and renew me. How can I say anything is good but You? You fill me like no one in this world can fill me. *You alone* are the real joy giver. Please remove from my heart any desire for anyone or anything but You. Thank You, in Jesus, Name. Amen.

# MAY 2

Dear Friend, Kept by the Watchman,

When I remember thee upon my bed, *and* meditate on thee in the *night* watches. Because thou hast been my help, therefore in the shadow of thy wings will I rejoice. My soul followeth hard after thee: thy right hand upholdeth me.

Psalm 63:6–8 KJV

Lord,

So often I plow through my day, practically forgetting that You exist. Forgive me for forgetting You throughout the day. I know, when I lay down at night with a mind still racing full speed ahead, I need You. Help me to ever meditate on You. When I slow down and reflect, I know You are ever leading, guiding, and protecting me. You give me wisdom and words needed at that moment. You stop my tongue before it lashes out its damaging rays. You send help just the moment I need it. You supply my every breath and heartbeat. I rejoice in You. You are my God. Amen.

## MAY 3

Dear Friend, Blessed by the Lord,

Make a joyful shout to God, all the earth! Sing out the honor of His name; make His praise glorious. Say to God, "How awesome are Your works! Through the greatness of Your power Your enemies shall submit themselves to You. All the earth shall worship You and sing praises to You; they shall sing praises *to* Your name." Selah.

Psalm 66:1–4

Lord,
When I think about what You have done for me, I want to make a joyful shout that can be heard around the globe! How awesome are Your works! Your goodness and love permeate my soul. No one can stand against You. Your love will draw them to You, or You will literally love them to death—to their death that they have foolishly chosen when they rejected You. You will never cease to love us. What a day it will be when every knee shall bow and every tongue shall confess that You are righteous and worthy of praise. Let my life be praise to You both now and forevermore. Amen.

# MAY 4

Dear Friend, Precious Treasure of God,

How lovely *is* Your tabernacle, O Lord of hosts! My soul longs, yes, even faints for the courts of the Lord; my heart and my flesh cry out for the living God. *Even* the sparrow has found a home, and the swallow a nest for herself, where she may lay her young—even Your altars, O Lord of hosts, my King and my God. Blessed *are* those who dwell in Your house; they will still be praising You.

Psalm 84:1–4

Lord,
Nothing is lovelier than to be in Your presence. You allow us to build buildings that we call Your house so that we can feel closer to You, and You long to dwell in our hearts. During King David's time, You visited men in the tabernacle, the holy and most holy places being the most sacred. A priest entered the most holy place with fear and trepidation, repenting, fasting, and praying that he might be acceptable in Your sight. Yet the birds flew in and out, building their nests in the safety of Your tabernacle. Lord, I long to be a trusting sparrow; building my nest in the safety of Your care and dwelling with You. Please make my heart Your tabernacle. Cleanse me and make me Your holy place. Let me consider coming into Your presence a very serious and sacred matter. Amen.

# MAY 5

Dear Friend, Daughter/Son of the King,

I will sing of the mercies of the Lord forever; with my mouth will I make known Your faithfulness to all generations. For I have said, "Mercy shall be built up forever; Your faithfulness You shall establish in the very heavens. I have made a covenant with My chosen, I have sworn to My servant David: 'Your seed I will establish forever, and build up your throne to all generations.'"

Psalm 89:1–4

Lord,
You are so merciful! I cry to You and You hear me. You rescue me from the trouble I have steeped myself in. And when I then turn from You and drift into my own ways You persistently woo me. You patiently allow me to wallow in my own selfish dung, though it pains You so deeply. You wait eagerly for my mournful wail of misery. Joyfully, You rescue me and wash me again. Your mercy and faithfulness endure forever. You have kept Your covenant. You have established Christ forever. Please fulfill Your covenant in me. Let Christ live in me forever. O how awesome is Your healing power! Praise Your Name forever, merciful God! Amen.

# May 6

Dear Friend, Chosen by God,

My covenant I will not break, nor alter the word that has gone out of My lips. Once I have sworn by My holiness; I will not lie to David: "His seed shall endure forever, and his throne as the sun before Me; It shall be established forever like the moon, even *like* the faithful witness in the sky."

Psalm 89:34–37

Lord,

Thank You for establishing Your holy covenant. It is so unlike the covenants and promises that I make. My promises are indeed as ropes of sand. Your covenant is a sure promise that needs only to be believed and surrendered to. Please forgive me for trying to change or even add my two cents to it. *You, Jesus,* are David's Seed, and Your throne will endure forever. Praise You, Jesus, for being a powerful, faithful witness in heaven. You have shown what the matchless agape love and grace of God can do. Please help me to depend completely on You and never on my own wisdom. I am nothing. You are everything. Please fulfill Your covenant in me. In Jesus' Name, Amen.

# MAY 7

Dear Friend, Loved by the Almighty,

He that dwelleth in the secret place of the most High shall abide under the shadow of the Almighty. I will say of the Lord, "*He is* my refuge and my fortress: my God; in him will I trust." Surely he shall deliver thee from the snare of the fowler, *and* from the noisome pestilence. He shall cover thee with His feathers, and under His wings shalt thou trust: His truth *shall be thy* shield and buckler.

Psalm 91:1–4 KJV

Lord,

Let me ever dwell in Your secret place. O to be in Your shadow! You are indeed my refuge and my fortress. It is the protective hedge of Your love and goodness and the beautiful tower of Your sacrifice that keeps my wicked heart from sinning. Lord, I am nothing. You are everything. Please cover me with the feathers of Your mighty power. I trust in Your strength alone. Your very truth keeps me alive; it is the source of my every breath. You are Truth! Thank You Father! Thank You Spirit! Thank You Jesus! I love You, Almighty, Most High God! Amen.

# MAY 8

Dear Friend, Protected by the Father,

Thou shalt not be afraid for the terror by night; *nor* for the arrow *that* flieth by day; *Nor* for the pestilence *that* walketh in darkness; *nor* for the destruction *that* wasteth at noonday. A thousand shall fall at thy side, and ten thousand at thy right hand; *but* it shall not come nigh thee. Only with thine eyes shalt thou behold, and see the reward of the wicked.

Psalm 91:5–8 KJV

Lord,
All around me terror reigns. It is on the news, in the town. It can be so utterly depressing, not to mention outright scary. Arrows of spiritual, mental, and physical sickness assail me daily. Thank You that I can rest peacefully in Your care as things seem to fall apart in and around me. Though this mortal body may fail me, *You never fail.* I am eternally secure in Your love and grace. You protect my heart. It is safe in You. Lord, give me the strength to stand tall spiritually for Your sake, even when those close to me fall. I need not fear, though the heavens fall and the earth be removed. Thank You Jesus! Amen.

# MAY 9

Dear Friend, Child of God,

Because thou hast made the Lord, *which is* my refuge, *even* the most High, thy habitation; There shall no evil befall thee, neither shall any plague come nigh thy dwelling. For He shall give His angels charge over thee, to keep thee in all thy ways. They shall bear thee up in *their* hands, lest thou dash thy foot against a stone.

Psalm 91:9–12 KJV

Lord,

How You surround me with Your perfect love! You long for me to fully surrender *all* to You. You are able to uphold my mind, body, and spirit with Your mighty hand. Angels stand on guard to protect me. How easy it is to give You my feeble, worn-out body; yet how difficult it seems to give You my stubborn, selfish spirit. Father, please help me to completely believe in Your awesome, redemptive power, Your covenant promises that You will protect and redeem my heart. Thank You for Your promise. I believe You. Please keep the evil plagues of pride and unbelief from my heart. Thank You for the angels that bear me up to You. Amen.

# MAY 10

Dear Friend, Loved of the Father,

Thou shalt tread upon the lion and the adder: the young lion and the dragon shalt thou trample under feet. Because he hath set his love upon me, therefore will I deliver him: I will set him on high, because he hath known my name. He shall call upon me, and I will answer him: I *will be* with him in trouble; I will deliver him, and honor him. With long life will I satisfy him, and shew him my salvation.

Psalm 91:13–16 KJV

Lord,
*You* have defeated Satan—the roaring lion, the crafty serpent, the dragon. You deliver me from his snares with Your love. Jesus, I call upon You to cleanse and renew my heart. I surrender all to You, my Redeemer. Please set my love ever upon You. Replace my pitiful selfish love, with Your everlasting agape love. I believe that You will deliver my sinful, selfish heart from its disease of unbelief. Throughout eternity You will continue to reveal the beautiful mysteries of Your salvation. Wow! You are so awesome! Amen.

# MAY 11

Dear Friend, Daughter/Son of the King,

O come, let us sing to the Lord: let us make a joyful noise to the rock of our salvation. Let us come before His presence with thanksgiving, and make a joyful noise unto him with psalms. For the Lord *is* a great God, and a great King above all gods. In his hand *are* the deep places of the earth: the strength of the hills *is* his also. The sea *is* his, and he made it; and his hands formed the dry *land*.

Psalm 95:1–5 KJV

Lord,

Praise be to You for ever and ever! O how I love You! You have saved my soul and blessed me more and more each day with innumerable blessings. You are beautiful. You are the Creator of beautiful things. How wondrous are the hills and the rivers; the lofty trees and the mighty seas. You have filled the land with more variety of trees and flowers, fruits and nuts and seeds than can fit in a book. Man cannot take credit for creating these things no matter how much knowledge we acquire or experiments we accomplish. *All* life comes from You. Forgive us for thinking to improve on Your creative power. Thank You for Your merciful blessings. Thank You for filling my heart. Amen.

# MAY 12

Dear Friend, Servant of the Lord,

Make a joyful noise unto the Lord, all ye lands. Serve the Lord with gladness: come before his presence with singing. Know ye that the Lord he *is*
God: *it is* He *that* hath made us, and not we ourselves; *we are* his people,
and the sheep of his pasture. Enter into his gates with thanksgiving, *and*
into his courts with praise: be thankful to him, *and* bless his name. For
the Lord *is* good; his mercy *is* everlasting; and His truth *endureth* to all
generations.

Psalm 100 KJV

Lord,
Blessed be Your Name forever and ever! How joyful I am when I look
at all You have created and what You have done for me! My heart sings
with excited adoration for Your wonderful love for me. You are God. You
have created us in Your image—how incredibly special! I am thrilled to
be Your little lamb in Your pasture. Let me praise You with all my being.
Fulfill Your covenant in me, Lord. I want to praise You face to face!
Hallelujah! Amen.

# MAY 13

Dear Friend, Redeemed by the Lamb,

Bless the Lord, O my soul: and all that is within me, *bless* his holy name. Bless the Lord, O my soul, and forget not all his benefits: Who forgiveth all thine iniquities; who healeth all thy diseases; Who redeemeth thy life from destruction; who crowneth thee with lovingkindness and tender mercies; Who satisfieth thy mouth with good *things;* so *that* thy youth is renewed like the eagle's. The Lord executeth righteousness and judgment for all that are oppressed. He made known his ways unto Moses, his acts unto the children of Israel. The Lord *is* merciful and gracious, slow to anger, and plenteous in mercy.

Psalm 103:1–8 KJV

Lord,

My soul is full to overflowing with the ever abundant supply of good things You have bestowed upon me: fresh air, beautiful sky, abundance of delicious food, walks in the country, talks with family and friends, health, and healing for my diseased mind and spirit. You have redeemed me from the very depths of hell. You are so loving and beautiful beyond description. Lord, You execute righteousness and judgment for me. All will bow before Your holy face. I am concerned for Your perfect character. You have made Yourself known to Moses, and You make Yourself known to me. May I be a true and just reflector of Your mercy and grace. Amen.

# MAY 14

Dear Friend, Daughter/Son of God,

For as the heaven is high above the earth, *so* great is his mercy toward those who fear him; As far as the east is from the west, *so* far hath he removed our transgressions from us. Like as a father pitieth *his* children, so the Lord pitieth them that fear him. For he knoweth our frame; he remembereth that we *are* dust.

Psalm 103:11–14 KJV

Lord,
Your mercy is beyond my comprehension. You have been portrayed as such a vengeful God, but You are totally the opposite. You long to free us from our bondage to sin. You do not wish to bring up my mistakes again and again. You know my frailty. You know I am weak in body, mind, and spirit. Jesus, You have experienced everything I have and will experience, and You have conquered all of it. Lord, I surrender to Your mercy. Please remove my transgression from me. Fill me with Your love and peace. I love You, Lord. Amen.

# MAY 15

Dear Friend, Seeker of God,

O give thanks unto the Lord; call upon his name; make known his deeds among the people. Sing unto him, sing psalms unto him: talk ye of all his wondrous works. Glory ye in his holy name: let the heart of them rejoice that seek the Lord. Seek the Lord, and his strength: seek his face evermore. Remember his marvelous works that he hath done; his wonders, and the judgments of His mouth; O ye seed of Abraham his servant, ye children of Jacob his chosen.

Psalm 105:1–6 KJV

Lord,
Thank You for the wonderful things You have done in my life. You give me breath. You give me sight that I may see the beauty around me and ears to hear the beautiful, sweet songs the birds sing each morning. You sustain me every day. My belly is full to overflowing. You have given me a family and friends, clothes, and a roof over my head. You have given me forgiveness and a hope. May I seek Your face evermore. Let me contemplate Your amazing love for me day and night. You, Jesus, the second Adam, have made me Your chosen seed by adoption through identifying Yourself forever with humanity. How amazing! How marvelous! Wow! Amen.

# MAY 16

Dear Friend, Kept by the Father's Love,

I will lift up mine eyes unto the hills, from whence cometh my help. My help *comes* from the Lord, which made heaven and earth. He will not suffer thy foot to be moved: he that keepeth thee will not slumber. Behold, he that keepeth Israel shall neither slumber nor sleep. The Lord *is* thy keeper: the Lord *is* thy shade upon thy right hand. The sun shall not smite thee by day, nor the moon by night. The Lord shall preserve thee from all evil: He shall preserve thy soul. The Lord shall preserve thy going out and thy coming in from this time forth, and even forevermore.

Psalm 121 KJV

Lord,
When I take in the massive beauty of the mountains, it reminds me of Your almighty power. With a word, You created the beauty that surrounds me. It makes it easy to believe in Your protective promises as I stare awed and amazed at Your handiwork. Thank You for the love You have for me that compels You to continually protect and woo the likes of me. I slumber and sleep. I drift into long periods of spiritual hibernation, but You are still keeping me, protecting me, and waiting for me to wake up. You are a patient, faithful God. Thank You for preserving my soul. You preserve me with the sacrifice of Yourself. How I love You, my Help! Amen.

## MAY 17

Dear Friend, Beautiful Creation of Christ,

Behold, bless ye the Lord, all *ye* servants of the Lord, which by night stand in the house of the Lord. Lift up your hands *in* the sanctuary, and bless the Lord. The Lord that made heaven and earth bless thee out of Zion.

Psalm 134 KJV

Lord,
What a blessing it is to stand in Your house and feel Your presence. I lift up my hands to You in thanksgiving, and You fill them with good things! You are marvelous! Your goodness only increases. It is a privilege beyond compare to be Your servant. You, my Master, have served me completely; You have served me beyond what I could think, ask, or imagine. Help me to serve You with the same spirit with which You have served me. You made heaven and earth—You, my holy God. I will look to You and praise Your Name forever! Amen.

# MAY 18

Dear Friend, Loved by the Father,

O give thanks unto the Lord; for *he is* good: for his mercy *endureth* for ever. O give thanks unto the God of gods: for his mercy *endureth* for ever. O give thanks to the Lord of lords: for his mercy *endureth* for ever. To him who alone doeth great wonders: for his mercy *endureth* for ever. To him that by wisdom made the heavens: for his mercy *endureth* for ever. To him that stretched out the earth above the waters: for his mercy *endureth* for ever.

Psalm 136:1–6 KJV

Lord,

May my praise echo that of the psalmist, for surely Your mercy does endure forever. You alone are Creator and God. You speak, and it is so. You have made everything we need and led us through every tribulation. Just as You led the children of Israel through the desert, You still lead us today. It is You who provides for our every need. Thank You, Father, for Your unfailing mercy. Without Your mercy, we would all be dead and without hope. I am nothing, Lord. *You are everything*! Your mercy endures forever. Amen.

## MAY 19

Dear Friend, Loved by the Father,

Where can I go from Your Spirit? Or where can I flee from Your presence? If I ascend into heaven, You are there; if I make my bed in hell, behold, You *are there*. *If* I take the wings of the morning, *and* dwell in the uttermost parts of the sea, even there Your hand shall lead me, and Your right hand shall lead me. If I say, "Surely the darkness shall fall on me," even the night shall be light about me; Indeed, the darkness shall not hide from You, but the night shines as the day; the darkness and the light *are* both alike *to You*. For You formed my inward parts; You covered me in my mother's womb.

Psalm 139:7–13

Lord,

When I hide from everyone else, I am in Your loving presence. You know my thoughts, my heart. You woo me at all times. Day by day You show me how deeply You care for every part of me. Father, forgive me for running from You, for thinking that I could ever do without You, or worse yet, that I would want to live without You. Thank You for pursuing me so intimately and adamantly. I love Your awesome love for me. You draw me as You have since I was in my mother's womb. I love You, Lord. Amen.

# MAY 20

Dear Friend, Created with Love,

I will praise thee; for I am fearfully *and* wonderfully made: marvelous are thy works; and *that* my soul knoweth right well . . . How precious also are thy thoughts unto me, O God! how great is the sum of them! *If* I should count them, they are more in number than the sand: when I awake, I am still with thee . . . Search me, O God, and know my heart: try me, and know my thoughts: And see if *there be any* wicked way in me, and lead me in the way everlasting.

Psalm 139:14, 17–18, 23–24 KJV

Lord,
Praise be to Your holy and magnificent Name! I am not the product of some accident, whim, or fancy. It is a marvelous mystery to me: the thought, the planning, and the love You put into creating me. I am simply awed at Your handiwork. It encourages my heart endlessly to know that You have been, are, and will be thinking of me. O to know and understand Your precious thoughts for me! Lord, You know there are wicked ways in me. Please reveal them at Your mercy, and cleanse me from my sin. How beautiful You are to me, Lord. You are beautiful! Amen.

# MAY 21

Dear Friend, Child of the King,

Trust in the Lord with all your heart, and lean not to your own understanding; In all your ways acknowledge Him, and He shall direct your paths. Do not be wise in your own eyes; fear the Lord and depart from evil. It will be health to your flesh, and strength to your bones. Honor the Lord with your possessions, and with the firstfruits of all your increase; So your barns will be filled with plenty, and your vats will overflow with new wine.

Proverbs 3:5–10

Lord,

I have been trained to "use the brain the good Lord gave me" to figure things out, and so I naturally do, forgetting that the God, who created my now faulty, sinful brain, is all-knowing. Lord, You have all understanding. You have a plan for me. You are all-wise. Please forgive me for assuming that my wisdom and judgment is as good as Yours. My flesh and my bones suffer because of my pride that keeps me from submitting completely to You. Thank You for reminding me that everything I have is a gift from You. The firstfruits of everything I am and everything I have belong to You. Please fill my heart to overflowing with Your love and grace. May Your mercy flow through me to all who cross my path. You are Almighty God. Amen.

# MAY 22

Dear Friend, Loved by the Father,

My son, do not despise the chastening of the Lord, nor detest His correction; For whom the Lord loves, He corrects, just as a father the son *in whom* he delights.
Proverbs 3:11–12

Lord,
As a child, I never learned to appreciate correction. I always felt that those who were correcting me just didn't understand and just didn't know what I knew—they just "didn't get it" like I did. I am from birth prideful and arrogant. I just want my own way because it clearly makes the most sense, of course. Father, please forgive me for my insulting attitude. Touch my heart. Let me now become a teachable child. Guard my heart from the foolish wisdom of men and from my own devising. Cause me to walk in Your paths, to trust You, and to rest in Your wisdom and care. Correct me, Father. Correct my wayward, stubborn, unbelieving heart with Your unfailing agape love. Take all of me. I surrender my life to You. I surrender my heart to You. I surrender my will to You. Thank You for Your endless love for Your erring child. Amen.

# MAY 23

Dear Friend, Loved of God,

My son, attend to my words; incline thine ear unto my sayings. Let them not depart from thine eyes; keep them in midst of thine heart. For they *are* life unto those that find them, and health to all their flesh. Keep thy heart with all diligence; for out of it *are* the issues of life.

Proverbs 4:20–23 KJV

Lord,

Thank You so much for Your loving instruction. I need *Your* words of wisdom in this world. Help me to keep Your Word ever in my heart and before my eyes. Jesus, indeed meditation on You brings true healing to my body, mind, and spirit. I need You to be the sole keeper of my heart. I need You to fill me and consume me with Your love. Fulfill Your covenant in me. Touch my ears, that they may ever be attuned to Your sweet voice. Amen.

# MAY 24

Dear Friend, Child of God,

The fear of the Lord *is* the beginning of wisdom, and the knowledge of the Holy One *is* understanding. For by me your days will be multiplied, and years of your life will be added unto you. If you are wise, you are wise for yourself, and *if* you scoff, you will bear *it* alone.

Proverbs 9:10–12

Lord,
Please forgive me for looking to man for wisdom and understanding. Nothing can compare to You and the wisdom and understanding that comes from dwelling on and in You. I am nothing. You are everything. My days on this earth are but few, but You want to give me an eternity of days to be with You. Make me wise with the knowledge and understanding of Your holy character. Forgive me for scoffing at Your promises. I embrace Your holy Word as the truth about You and as Your almighty covenant with me. Lord, I believe in You and in Your promises. This is the beginning of wisdom. Amen.

## MAY 25

Dear Friend, Bought by the Blood,

*There was* a little city, and few men within it; and there came a great king against it, and besieged it, and built great bulwarks against it: Now there was found in it a poor wise man, and he by his wisdom delivered the city; yet no man remembered that same poor man. Then said I, Wisdom *is* better than strength: nevertheless the poor man's wisdom *is* despised, and his words are not heard. The words of wise *men are* heard in quiet more than the cry of him that ruleth among fools. Wisdom *is* better than weapons of war: but one sinner destroyeth much good.

Ecclesiastes 9:14–18 KJV

Lord,

Earth is but a "little city." Satan has come against it and besieged it. He has built great bulwarks of unbelief and falsehoods about Your perfect character of love. Jesus, You came as a poor Man among us, though You had indeed been living among us all along as our Creator and God. Thank You, Jesus, for Your wisdom—a wisdom that comes from the heart of the Father to all who will hear. Thank You for delivering us from the enemy. You have conquered. Lord, I claim Your complete deliverance from sin in my life. May I never think to be wise of myself. Help me to listen to Your quiet words of wisdom. Stop the foolish cries that belch from my mouth. Save me from destroying Your good. Faith is the victory! I am Yours. Amen.

## MAY 26

Dear Friend, Loved by the Beloved,

The song of songs, which is Solomon's. Let him kiss me with the kisses of his mouth—For your love is better than wine. Because of the fragrance of your good ointments, your name is ointment poured forth; therefore the virgins love you. Draw me away! We will run after you. The king has brought me into his chambers. We will be glad and rejoice in you. We will remember your love more than wine. Rightly do they love you.

Song of Solomon 1:1–4

Lord,
O what a beautiful picture of you! O how beautiful to be your bride! Indeed, the name of Jesus is sweet to the senses. Those, who have known no other, love you deeply. Jesus, you kiss me with blessing after blessing after sweet blessing. You have even given me the most precious blessing of all—You have brought me into Your chambers, Your most holy place, to cleanse me within and without, fulfilling Your covenant in me and making me like You. Nothing compares to the holy and selfless love with which You draw me. Please don't ever let me get away. I want to be Yours forever. I want all to rejoice with me and be glad in You. Let me love You with the same love with which You love me. Your love lasts forever. Amen.

# MAY 27

Dear Friend, Purchased of God,

Come now, and let us reason together, saith the Lord: though your sins be as scarlet, they shall be as white as snow; though they be red like crimson, they shall be as wool. If ye be willing and obedient, ye shall eat the good of the land: But if ye refuse and rebel, ye shall be devoured with the sword: for the mouth of the Lord hath spoken *it*.

Isaiah 1:18–20 KJV

Lord,

You are amazing! You alone can change my heart. You have been willing and obedient to the penalty of my sins. You have not only supplied the good of the land— *You are* the good of the land! Lord, take away my crimson desires. Fill me with Your pure, snow-white desires for my heart. I am willing, Father. Make me obedient. Fulfill Your covenant in me. Fix my eyes on You. Cleanse my rebellious heart that leads to certain destruction. Give me Your holy reasoning. Fill me with the mind of Christ Jesus, my precious Savior, Brother, Husband, and Friend. Hallelujah! Praise the Lord! Amen.

## MAY 28

Dear Friend, Heir with the Prince of Peace,

For unto us a child is born, unto us a son is given: and the government shall be upon his shoulder: and his name will be called Wonderful, Counselor, The mighty God, The everlasting Father, The Prince of Peace.

Isaiah 9:6 KJV

Lord,
Thank You for Your ever amazing love. Thank You for the Child, the Son, the Servant/King who has taken the government of heaven and earth upon His shoulder. You allowed an earthly government to weigh on Your shoulder, to crush Your very heart, so that You could reclaim eternally the government of this poor, lost world. How magnificent is Your Name! You have given us Your most precious possession—Yourself. Truly You are wonderful. To whom could I go for counsel but to You, my Creator and Redeemer? You are indeed a mighty God; Your mercies endure forever. My heart overflows with gratitude for Jesus, the Prince of Peace, who has bonded Himself to me, and me to Himself. Hallelujah! Amen!

# MAY 29

Dear Friend, Created by God,

Thou wilt keep *him* in perfect peace, *whose* mind *is* stayed *on thee:* because he trusteth in thee. Trust ye in the Lord for ever: for in the LORD JE-HO-VAH *is* everlasting strength:

Isaiah 26:3–4 KJV

Lord,

My heart yearns and longs and aches for Your perfect peace. It seems impossible to have peace in this messed-up crazy world of hate and violence as I race to have it my way without any harm or inconvenience to me. Please give me Your perfect peace today by bringing thoughts of You to my mind throughout the day. Fulfill Your covenant in me. Consume me with thoughts of You. Encourage me to trust in You deeper and deeper still. You are my strength. You are my Jehovah. I believe You can give my heart peace, even while I weep and pray for my fellow man. Thank You for this assurance: that You are Sovereign God, that Your tears of love and pity are far larger than mine, and that You have gained the victory of peace! I love You, Lord Jesus. Amen.

# MAY 30

Dear Friend, Wooed by the Almighty,

And therefore will the LORD wait, that he may be gracious unto you, and therefore will he be exalted, that he may have mercy upon you: for the LORD *is* a God of judgment: blessed *are* all they that wait for him.

Isaiah 30:18 KJV

Lord,
You are a patient and merciful God. You do not delight in the destruction of the wicked. We are all wicked in our hearts, Lord. Your Spirit has revealed my wickedness to me. Forgive me, Lord, for causing You so much pain with my stubborn unfaithfulness. Thank You for Your graciousness. Thank You for allowing as many calamities as it takes to draw me close to You for complete healing. Be exalted in my life, Jesus. Let Your mercy and justice shine forth in harmony in my life. Help me to always wait for You and to let You reign in my heart in Your mighty way. Amen.

# MAY 31

Dear Friend, Comforted by God,

Comfort ye, comfort ye my people, saith your God. Speak ye comfortably to Jerusalem, and cry unto her, that her warfare is accomplished, that her iniquity is pardoned: for she hath received of the Lord's hand double for all her sins. The voice of him that crieth in the wilderness, Prepare ye the way of the LORD, make straight in the desert a highway for our God. Every valley shall be exalted, and every mountain and hill shall be made low: and the crooked shall be made straight, and the rough places plain: And the glory of the LORD shall be revealed, and all flesh shall see *it* together: for the mouth of the LORD hath spoken *it*.

Isaiah 40:1–5 KJV

Lord,

You are my comfort. You supply all my physical comforts, and You are my spiritual Comforter. You have accomplished my spiritual warfare. You have purchased my pardon. You have provided a way of escape from sin for me. As John proclaimed Your Name in the wilderness, may I proclaim Your Name in the wilderness of this world. Lord, may I be like a valley, low in this world, as You were. Make my crooked ways straight with Your love and grace. May Your glory be revealed in my life today. Amen.

# JUNE 1

Dear Friend, Bride of Christ,

He gives power to the weak, and to *those who have* no might He increases strength. Even the youths shall faint and be weary, and the young men shall utterly fall, but those who wait on the Lord shall renew *their* strength; they shall mount up with wings like eagles, they shall run and not be weary, they shall walk and not faint.

Isaiah 40:29–31

Lord,

When I feel faint, it reminds me that *all* strength comes from You. You have said, "Blessed are the poor in spirit, for theirs is the kingdom of God." I need Your faith to help me wait upon You. Please forgive me for running ahead on my own. I am truly weak, especially when I think I'm strong. I faint, I'm weary, and I have utterly fallen. But I will rest in You, my Creator and Redeemer, You who renew me. It is in You that I can walk or run and not faint. Fulfill Your covenant in me. Give me Your strength and Your faith that is to my heart the wings of eagles—a faith that causes me to soar closer and closer to You, leaving this world and its selfish cares behind, and flying with You in Your love and redemptive concern for Your creatures. Renew me in You. Amen.

# JUNE 2

Dear Friend, Upheld by His Right Hand,

Fear thou not; for I *am* with thee: be not dismayed; for I *am* thy God: I will strengthen thee; yea, I will uphold thee with the right hand of my righteousness. Behold, all they that were incensed against thee shall be ashamed and confounded: they shall be as nothing; and they that strive with thee shall perish. Thou shalt seek them, and shalt not find them, *even* them that contended with thee: they that war against thee shall be as nothing, and as a thing of naught. For I the LORD thy God will hold thy right hand, saying unto thee, Fear not; I will help thee.

Isaiah 41:10–13 KJV

Lord,

Your promises are absolutely incredible! You have promised to be my strength and uphold me with Your righteous right hand. You have promised to shame and disgrace those who are against me; they will perish. You have promised to make those who persecute me as a nonexistent thing. Wow! Why on earth am I still trying to fight battles myself? Lord, help me! You have promised to help me. Help me to believe what You have promised. Stuff me to overflowing with Your faith so that I can be rid of this bondage way of thinking. I claim Your promises for my life, my family's lives, the lives of my friends, and the nation. Father, fill us all with true belief in Your promises. Amen.

# JUNE 3

Dear Friend, Redeemed by the Lamb,

But now, thus says the Lord, who created you, O Jacob, and He who formed you, O Israel: "Fear not, for I have redeemed you; I have called *you* by your name; You *are* Mine. When you pass through the waters, I *will be* with you; and through the rivers, they shall not overflow you. When you walk through the fire, you shall not be burned, nor shall the flame scorch you. For I *am* the Lord your God, the Holy One of Israel, your Savior; I gave Egypt for your ransom, Ethiopia and Seba in your place."

Isaiah 43:1–3

Lord,
Thank You for creating me. You have tenderly formed me with Your hand. All Your other creations You spoke into existence, but man You formed in Your own image. You have known my name from eternity past. I am Yours. How precious are Your promises to me! What is this disease of my heart that causes me to trust in man's devices rather than Your sovereign Word? Please forgive me for my continual, blatant unbelief. Lord, cleanse me; give me the beautiful faith of Jesus. You are the Lord my God, the Holy One of Israel, my Savior. Hallelujah! Amen.

# JUNE 4

Dear Friend, Redeemed by the Lamb,

Therefore the redeemed of the LORD shall return, and come with singing unto Zion; and everlasting joy *shall be* upon their head: they shall obtain gladness and joy; *and* sorrow and mourning shall flee away.

Isaiah 51:11 KJV

Lord,

Thank You for redeeming me. Let me return unto You, Lord Jesus. My heart is full of singing because of Your great love. Thank You for true joy that is indeed everlasting. You, and You alone, can cause my sorrow and mourning to flee. O what beautiful promises You have bestowed upon all of Your creatures! Lord, how beautiful it will be for You on the day when Your sorrowing and sighing for Your wayward children can end. Your patience is indeed everlasting. Jesus, I hope with You for that beautiful day. May Your heart, Your character of love, be lifted up in my life. Use me, Father, to reveal Yourself to all. I sing praise to Your awesome and powerful Name! Amen.

# JUNE 5

Dear Friend, Loved by the Eternal God,

Who has believed our report? And to whom has the arm of the Lord been revealed? For He shall grow up before Him as a tender plant, and as a root out of dry ground, He has no form or comeliness; and when we see Him, *there is* no beauty that we should desire Him. He is despised and rejected by men, a Man of sorrows and acquainted with grief. And we hid, as it were, *our* faces from Him; He was despised, and we did not esteem Him. Surely He has borne our griefs and carried our sorrows; yet we esteemed Him stricken, smitten by God, and afflicted. But He was wounded for our transgressions, *He was* bruised for our iniquities; the chastisement for our peace *was* upon Him, and by His stripes we are healed.

Isaiah 53:1–5

Lord,
You have loved me from before the foundation of the world, yet I have despised and rejected You in favor of my own ideas, my own pride, and my own self-centeredness. You have been bearing my sorrows and grief forever, yet I accuse You of not caring or understanding. Please forgive me, Lord. Thank You for the healing that You have provided in Jesus. Please don't let me hide my face from You. I long for Your presence. I need You desperately. O, what a most eternally horrible thing to reject You. My heart feels sorrow for the pain I have caused You from eternity past. Let me bring You joy and peace forevermore. Let me allow You to heal me. Amen.

# JUNE 6

Dear Friend, Loved by the Lamb,

All we like sheep have gone astray; we have turned, every one, to his own way; and the Lord has laid on Him the iniquity of us all. He was oppressed and He was afflicted, yet He opened not His mouth; He was led as a lamb to the slaughter, and as sheep before its shearers is silent, so He opened not His mouth.

Isaiah 53:6–7

Lord,

Please forgive me for thoughtlessly laying my iniquity upon You day after day. I carry on as if there is no consequence. O Jesus, I am so sorry for torturing You so—You the One who allowed Yourself to be led like a lamb to the slaughter. I am in awe of Your love for me, Jesus; a love that caused You to silently bear the shame and humiliation that was heaped upon You. I am forever amazed when I think of how You sweat great drops of blood in deep emotional and spiritual agony in the Garden of Gethsemane. You abhorred sin, and You loved Your Father so much, yet You willingly chose to be separated for eternity from the Father because of Your love for us and because of Your love for the Father. Please fill me with this amazing love! Praise Your Name! You, the Lamb, are also the Shepherd. Lead me to You, Lord. May I be a helpless lamb in Your arms. Amen.

## June 7

Dear Friend, Sustained by the Water of Life,

Ho, every one that thirsteth, come ye to the waters, and he that hath no money: come ye, buy and eat; yea, come, buy wine and milk without money and without price. Wherefore do ye spend money for *that which is* not bread? and your labour for *that which* satisfieth not? Hearken diligently unto me, and eat ye *that which is* good, and let your soul delight itself in fatness. Incline your ear, and come unto me: hear, and your soul shall live; and I will make an everlasting covenant with you, *even* the sure mercies of David.

Isaiah 55:1–3 KJV

Lord,

My soul is so thirsty. I drink, but I thirst again because I am not drinking the pure Water of Life that comes solely from You. I am nothing and can only offer You a broken, sin-sick heart. Please forgive me for wasting my time and thoughts on things that are not the Bread of Life. As You said, Lord, it does not satisfy. Thank You for the fresh, endless supply of Your Living Water and Bread. I surrender my ear and soul to Your everlasting covenant and mercies. *You, alone,* keep Your promises. My words are as dust in the wind and my promises as ropes of sand. Fulfill Your covenant in me, Lord. Fill me to overflowing with Your precious words of life. Amen.

# JUNE 8

Dear Friend, Seeker of the Lord,

Seek ye the LORD while he may be found, call ye upon him while he is near: Let the wicked forsake his way, and the unrighteous man his thoughts: and let him return unto the LORD, and he will have mercy upon him; and to our God, for he will abundantly pardon.

Isaiah 55:6–7 KJV

Lord,

Cause my heart to seek You. Give me the wisdom to turn to You, to seek You, instead of the wisdom and opinions of man. Remove from my thinking the idea that You have given me a brain and have set me on my own to use it, calling You only in situations that are "out of my league." Forgive me for insulting Your love and Your promises so continually. Father, let me forsake my wicked foolishness and return wholly to Your mercies. My heart is grateful for Your pardon and mercies. Bury Your thoughts deep in my heart, and let them grow to overflowing throughout my life. Be Thou my wisdom. I will ever seek You. Amen.

## JUNE 9

Dear Friend, Loved by the Father,

For my thoughts *are* not your thoughts, neither *are* your ways my ways, saith the LORD. For *as* the heavens are higher than the earth, so are my ways higher than your ways, and my thoughts than your thoughts. For as the rain cometh down, and the snow from heaven, and returneth not thither, but watereth the earth, and maketh it bring forth and bud, that it may give seed to the sower, and bread to the eater: So shall my word be that goeth forth out of my mouth: it shall not return unto me void, but it shall accomplish that which I please, and it shall prosper *in the thing* whereunto I sent it. For ye shall go out with joy, and be led forth with peace: the mountains and the hills shall break forth before you into singing, and all the trees of the field shall clap *their* hands.

Isaiah 55:8–12 KJV

Lord,
My thoughts can never compare with the thoughts You have for me. May my thoughts vanish away as You fill me with Your holy thoughts. Jesus, You are the Word that comes from the Father. You have accomplished, are accomplishing, and will accomplish that which You please. Lord; do not let Your Word return void from me. Accomplish Your purpose in me. May You prosper in my life. You are my joy and my peace. How I love to listen to the mountains and the hills sing Your praises. Let me join them. All nature bows before You as the trees loudly resound Your awesome majesty. Hallelujah! Amen.

# JUNE 10

Dear Friend, Precious to God,

O that You would rend the heavens! That You would come down! That the mountains might shake at Your presence—As fire burns brushwood, as fire causes water to boil—to make Your name known to Your adversaries, *that* the nations may tremble at Your presence! When You did awesome things *for which* we did not look, You came down, the mountains shook at Your presence. For since the beginning of the world *men* have not heard nor perceived by the ear, nor has the eye seen any God beside You, who acts for the one who waits for Him. You meet him who rejoices and does righteousness, *who* remembers You in Your ways. You are indeed angry, for we have sinned—in these ways we continue; and we need to be saved.

Isaiah 64:1–5

Lord,

You desperately wanted to come down and talk to the children of Israel at Mt. Sinai, but they were afraid of You. Father, sometimes I wish that You would show up and speak to me face to face. Thank You for not doing that; I would indeed be consumed by Your presence. I am wicked to the core—proud, selfish, and unbelieving. My sinfulness cannot hear or see You by my side, loving, guiding, and protecting me. Father, thank You for Your presence in my life. Thank You, Holy Spirit, for teaching me, showing me my condition and need, and pointing me to Jesus, my Savior. Let me wait for You, Lord. Forgive me for trying to be my own god and savior. I am steeped in sin. I know You hate for me to remain in this condition. I need to be saved from my habitual sinning. I rejoice in Your righteousness. Amen.

# JUNE 11

Dear Friend, Consumed by His Love,

But we are all like an unclean *thing*, and all our righteousnesses *are* like filthy rags; we all fade as a leaf, and our iniquities, like the wind, have taken us away. And *there is* no one who calls on Your name, who stirs himself up to take hold of You; for You have hidden Your face from us, and have consumed us because of our iniquities.

Isaiah 64:6–7

Lord,

I am truly an unclean thing. I think that my good deeds make me look good, but I cannot so much as take a breath of my own accord. I soak helplessly in my iniquities. I am drowning and cannot get out. Even in my hopeless wretchedness I forget that You are ever near, weeping in agony for me as I refuse to let You save me from my sinfulness. You do not wish to consume me by fatal fire. God, I do know this about You. You long to consume me with Your agape love. Consume me, Lord. Consume me with Your power of repentance and forgiveness. Consume me with victory over the bondage of my sin. Consume me with Your everlasting covenant of love. Amen.

# JUNE 12

Dear Friend, Child of God,

But now, O Lord, You *are* our Father; we *are* the clay and You our Potter; and all we *are* the work of Your hand. Do not be furious, O Lord, nor remember iniquity for ever; indeed, please look — we all *are* Your people! Your holy cities are a wilderness, Zion is a wilderness, Jerusalem a desolation. Our holy and beautiful temple, where our fathers praised You, is burned up with fire; and all our pleasant things are laid waste. Will You restrain Yourself because of these *things*, O Lord? Will You hold Your peace, and afflict us very severely?

Isaiah 64:8–12

Lord,

Thank You for being my Father. I can imagine how I am like a stubborn lump of clay that does not cooperate with the Potter's hands. I lump up in pride, and I collapse in unbelief and self-pity. You are so patient with me. You do not throw out the clay but begin again and again to mold me. Please forgive me for allowing Your cities to become a wilderness. Your church is often a wilderness where we roam to and fro, looking for conscience appeasement instead of looking to You. We wander forty years at a time, trying to do things our own way. Forgive me, Jesus, for making Your holy and beautiful temple, my body, a place of waste. I have allowed my body, mind, and spirit to be consumed with iniquity. Father, Your discipline is love. You long to draw me near to Yourself. Fulfill Your covenant in me. Mold me into Jesus. Make me like You. Amen.

## JUNE 13

Dear Friend, Daughter/Son of God,

"It shall come to pass that before they call, I will answer; and while they are still speaking, I will hear. The wolf and the lamb shall feed together, the lion shall eat straw like the ox, and dust *shall be* the serpent's food. They shall not hurt nor destroy in all My holy mountain," says the Lord.

Isaiah 65:24–25

Lord,

Before time began, You knew what I would pray today. You foresaw all my needs, and You have already made provisions for every detail of my life now and through eternity. What can I say in comparison of what You have done for me? Your loving care is absolutely matchless, even to description. You have redeemed this world from the enemy who terrorizes us because he hates You so. You have provided a way of escape from his ugly snares. Who am I that I think my "God-given wisdom" is enough to go on? Is my mind as full of wisdom and knowledge as Yours? Most obviously, absolutely not! Jesus, forgive me for not relying *totally* on You. Help me to trust You with my whole life, as You certainly know far better than I what I need. Thank You for Your lovingkindness and patience towards Your erring creatures. Amen.

## JUNE 14

Dear Friend, Called of God,

Then the word of the Lord came to me, saying: "Before I formed you in the womb I knew you; before you were born I sanctified you; I ordained you a prophet to the nations." Then said I: "Ah, Lord God! Behold, I cannot speak, for I *am* a youth." But the Lord said to me: "Do not say, 'I am a youth.' For you shall go to all to whom I send you, and whatever I command you, you shall speak. Do not be afraid of their faces, for I *am* with you to deliver you," says the Lord.

Jeremiah 1:4–8

Lord,
I often forget that before I was formed in the womb, You knew me. Sometimes I feel somewhat lost in the crowd. Thank You for reminding me that I am always special in Your eyes. Thank You that You have an awesome plan for me. Whatever You want me to do, Father, You have all the power and wisdom I need to do it. Just as You called Jeremiah in his youth and promised to give him words and direction, You have done the same for me. I do not feel like I can go or speak or endure the ridicule of others, but You have promised to deliver me. I believe Your promise. Please fulfill Your covenant in me. Make me usable for Your service. May every thought, word, and action be guided by Your Spirit. Amen.

## JUNE 15

Dear Friend, Precious Child of God,

For I know the thoughts that I think toward you, saith the Lord, thoughts of peace, and not of evil, to give you an expected end. Then shall ye call upon me, and ye shall go and pray unto me, and I will hearken unto you. And ye shall seek me, and find *me*, when ye shall search for me with all your heart. And I will be found of you, saith the Lord: and I will turn away your captivity.

Jeremiah 29:11–14 KJV

Lord,
Please help me to believe that the plans You have for me will give me peace. Forgive me for thinking that my own plans make more sense. Forgive me for compromising in my mind, thinking that what I think is always from You if it makes sense to me. Forgive me for thinking that the mentality that "God understands" is an acceptable excuse for doing things that I really know deep inside are not what You want for me. O Lord Jesus, help me to call upon You, to seek *You first and always*. May all of my thoughts be surrendered to You. Fill me with Your thoughts. Bring me back from the captivity of my stubborn unbelief. Amen.

# JUNE 16

Dear Friend, Eternally Loved,

The Lord hath appeared of old to me, *saying,* Yea, I have loved thee with an everlasting love: therefore with lovingkindness I have drawn thee.

Jeremiah 31:3 KJV

Lord,

How is it that You have loved me from eternity past? How can I ever doubt this kind of love? Fulfill Your covenant in me, Lord. Thank You for Your lovingkindness that draws me ever closer to You. I want to be with You, Lord. Forgive my selfish spirit that puts me before You. I am nothing. *You are everything.* An everlasting love is beyond my comprehension. I cannot recall so much as the day I was born or my time in the cradle, yet to You it is something You have known forever. Before there was time, You gave an everlasting promise; You gave Yourself to this entire sinful race through a most beautiful, redemptive plan. Draw me close to Yourself, Lord. Draw me closer and closer. I really want to come. Thank You for Your everlasting love. Amen.

## JUNE 17

Dear Friend, Loved by the Father,

*Through* the Lord's mercies we are not consumed, because His compassions fail not. *They are* new every morning; great *is* Your faithfulness. "The Lord *is* my portion," says my soul, "Therefore I hope in Him."

Lamentations 3:22–24

Lord,

It is because of Your mercies that I live and breathe. Please remind me of this continually as I deal with my brothers and sisters. Your compassion warms and encourages my heart in this cold-hearted world. Help me to ever keep in mind how deep and compassionate Your love is for me. Keep in the forefront of my mind how much You love each and every person that ever crosses my path. Work through me to reveal Your love to *everyone* no matter how lovely or frustrating they are to me. You are faithful even when I pay You no attention. Fulfill Your covenant in me. I desperately want to be like You, to reflect the love of the Father to a hateful world, unaware of Your true character of agape love. Lord, You are my hope! I praise You for Your faithfulness! Amen.

# JUNE 18

Dear Friend, Loved in His Justice,

Therefore say to the house of Israel, "Thus says the Lord God: I do not do *this* for your sake, O house of Israel, but for My holy name's sake, which you have profaned among the nations wherever you went. And I will sanctify My great name, which has been profaned among the nations, which you have profaned in their midst; and the nations shall know that I *am* the Lord,' says the Lord God, 'when I am hallowed in you before their eyes. For I will take you from among the nations, gather you out of all the countries, and bring you into your own land. Then I will sprinkle clean water on you, and you shall be clean; I will cleanse you from all your filthiness and from all your idols."

Ezekiel 36:22–25

Lord,

Please forgive me for profaning Your name. I have not rightly represented You at all. It is indeed crucial that Your great and holy Name, which is Your great and holy character, be rightly and clearly made known throughout the world and throughout the universe. We are so confused as to who You really are. Father, I want You to make me holy. I want You to gather me to Yourself for Your holy purpose. Cleanse me with Your Living Water—Your holy character of selfless love. Cleanse me from my filthiness, my pride, my unbelief, and my desire to depend on myself. Remove the idols of tradition, other people's opinions, and my stubborn selfish will from my heart. Let me be a true reflection of You to the nations. Amen.

## JUNE 19

Dear Friend, Blessed by the Everlasting Covenant,

I will give you a new heart and put a new spirit within you; I will take the heart of stone out of your flesh and give you a heart of flesh. I will put My Spirit within you and cause you to walk in My statutes, and you will keep My judgments and do *them*. Then you shall dwell in the land that I gave to your fathers; you shall be My people, and I will be your God. I will deliver you from all your uncleanness. I will call for the grain and multiply it, and bring no famine upon you.

Ezekiel 36:26–29

Lord,

Thank You for Your promise of a new heart. How I long to have Your Spirit in me. Truly, my heart is stone. I do not have Your love, Your compassion, repentance, forgiving spirit, and mercy in and of myself. Fulfill Your everlasting covenant in me. Write Your law on my heart, O God. Fulfill Your purpose in my life. Thank You for adopting me. Deliver me from my uncleanness. Cause me to walk in Your paths. Fill me with Yourself. I long to dwell with You in that land, the new earth, that You have promised. What a joy and a privilege to be counted as Your child and to acknowledge You as my God. Praise be to You forever! Amen.

## June 20

Dear Friend, Kept by His Promises,

Shadrach, Meshach, and Abed-Nego answered and said to the king, "O Nebuchadnezzar, we have no need to answer you in this matter. If that *is the case,* our God whom we serve is able to deliver us from the burning fiery furnace, and He will deliver us from your hand, O king. But if not, let it be known to you, O king, that we do not serve your gods, nor will we worship the image which you have set up."

Daniel 3:16–18

Lord,

Help me to trust Your Word and Your promises in every situation. If I do not trust You with the little details of my life, how can I expect to trust You when my life is at stake? I want to serve You faithfully in every way. Help me not to look at this world as my inheritance. Keep my focus on Jesus, my real inheritance. Remind me continually that this life is but a moment in eternity. Whether I live long or only briefly on this earth does not really matter. What matters is my need to perfectly reflect Your character to those around me. Father, fill me with Your Spirit. Let Jesus rule my life completely. I want to worship You, and You alone. May I boldly and steadfastly serve You, and You *only.* Amen.

# JUNE 21

Dear Friend, Tried with the True Witness,

Then Nebuchadnezzar was full of fury, and the expression on his face changed toward Shadrach, Meshach, and Abed-Nego. He spoke and commanded that they heat the furnace seven times more than it was usually heated. And he commanded certain mighty men of valor who *were* in his army to bind Shadrach, Meshach, and Abed-Nego, *and* cast *them* into the burning fiery furnace. Then these men were bound in their coats, their trousers, their turbans, and their *other* garments, and were cast into the midst of the burning fiery furnace. Therefore, because the king's command was urgent, and the furnace exceedingly hot, the flame of the fire killed those men who took up Shadrach, Meshach, and Abed-Nego.

Daniel 3:19–22

Lord,
You were drawing King Nebuchadnezzar to Yourself. You used three willing men to show the king who You are. May I be willing to be used by You to draw others to Your loving grace. Jesus, You said that we need to be tried in the fire of trials that we may become as pure gold. I want to have a character as pure as gold. Help me to remember this when things become difficult and fearful. I need Your Spirit to reveal and remove the impurities of my character. Those that do not trust in You will be consumed as the mighty men of valor were consumed by the heat of the furnace. Fulfill Your covenant in me, Lord. Remove my wicked heart and create in me a clean heart. Amen.

# JUNE 22

Dear Friend, Brother/Sister of Christ,

And these three men, Shadrach, Meshach, and Abed-Nego, fell down bound into the midst of the burning fiery furnace. Then King Nebuchadnezzar was astonished; and he rose in haste and spoke, saying to his counselors, "Did we not cast three men bound into the midst of the fire?" They answered and said to the king, "True, O king." "Look!" he answered, "I see four men loose, walking in the midst of the fire; and they are not hurt, and the form of the fourth is like the Son of God."

Daniel 3:23–25

Lord,

When the fiery trials of life make me fall down, may I fall on my knees into Your arms. What an incredible encouragement this story is to me. How beautiful, Jesus, that You were already in the midst of the fire! You walked with the three Hebrews in their fiery trials, and You walk with me as well. How awesome that King Nebuchadnezzar recognized You in the fire. Is it because he already had a clear glimpse of Your character through the lives of three captives? When You are clearly lifted up, no one can mistake You for anyone else. The world desperately needs a clear picture of You. Use me, Lord, to show others who You really are. You honor those who honor You. Thank You, Jesus, for walking with me. Amen.

# JUNE 23

Dear Friend, Loved by the Everlasting,

Then Nebuchadnezzar went near the mouth of the burning fiery furnace *and* spoke, saying, "Shadrach, Meshach, and Abed-Nego, servants of the Most High God, come out, and come *here*." Then Shadrach, Meshach, and Abed-Nego came from the midst of the fire. And the satraps, administrators, governors, and the king's counselors gathered together, and they saw these men on whose bodies the fire had no power; the hair of their head was not singed nor were their garments affected, and the smell of fire was not on them. Nebuchadnezzar spoke, saying, "Blessed be the God of Shadrach, Meshach, and Abed-Nego, who sent His Angel and delivered His servants who trusted in Him, and they have frustrated the king's word, and yielded their bodies, that they should not serve nor worship any god except their own God!"

Daniel 3:26–28

Lord,
Someday, those who have chosen to trust in themselves and in the inventions of man instead of putting their trust in You will be destroyed by fire. You do not want anyone to be destroyed. This fire will have no power over those who have put their lives wholly in Your care. Father, I want to serve You with my whole body, my whole mind, and my whole heart. You have promised over and over that You will protect those who put their trust in You. I trust in You, Lord. Blessed be Your name, Jesus, who came to deliver me from the destructive power of sin. Let me worship You and no other. Let me worship You in spirit and in truth. Amen.

# JUNE 24

Dear Friend, Loved by the King of kings,

Nebuchadnezzar the king, unto all people, nations, and languages, that dwell in all the earth; Peace be multiplied unto you. I thought it good to shew the signs and wonders that the high God hath wrought toward me. How great *are* his signs! and how mighty *are* his wonders! his kingdom *is* an everlasting kingdom, and his dominion *is* from generation to generation . . . Now I Nebuchadnezzar praise and extol and honour the King of heaven, all whose works *are* truth, and his ways judgment: and those that walk in pride he is able to abase.

Daniel 4:1–3, 37 KJV

Lord,
Nebuchadnezzar's testimony is awesome. He thought to defy You and rule the world, but You loved him and had much greater plans for him. You would not let him go, even if it meant letting him eat grass in the field for seven years like a wild beast. You gave him dreams and visions of the future. You gave him Daniel, the prophet, who let You use him to interpret his dreams. Nebuchadnezzar learned that Your love is much greater than pride and unbelief. Help me to remember Nebuchadnezzar when I feel tempted to judge that someone is too hard or cold to be affected by Your love. No one is beyond the reach of Your infinite love. Amen.

# JUNE 25

Dear Friend, Chosen of God,

It pleased Darius to set over the kingdom one hundred and twenty satraps, to be over the whole kingdom; And over these, three governors, of whom Daniel was one, that the satraps might give account to them, so that the king would suffer no loss. Then Daniel distinguished himself above the governors and satraps, because an excellent spirit was in him; and the king gave thought to setting him over the whole realm.

Daniel 6:1–3

Lord,
You chose Daniel to bring good news to a heathen nation. Daniel stood out as a light on a hill. He remained faithful to You. He kept his eyes on You and looked to You for guidance. He was a just ruler, and those under him were to give an account to him. Jesus came to bring good news to a fallen world. Jesus stood out like a beacon of light. Jesus, You are the Light. You kept Your focus on Your Father, ever trying to reflect His love to a dying world. And Your Father sought to set You over the whole realm. You are King of the Universe. Those under You will give an account to You. I want to be found worthy, Jesus. You make me worthy. Fill me with Your spirit as You filled Daniel. May I be like You, a beacon of light on a hill that cannot be hid. Amen.

## JUNE 26

Dear Friend, Protected by the Almighty,

So the governors and satraps sought to find *some* charge against Daniel concerning the kingdom; but they could find no charge or fault because he *was* faithful; . . . Then these men said, "We shall not find any charge against this Daniel unless we find *it* against him concerning the law of his God." So [they] thronged before the king, and said thus to him, "King Darius, live forever! All the governors of the kingdom, . . . have consulted together to establish a royal statute and to make a firm decree, that whoever petitions any god or man for thirty days, except you, O king, shall be cast into the den of lions. Now, O king, establish the decree and sign the writing, so that it cannot be changed, according to the law of the Medes and Persians, which does not alter. Therefore King Darius sign the written decree."

Daniel 6:4–9

Lord,
Did Daniel know what a parallel to Christ his life was? The priests and rulers sought to find a charge against Jesus concerning the kingdom. They did not believe that His kingdom is not of this world. The rulers could not find any fault in Him. They tested Him repeatedly on the laws of God and man. Little did they realize that they were testing the Author of the Law. They then appealed to the pride of Pilate and Herod. They thought to put the laws of man above the Law of God. The Law of God leads to life, but the laws of man lead to destruction. Forgive me, Lord, for thinking that my own rules and ideas are above Yours. Your purity magnifies my filth. Cleanse me and fill me with Your Spirit. May I serve You forever. Amen.

# JUNE 27

Dear Friend, Loved by the Faithful Witness,

Now when Daniel knew that the writing was signed, he went home. And in his upper room, and his windows open toward Jerusalem, he knelt down on his knees three times that day, and prayed and gave thanks before his God, as was his custom since early days. Then these men assembled and found Daniel praying and making supplication before his God. And they went before the king, and spoke concerning the king's decree: "Have you not signed a decree that every man who petitions any god or man within thirty days, except you, O king, shall be cast into the den of lions?" The king answered and said, "The thing is true, according to the law of the Medes and Persians, which does not alter."

Daniel 6:10–12

Lord,
Please forgive me for letting the laws and traditions of men alter my belief in and faithfulness to You. I am so weak and selfish. This brings fearfulness. Jesus, You *never* altered Your constant communication with Your Father. You knew full well, there were those who sought to take Your life. Your belief in the Father's love was stronger than anything. You did not waver. Fulfill Your covenant in me. Draw me to Yourself and fill me with Your Spirit. I want to serve You always. Man has largely disregarded Your Law, but I ask You to let it reign supreme in my heart. Forgive me for hiding my belief in You to avoid commotion or conflict. Let me never be ashamed to be seen or heard speaking with or for You. Thank You for being my God! Amen.

# JUNE 28

Dear Friend, Connected with Jesus,

So they answered . . . the king, "That Daniel, who is one of the captives from Judah, does not show due regard for you, O king, or for the decree that you have signed, but makes his petition three times a day." . . . when [the king] heard [this], he was greatly displeased with himself, and set *his* heart on Daniel to deliver him; and he labored until the going down of the sun to deliver him. Then these men . . . said to the king, "Know, O king, that *it is* the law of the Medes and Persians that no decree or statute which the king established may be changed."

Daniel 6:13–15

Lord,

You came not just *for* me, but *as* me. The Babylonian rulers despised Daniel and wished to have his position for themselves. I have despised and rejected my Creator and Savior, wishing that You would do things my way, or essentially, that *my* word would reign. You are indeed a God of longsuffering and grace to forgive my obviously hateful attitudes toward You, the innocent and holy One who has given all for me. Forgive me, Jesus, for despising and rejecting You in exchange for man's approval. Forgive me for trying to improve on Your holy and just laws. May I never be ashamed to call on Your name, and to declare Your sovereign majesty. And Lord, like Darius, I have sold out my friends for my own selfishness and pride. Forgive me for such inexcusable insensitivity. Help me to considerer the consequences of my actions *before* speaking. Amen.

# JUNE 29

Dear Friend, Redeemed by the Lamb,

So the king gave the command, and they brought Daniel and cast *him* into the den of lions. *But* the king spoke, saying to Daniel, "Your God whom you serve continually, He will deliver you." Then a stone was brought and laid at the mouth of the den, and the king sealed it with his own signet ring . . . that the purpose concerning Daniel might not be changed.

Daniel 6:16–17

Lord,

Like Darius, I have gotten myself into difficult situations because of my pride. I have had to choose between saving my own face or saving a friend. Just as King Darius knew Daniel was an innocent man who trusted in You, so Pilate knew that Christ was innocent, although His accusers shouted, "We have a law!" I am Your accuser. O Jesus, how horrible that I judge You by my own standards. Please forgive me for accusing You of evil acts of which You are not guilty. You were condemned to die, and, though innocent, willingly laid down Your life. Daniel was put in a "tomb" with a stone and a seal. You, too, were placed in a tomb, and a seal was put on the stone that men thought would hold You in. But the story does not end there! Your faithfulness is more powerful than death! O hallelujah! Amen.

# June 30

Dear Friend, Loved by the Risen Savior,

Now the king went to his palace and spent the night fasting; and no musicians were brought before him. And his sleep went from him. Then the king arose very early in the morning and went in haste to the den of lions. And when he came to the den, he cried out with a lamenting voice to Daniel . . . "Daniel, servant of the living God, has your God, whom you serve continually, been able to deliver you from the lions?" Then Daniel said to the king, "O king, live forever! My God sent His angel and shut the lions' mouths, so that they have not hurt me, because I was found innocent before Him; and also, O king, I have done no wrong before you." Now the king was exceedingly glad for him, and commanded that they should take Daniel up out of the den. So Daniel was taken . . . out, and no injury whatever was found on him, because he believed in his God.

Daniel 6:18–23

Lord,
Those who believe that Jesus is the Son of God spend many sleepless hours fasting and praying. Mary, like King Darius, arose early and ran to the tomb. The king found Daniel alive and well, protected by the angel of the Lord. Mary found Jesus alive and well, called forth from the tomb. The devil walks about as a roaring lion, seeking whom he may devour. You have proven time and again, Lord, that Satan, the roaring lion, is *no* match for Your loving power . Please help me to remember this when I am tempted. Help me trust wholly in You. May I be found innocent before You. As Daniel was lifted out of the den of lions, may I be lifted out of this pit of sin. Thank You Jesus! Amen.

# JULY 1

Dear Friend, Bride of Christ,

When the Lord began to speak by Hosea, the Lord said to Hosea: "Go, take yourself a wife of harlotry, for the land has committed great harlotry *by departing* from the Lord." So he went and took Gomer the daughter of Diblaim, and she conceived and bore him a son. Then the Lord said to him: "Call his name Jezreel, for in a little *while* I will avenge the blood of Jezreel on the house of Jehu, and bring an end to the kingdom of the house of Israel. "It shall come to pass in that day that I will break the bow of Israel in the valley of Jezreel."

Hosea 1:2–5

Lord,
How desperately You want to sit down and reason with me, but I am so stubborn and set in my own ways. You go to great lengths to show how endless and painfully patient Your love is for me. You used Hosea as an object lesson of how much You love Your adulterous people; how faithful You are to me while I am faithlessly living for myself. The only thing I seem to be willing to do is avenge the blood of my fellow men for Your sake. I am readily available to criticize, bring down, and kill the heart of those who are rejecting You in a more open way than my subtle rejection of Your grace. Father, please fill me with Your redeeming agape love that draws all men to Yourself. Please forgive my adulterous heart that laps up every blessing You lavish on me and ignores You while using these blessings for my own purposes. Thank You for marrying an unfaithful, adulterous harlot like me. My heart longs for You. Amen.

# JULY 2

Dear Friend, Loved by the Everlasting,

And she conceived again and bore a daughter. Then *God* said to him: "Call her name Lo-Ruhamah, for I will no longer have mercy on the house of Israel, but I will utterly take them away. Yet I will have mercy on the house of Judah, will save them by the Lord their God, and will not save them by bow, nor by sword or battle, by horses or horsemen." Now when she had weaned Lo-Ruhamah, she conceived and bore a son. Then *God* said: "Call his name Lo-Ammi, for you *are* not my people, and I will not be your God."

Hosea 1:6–9

Lord,
Please help me to understand the gravity of rejecting You. You don't ever want to leave me or forsake me, but if I determine that I want none of You and want only my own way, as did Israel, then You must, because of my will, leave and forsake me. How painful this is for me does not reflect the even deeper pain that You experience when I reject You. Father, have mercy on me as on the house of Judah. Spare me the final results of my sins. Pull me from the miry clay of my faithless selfishness. Redeem me not through the means of men, but through Jesus and His faith in Your holy promises. I want to be Your child, my Father. I want *You, and You alone*, to be my God. Draw my adulterous heart ever closer to Your pure heart of true and holy love. Amen.

# JULY 3

Dear Friend, Restored by the Lord,

Yet the number of the children of Israel shall be as the sand of the sea, which cannot be measured or numbered; and it shall come to pass, *that* in the place where it was said unto them, Ye *are* not my people, *there* it shall be said unto them, *Ye are* sons of the living God. Then shall the children of Judah and the children of Israel be gathered together, and appoint themselves one head, and they shall come up out of the land: for great *shall be* the day of Jezreel.

Hosea 1:10–11 KJV

Lord,
Your promises never fail. Your everlasting love never wavers. There is no end to the lengths of Your restoring mercy and grace. Though I fail You again and again, though I wallow in the pit of my selfish pride, You patiently woo me back to Yourself with Your sweet, disciplining love. Lord, I can feel the power of Your precious love longing to remove *all* the deadly sin of unbelief from my heart. How desperately You desire to unite Your children under one Head—Jesus Christ. O to be a grain of sand in the sea of Your kingdom! Cleanse me, Father. Fulfill Your covenant in me. Restore Your kingdom in my heart. Reign supreme in every word and deed that comes out of me. Holy Spirit, set up house permanently in my heart. Magnify the Most High through my life. I desire Your redemptive power. Amen.

# JULY 4

Dear Friend, Precious to God,

"Now therefore," says the Lord, "Turn to Me with all your heart, with fasting, and weeping, and with mourning." So rend your heart, and not your garments; return to the Lord your God, for He *is* gracious and merciful, slow to anger, and of great kindness; and He relents from doing harm. Who knows *if* He will turn and relent, and leave a blessing behind Him—a grain offering and a drink offering for the Lord your God?
Joel 2:12–14

Lord,
I am happy to give You my surplus and all the problems I can't solve, but I balk at surrendering my will. Father, cause me to fast and weep and mourn. Let me eat no selfish thoughts. Let my heart be anguished because of the injustice and hate I have had toward You—toward Your perfect will for me. Please forgive me for thinking that You are fooled by my stingy, faithless offerings; as if doing some good things will appease Your true desire for my heart. Were it not for Your sweet graciousness and deep mercy, I would indeed be consumed—consumed by my rancid selfishness in the light of Your loving kindness. Thank You for the countless blessings You shower on an undeserving wretch like me. Amen.

# JULY 5

Dear Friend, Convicted by the Spirit,

Blow the trumpet in Zion, sanctify a fast, call a solemn assembly: Gather the people, sanctify the congregation, assemble the elders, gather the children, and those that suck the breasts: let the bridegroom go forth of his chamber, and the bride out of her closet. Let the priests, the ministers of the LORD, weep between the porch and the altar, and let them say, Spare thy people, O LORD, and give not thine heritage to reproach, that the heathen should rule over them: wherefore should they say among the people, Where *is* their God?

Joel 2:15–17 KJV

Lord,
Your love and Your mercy cannot allow wickedness to continue in this world forever. You have overcome this world, and now the victory is mine. How You long to fulfill that victory in my heart, Jesus! All the well-meaning moral and religious laws established by the land will *never* accomplish what Your Spirit longs to accomplish in my heart. Father, let me gather with those who want to seek You with *all* of their heart. Let me put aside all earthly activity and weep for Your people. Let me fast and pray for Your chosen ministers that they may weep before You and that they may be totally emptied so You may fill them completely. Fulfill Your covenant in me, Lord. Take away my reproach and let me be a banner of Your love and sanctifying power. Cause my life to proclaim, "The Lord is my God! Jesus is my Savior! His Spirit has residence in my heart! Hallelujah!" Amen.

# July 6

Dear Friend, Restored by the Lord,

"Behold, the days are coming," says the Lord, "When the plowman shall overtake the reaper, and the treader of grapes him who sows seed; the mountains shall drip with sweet wine, and all the hills shall flow *with it*. I will bring back the captives of My people Israel; they shall build the waste cities and inhabit *them;* they shall plant vineyards and drink wine from them; they shall also make gardens and eat fruit from them. I will plant them in their land, and no longer shall they be pulled up from the land I have given them," says the Lord Your God.

Amos 9:13–15

Lord,
You are so patient with me. I know You must really long to take this wicked, adulterous heart from me and give me a new, clean, pure heart. Like the children of Israel, I have forsaken You and become a captive of sin. Please fulfill Your covenant in me, Lord. Bring me back to You. Turn the wasted city of my heart and mind into Your habitation. Fill me with the fruit of Your Spirit. I long for the day when You will plant me in the earth made new; the day when all evil, all death, and all sin, will be forever abolished. Come, Lord Jesus. Amen.

# JULY 7

Dear Friend, Child of God,

But upon mount Zion shall be deliverance, and there shall be holiness; and the house of Jacob shall possess their possessions. And the house of Jacob shall be a fire, and the house of Joseph a flame, and the house of Esau for stubble, and they shall kindle in them, and devour them; and there shall be not *any* remaining of the house of Esau; for the LORD hath spoken it.

Obadiah 17–18 KJV

Lord,
The house of Esau are those who have rejected You, and Your beautiful gift of redemption. Esau despised his inheritance. He preferred to be gratified here and now. His descendants refused to help the descendants of his brother, Jacob. The Edomites despised the Israelites and would not help them. Those who hate You refuse to help those who love You. Father, my heart is like Esau's; I am living for myself—which is hate toward Your perfect love for me. Please give me a heart like Jacob's. Let me wrestle with You until You win completely in my heart. Thank You for the deliverance that You provide, Jesus. You deliver me from my selfish chains of sin, as well as from this world. Holy Spirit, please bring Your holiness into my heart. Let Your fire and Your flame burn through my heart and my life. Amen.

# JULY 8

Dear Friend, Loved to the Uttermost,

Then I said, I am cast out of thy sight; yet I will look again toward thy holy temple. The waters compassed me about, *even* to the soul: the depth closed around me round about, weeds were wrapped about my head. I went down to the bottoms of the mountains; the earth with her bars *was* about me for ever: yet hast thou brought up my life from corruption, O LORD my God. When my soul fainted within me I remembered the LORD: and my prayer came in unto thee, into thine holy temple. They that observe lying vanities forsake their own mercy. [9] But I will sacrifice unto thee with the voice of thanksgiving; I will pay that *that* I have vowed. Salvation *is* of the LORD.

Jonah 2:4–9 KJV

Lord,
There is no limit to what You in Your mercy will do to save one of Your children. There is no way to hide from Your tender wooing. Like Jonah, I sometimes think I am actually running away from You—out of sight out of mind, I guess. But I am never out of Your sight or mind or heart, no matter how far I try to run from You. Thank You, Lord, for pursuing me to the very ends and depths of the earth. Thank You for hearing my pitiful prayers and responding with Your miraculous mercy. Salvation is of the Lord. Amen.

# JULY 9

Dear Friend, Redeemed by His Mercy,

Wherewith shall I come before the LORD, *and* bow myself before the high God? shall I come before him with burnt offerings, with calves a year old? Will the Lord be pleased with thousands of rams, *or* with ten thousands of rivers of oil? shall I give my firstborn *for* my transgression, the fruit of my body *for* the sin of my soul? He hath shewed thee, O man, what *is* good; and what doeth the LORD require of thee, but to do justly, and to love mercy, and to walk humbly with thy God?

Micah 6:6–8 KJV

Lord,
Forgive me for offering You tithes and offerings of money, time in church activities, devotional time squeezed into a few rushed minutes or cut short by the fact that I've gone to sleep, items for charity drives, and all the other things I think I so graciously offer. These are all too often an attempt to ease a conscience that is being wooed by the Spirit. Giving You things while holding on to my heart is not good for You or for me. Jesus, You have shown me what is good—a heart transformation that truly understands and believes in Your justice and mercy; a humble heart that is totally surrendered to Your ways. Take my heart as an offering. It is the most broken and messed up thing I have, but it is what You want most. Redeem it for Yourself. Live Your life in me. Amen.

# JULY 10

Dear Friend, Loved by the Everlasting,

The Lord *is* good, a stronghold in the day of trouble; and He knows those who trust in Him. But with an overflowing flood He will make an utter end of its place, and darkness will pursue His enemies. What do you conspire against the Lord? He will make an utter end of *it*. Affliction will not rise up a second time. For while tangled *like* thorns, and while drunken *like* drunkards, they shall be devoured like stubble fully dried.

Nahum 1:7–10

Lord,
You will never forsake those who put their trust in You. Though it would seem that the whole world forsakes You, there are always those who stand as witnesses of Your everlasting power and love. Fulfill Your covenant in me, Lord. Let me walk in Your Light and in Your faith. As Judah longed for the day when You would utterly destroy their enemy, so I long for the day when You will come and put an end to the wickedness of this world. I long for the day when You will come and claim Your faithful children. How beautiful will be the day when You cleanse this old earth with fire and utterly consume and eternally end sin. You will not allow affliction to rise a second time. Jesus, be my stronghold in these days of trouble. Be my Shield and Protector while the enemy still rages against You. Thank You for being the Redeemer of my heart and for being the Redeemer of this sin-sick world. Amen.

# JULY 11

Dear Friend, Witness of the True Witness,

Thus says the Lord: "Though *they are* safe, and likewise many, yet in this manner they will be cut down when he passes through. Though I have afflicted you, I will afflict you no more; For now I will break off his yoke from you, and burst your bonds apart." The Lord has given a command concerning you: "Your name shall be perpetuated no longer. Out of the house of your gods I will cut off the carved image and the molded image. I will dig your grave, for you are vile." Behold, on the mountains the feet of him who brings good tidings, who proclaims peace! O Judah, keep your appointed feasts, perform your vows. For the wicked one shall no more pass through you; he is utterly cut off.
Nahum 1:12–15

Lord,
When people cry "peace and safety," then shall sudden destruction and the end come. Now, as in Ninevah, there is a false security among many. The majority trample the minority to further their own cause. But You will not allow this to go on forever. When all have heard Your gospel of peace declared and all have chosen to claim Your free gift of salvation or reject it, You will allow wickedness to perpetuate no longer. You long to burst the bonds of sin from our hearts. I know the destruction of the wicked is painful to You. You sent Jonah to Ninevah to alert them to their chosen destiny of destruction. They heeded Your pleas but for a hundred years. Father, let my feet bring good tidings and proclaim the peace that trust in You brings. Cause me to live as a faithful one. You do not delight in the destruction of the wicked. Amen.

# JULY 12

Dear Friend, Cared for by the Father,

But the Lord *is* in His holy temple: let all the earth keep silence before him.
Habakkuk 2:20 KJV

Lord,

You are holy. You are the Almighty, Omnipotent Creator. You are my Savior and my King. Jesus, You are in Your holy temple. You are now interceding for me. Fulfill Your covenant in me. Let me keep silent before You. Please speak and let me listen. Let me hold my peace and stop asking for things I know You do not wish for me. May I just halt the rationalizations right now. Please keep me silent while *You* speak through me. Work Your work in me. Cleanse Your temple, and cleanse me, a temple for You. Cleanse my body, mind, and spirit. I stand in silent awe of Your love. Amen.

# JULY 13

Dear Friend, Redeemed by the Lamb,

"Therefore wait for Me," says the Lord, "Until the day I rise up for plunder; My determination is to gather the nations to My assembly of kingdoms, to pour on them My indignation, all My fierce anger; all the earth shall be devoured with the fire of My jealousy. For then I will restore to the peoples a pure language, that they may all call on the name of the Lord, to serve Him with one accord. From beyond the rivers of Ethiopia My worshippers, the daughters of My dispersed ones, shall bring My offering."

Zephaniah 3:8–10

Lord,
What a relief is Your promise that You will not leave this earth as it is, to continue forever. Your anger, the part of Your loving character that abhors evil, will meet those who reject You face to face. How sad that they will be consumed by Your very presence. How tragic is the future for those who reject Your mercy. How uplifting is Your promise that You will restore Your people. How I long for the company of those who call on Your name. Jesus, I know that You, by Your Spirit, are even now at work in my heart, restoring my soul to you, purifying my language. I bring my humble and pathetic offering, my wounded heart, to You. Take me, Lord. Let me serve Your purpose in this wicked world. In Jesus' name I plead. Amen.

# JULY 14

Dear Friend, Healed by the Great Physician,

In that day you shall not be shamed for any of your deeds in which you transgress against Me; for then I will take away from your midst those who rejoice in your pride, and you shall no longer be haughty in My holy mountain. I will leave in your midst a meek and humble people, and they shall trust in the name of the Lord. The remnant of Israel shall do no unrighteousness and speak no lies, nor shall a deceitful tongue be found in their mouths; for they shall feed *their* flocks and lie down, and no one shall make *them* afraid.

                                                          Zephaniah 3:11–13

Lord,

You will fulfill Your promise to restore the earth; to give it as an inheritance to the children of Abraham—all who believe in You, as Abraham did. You will cleanse the earth with fire and make all things new. It is my heart's desire, and choice to be among those who believe Your righteous sacrifice of Your Son. I believe that Christ's blood covers me. You have buried my transgressions deeper than the deepest sea. Fulfill Your covenant in me, Lord. Cleanse every selfish desire and ugly spot from my heart. Cause me to be meek and humble before You and before all men. Sanctify my life; purify my tongue. Fill me with Your perfect love that casts out all fear. Amen.

## JULY 15

Dear Friend, Temple of the Lord,

Then the word of the Lord came by Haggai the prophet, saying, "*Is it* time for you yourselves to dwell in paneled houses, and this temple *to lie* in ruins?" Now therefore, thus says the Lord of hosts: "Consider your ways! You have sown much, and bring in little; you eat, but do not have enough; you drink, but you are not filled with drink; you clothe yourselves, but no one is warm; and he who earns wages, earns wages to put into a bag with holes." Thus says the Lord of hosts: "Consider your ways!"

Haggai 1:3–7

Lord,

I have been trying to make a place for myself in this world so You can use me. I have filled myself with the education and traditions of men so that I can serve You better. What an insult! My Jesus, *I am so sorry*! Please forgive me for neglecting Your temple of my heart. I am very busy trying to accomplish good things, and I do not know You better. I eat like a glutton and do not even have the energy to do the things I like. I do not eat the Bread of Life. I drink, but I thirst from polluted drink because I do not drink the Water of Life. It is not the body that needs to be beautiful, but the heart. I clothe myself with socially acceptable habits, and there is no warm peace in my heart. Money comes, and money goes, and I have no treasure in heaven. Father, it is past time to build Your temple in my heart. Let me seek You first, and only. Amen.

# JULY 16

Dear Friend, Freed by the King of kings,

Rejoice greatly, O daughter of Zion! Shout, O daughter of Jerusalem! Behold, your King is coming to you; He *is* just and having salvation, lowly and riding on a donkey, a colt, the foal of a donkey.

Zechariah 9:9

Lord,

How beautiful was Jesus' entry into Jerusalem that Sunday, one week before His resurrection. Most heroes, who rode in triumph through the streets, were surrounded by bound captives, but not Jesus! He was surrounded by those whom He had set free from captivity—those who had been set free from disease of the body, mind, and spirit. Freely, they proclaimed Jesus as their King. What a foretaste of Christ's return. You will come, Lord Jesus, riding on a white horse in all Your glory and majesty! You will gather those whom You have freed from the bondage of sin. I claim You as my King. I claim the freedom from the bondage of sin that you give. Lord, O how I long for Your return! Amen.

# JULY 17

Dear Friend, Redeemed by the Lamb,

And I will pour upon the house of David, and upon the inhabitants of Jerusalem, the spirit of grace and of supplications: and they shall look upon me whom they have pierced, and they shall mourn for him, as one mourneth for *his* only *son*, and shall be in bitterness for him, as one that is in bitterness for *his* firstborn.

Zechariah 12:10 KJV

Lord,
Pour on me Your spirit of grace and supplication. Fill me with true repentance for the grief and heartache that I have caused You. You have loved me so much that You have willingly allowed me to kill You with my selfish arrogant unbelief. Jesus, only when I truly realize my evil, sin-sick condition, can You complete Your healing work in me. You *long* to heal me. Cleanse my soul. Fill me with Your spirit of grace and supplication. May I plead for my fellow man as You have pled for me. May I treat my fellow man as You treat me. I cannot do this on my own. Fill me now. Thank you, Jesus. Amen.

# JULY 18

Dear Friend, Friend of Jesus,

And *one* shall say unto him, What *are* these wounds in thine hands? Then he shall answer, *Those* with which I was wounded *in* the house of my friends.

Zechariah 13:6 KJV

Lord,

I have mortally wounded You, and You have called me Your friend. Who can explain such love? You, my absolutely guiltless Creator and Savior, took all my selfish hate, my arrogant sins, upon Yourself to free me eternally from my pride-ridden self. The wounds in Your hands and feet and side will ever remind me of a most costly and precious everlasting love. There are those who do not know You who will be utterly amazed at the length and height, and breadth and depth of Your agape love. You have stopped at nothing, Jesus, to reveal the heart of the Father to His erring children. O how I praise You for Your agape love! What a Friend we have in Jesus! O what an incredible, dear, sweet Friend! Hallelujah! Amen.

## JULY 19

Dear Friend, Rescued by the Almighty,

Behold, I will send my messenger, and he shall prepare the way before me: and the Lord, whom ye seek, shall suddenly come to his temple, even the messenger of the covenant, whom ye delight in: behold, he shall come, saith the LORD of hosts. But who may abide the day of his coming? and who shall stand when he appeareth? for he *is* like a refiner's fire, and like fullers' soap. And he shall sit *as* a refiner and a purifier of silver: and he shall purify the sons of Levi, and purge them as gold and silver, that they may offer unto the LORD an offering in righteousness.

Malachi 3:1–3 KJV

Lord,
Just as You sent John the Baptist to prepare the way for Your first coming, so also You will be sure the way is prepared for Your second coming. How anxious You are to come to Your temple! I am Your temple, Lord. I long for You to dwell in me eternally. But, O I am so impure and dirty. I cannot stand unless You refine me as silver and gold. You will be the Goldsmith who lets me heat up with trials so that my impurities come to the surface. You will be the One who lovingly scoops my impurities off. You will not let me scorch, but You will fill me with the faith to face increasing heat under Your watch-care. Jesus, scrub my filthy heart clean with Your soap of righteousness. Make me shine like a golden offering of righteousness. Amen.

# JULY 20

Dear Friend, Loved by the Changeless One,

Then shall the offering of Judah and Jerusalem be pleasant unto the LORD, as in the days of old, and as in former years. And I will come near to you to judgment; and I will be a swift witness against the sorcerers, and against the adulterers, and against false swearers, and against those that oppress the hireling in *his* wages, the widow, and the fatherless, and that turn aside the stranger *from his right,* and fear not me, saith the LORD of hosts. For I *am* the Lord, I change not; therefore ye sons of Jacob are not consumed. Even from the days of your fathers ye are gone away from mine ordinances, and have not kept *them*. Return unto me, and I will return unto you, saith the LORD of hosts. But ye said, Wherein shall we return?

Malachi 3:4–7 KJV

Lord,

Thank You for making my life an acceptable offering to You. You care deeply about Your children. You are offended when I am offended. No one practices sorcery or adultery, perjury or usury or discrimination without Your notice. You will call each into account. No one can stand before You except he be in Christ. Thank You for determining before the foundation of the world to save me. Thank You for never changing. Please forgive me for ignoring Your covenant and all the beautiful promises that are included in it. Please forgive me for barging off into my own misery. Father, let me return to You to be cleansed and renewed. Rebuild my heart. Show me how to return fully to You. Amen.

# JULY 21

Dear Friend, Blessed by the Lord,

"Will a man rob God? Yet you have robbed Me! But you say, 'In what way have we robbed you?' In tithes and offerings. You are cursed with a curse, for you have robbed Me, *even* this whole nation. Bring all the tithes into the storehouse, that there may be food in My house, and try Me in this," says the Lord of hosts, "If I will not open for you the windows of heaven and pour out for you *such* blessing that *there will* not *be room* enough to *receive it*."

Malachi 3:8–10

Lord,

Please forgive me for robbing You. I have not given You so much as a tenth of my time, my will, or my unbelieving heart. I have given to You my junk as an offering—my problems, my spare time, and my complaints. I return money but not my heart. I have robbed You of the joy You have when I allow You to take care of me. Please help me to give You all that I am that there may be the food of rejoicing in Your house. Let me try You. Lord, I know that You are anxious to cover me with Your precious blessings if and when I will ever let You. Father, I ask for forgiveness and restoration not just for myself, but because *we* have robbed You, even this whole nation. Please forgive our selfish, arrogant wastefulness of the resources that are truly Yours. You are everything! Everything we have, every breath we enjoy, is Yours. Please take it for Your honor and glory. Amen.

# July 22

Dear Friend, Brother/Sister of Christ,

The book of the genealogy of Jesus Christ, the Son of David, the Son of Abraham: Abraham begot Isaac, Isaac begot Jacob, and Jacob begot Judah and his brothers. Judah begot Perez and Zerah by Tamar, Perez begot Hezron, and Hezron begot Ram. Ram begot Amminadab, Amminadab begot Nahshon, and Nahshon begot Salmon. Salmon begot Boaz by Rahab, Boaz begot Obed by Ruth, Obed begot Jesse, and Jesse begot David the king, David the king begot Solomon by her *who had been the wife of* Uriah.

Matthew 1:1–6 KJV

Lord,

When I look at the earthly, human lineage that You chose to come through, I am amazed. Abraham and Isaac disbelieved You and lied about their wives in Egypt. Jacob was outright deceitful. Judah was despicable. Rahab was a harlot. David was a murderer and adulterer. Solomon married more heathen wives than he could sleep with in a year's time. When I look further down the genealogy I see Manasseh, the worst king Israel ever had. Jesus, these are the earthly roots and heritage You chose for Yourself. You have indeed proven that God is greater than all sin—even "hereditary sin." Thank You for making the way plain. I want to be like You. Help me to remember that Your strength is far greater than my sinful human tendencies. Amen.

# JULY 23

Dear Friend, Infinitely Loved,

Now the birth of Jesus Christ was on this wise: When as his mother Mary was espoused to Joseph, before they came together, she was found with child of the Holy Ghost. Then Joseph her husband, being a just *man*, and not willing to make her a publick example, was minded to put her away privily. But while he thought on these things, behold, the angel of the Lord appeared unto him in a dream, saying, Joseph, thou son of David, fear not to take unto thee Mary thy wife: for that which is conceived of her is of the Holy Ghost.

Matthew 1:18–20 KJV

Lord,
I cannot fathom how, not to mention why, You, God, remained God, yet became fully human and entered into the body of a virgin. Mary must have been absolutely astounded at the thought of carrying God Himself in her womb. In this day and age unplanned for and unwanted babies are discarded before birth. O Jesus! Forgive me for wanting to discard You before I even know who You really are. I nearly spiritually discarded myself before I could be born again. Help me to always accept everyone in every situation. You never discard Your children. Thank You Holy Spirit for putting Christ in me, filling my heart with His faith and righteousness. What a beautiful, beautiful Gift! Amen.

## JULY 24

Dear Friend, Daughter/Son of God,

And she shall bring forth a son, and thou shalt call his name JESUS: for he shall save his people from their sins. Now all this was done, that it might be fulfilled which was spoken of the Lord by the prophet, saying, Behold, a virgin shall be with child, and she shall bring forth a son, and they shall call his name Emmanuel, which being interpreted is, God with us. Then Joseph being raised from sleep did as the angel of the Lord had bidden him, and took unto him his wife: And knew her not till she had brought forth her firstborn son: and he called his name JESUS.

Matthew 1:21–25 KJV

Lord,

How beautiful! You were willing to come into a simple, willing woman with no advantages—for her or for You. You spoke of Your appearing through Your prophets long ago. You came through a sinful human like me. How beautiful! You came as Immanuel—God with us. How You long to be with us. Since we are not eager to come to You, You have come to us because You desire more than anything to be with us. Your desire is so strong that it caused You to walk away from your heavenly throne and become one with Your fallen creatures—anything to help me know beyond a shadow of a doubt how deeply and eternally You love me. Jesus, please give me the faith and grace to trust You *all* the time and *all* the way. Thank You so much for Your awesome gift of becoming us so we can be with You. How beautiful! How beautiful! How beautiful! Amen.

# July 25

Dear Friend, Loved of the Father,

Blessed *are* the poor in spirit: for theirs is the kingdom of heaven. Blessed *are* they that mourn: for they shall be comforted. Blessed *are* the meek: for they shall inherit the earth. Blessed *are* they which do hunger and thirst after righteousness: for they shall be filled.

Matthew 5:3–6 KJV

Lord,
Thank You for letting my spirit feel its true poorness, otherwise I would arrogantly ignore my desperate need for You. Thank You for a spirit of mourning, for now I more clearly see my drastic, pathetic condition and realize how You must mourn for Your erring children. Thank You for the comfort You give my hurting heart. Father, please make me meek like Jesus. Let me not grapple for an inheritance in this earth for Your kingdom is not of this world, and I so want to be with You. Fill my hungering and thirsting soul with Your righteousness. Thank You for the hunger and thirst that draw me to You and Your well-spring of righteousness. Thank You for promising to fill me. Amen.

# JULY 26

Dear Friend, Daughter/Son of God,

Blessed *are* the merciful: for they shall obtain mercy. Blessed *are* the pure in heart: for they shall see God. Blessed *are* the peacemakers: for they shall be called the children of God. Blessed are they which are persecuted for righteousness' sake: for theirs is the kingdom of heaven. Blessed are ye, when *men* shall revile you, and persecute *you*, and shall say all manner of evil against you falsely, for my sake.

Matthew 5:7–11 KJV

Lord,
Thank You for Your mercy. If it were not for Your mercy, I would be forever lost. Fulfill Your covenant in me. Make me pure that I may see You clearly and reflect You perfectly. Thank You for the eternal peace that Your forgiveness and cleansing love give. Fill me with Your Spirit of peace. Let me never be the source of contention. O to be worthy of being so like You that I am persecuted as You were and reflect the Father as You did. Thank You, too, for this blessing, that others may see a glimpse of You. May I reflect the character of Jesus, for Jesus' sake. Thank You for Your awesome blessings! Amen.

# JULY 27

Dear Friend, Child of God,

Ye are the salt of the earth: but if the salt have lost his savour, wherewith shall it be salted? It is henceforth good for nothing, but to be cast out, and to be trodden under foot by men. Ye are the light of the world. A city that is set on a hill cannot be hid. Neither do men light a candle, and put it under a bushel, but on a candlestick; and it giveth light unto all that are in the house. Let your light so shine before men, that they may see your good works, and glorify your Father, which is in heaven.

Matthew 5:13–16 KJV

Lord,

I well know that salt with no salty flavor is useless. So, a Christian with no flavor of Christ is also useless. Father, use me to bring out the beautiful godly flavors in others, as salt brings out the natural flavors in foods. Help me to not be overbearing, like too much salt that makes a person gag. Jesus, *You* are the true Light of the world. Shine through me to those near and far. Empty me and wash me of anything that would color or tint Your true light. Let everything I do reflect You, honor You, and glorify You, my magnificent and loving Father in heaven. I love You. Use me. Take *all* of me. Thank You, in Jesus' Name, Amen.

# July 28

Dear Friend, Purchased of God,

Think not that I am come to destroy the law, or the prophets: I am not come to destroy, but to fulfill. For verily I say unto you, Till heaven and earth pass, one jot or one tittle shall in no wise pass from the law, till all be fulfilled. Whosoever therefore shall break one of the least commandments, and shall teach men so, he shall be called least in the kingdom of heaven: but whosoever shall do and teach *them*, the same shall be called great in the kingdom of heaven.

Matthew 5:17–19 KJV

Lord,
Forgive me for separating Your mission from Your prophecies and Your law. Jesus, You are *the same* yesterday, today, and forever. Your law is but a reflection of Your character of love; a love that knows no bounds, a love that caused You to sacrifice Your very Self for those who disregard Your law — Your character of love. Father, help me to remember that Your laws are but *one* statement of love. Breaking one breaks all. Unbelief is what breaks Your law. Renew my unbelieving heart, Lord. Fulfill Your law in me. Amen.

# July 29

Dear Friend, Disciple of Christ,

After this manner therefore pray ye: Our Father which art in heaven, Hallowed be thy name. Thy kingdom come. Thy will be done in earth, as *it is* in heaven. Give us this day our daily bread. [12] And forgive us our debts, as we forgive our debtors. And lead us not into temptation, but deliver us from evil: For thine is the kingdom, and the power, and the glory, for ever. Amen.

Matthew 6:9–13 KJV

Lord,

Thank You for teaching me how to pray. Thank You for the Holy Spirit who interprets my feeble prayers. You alone are holy and worthy to be praised. Let your kingdom come into my heart. May Your will be done in every thought and every word that I utter. Give me the Bread of Life—the spiritual strength I need to glorify You today. Father, put Your forgiveness in my heart that I might forgive others as You forgive. Guide my choices, Lord, that I might not set myself up for disaster for you are God of the universe. Your word is power. May You be glorified forever. Amen.

# JULY 30

Dear Friend, Daughter/Son of the King,

But seek ye first the kingdom of God, and His righteousness; and all these things shall be added unto you. Take therefore no thought for the morrow: for the morrow shall take thought for the things of itself. Sufficient unto the day *is* the evil thereof.

Matthew 6:33–34 KJV

Lord,

Please give me the grace to put You *first* in my life. May I spend my day focused and rejoicing in Your goodness. May my heart sing your promise in Matthew 6 all day and through the night. Father, You love me more than tongue can tell. Thank You for that! Fill me with Your righteousness. Fill me with Your perfect love and Your faith—a love that casts out all fear and a faith that expels every doubt. Wake me in the morning with Your holy presence. Guide my every thought, word, and action throughout the day. Let me lay down in peace at night, knowing I have spent the *whole* day with You. Let me rest in Your loving protection. I am Yours, Lord Jesus. Please reign supreme in my heart. Thank You. Amen.

# JULY 31

Dear Friend, Loved by the Word,

The Centurion answered and said, "Lord, I am not worthy that Thou should come under my roof, but speak only a word, and my servant will be healed. For I also am a man under authority, having soldiers under me. And I say to this *one,* 'Go,' and he goes; and to another, 'Come,' and he comes; and to my servant, 'Do this,' and he does it." When Jesus heard it, He marveled, and said to those who followed, "Assuredly, I say to you, I have not found such great faith, not even in Israel!"

Matthew 8:8–10

Lord,

O to have the faith of the centurion—faith the size of a mustard seed! You are the Word. I need *You and You only.* Forgive me, Lord, for turning to plans and routines, fads and fashions, pills and potions instead of to You, the Master Creator and Healer. I need You to heal my unbelieving heart. Please keep me focused on You. Turn my eyes and my heart away from the world's proclaimed solutions, and focus my gaze upon You. I am nothing. *You are everything!* I believe Your Word accomplishes what it says, as it is said. I believe in Your healing Word. Speak, Lord, Your servant hears and believes! Amen.

# AUGUST 1

Dear Friend, Cherished by the Father,

And do not fear those who kill the body but cannot kill the soul. But rather fear him who is able to destroy both soul and body in hell. Are not two sparrows sold for a copper coin? And not one of them falls to the ground apart from your Father's will. But the very hairs of your head are all numbered. [31] Do not fear therefore; you are of more value than many sparrows.

Matthew 10:28–31

Lord,

I worry for my body that is but dust and let my soul be influenced by the devil and his schemes. Forgive me for being so petty and selfish. Please protect me from the enemy who tries at every pass to destroy my soul, though I live many years on this earth. Thank you for caring so dearly for the sparrows. How precious to me that You care so tenderly! Fulfill Your covenant in me. Replace my fear with the faith of Jesus. May I allow You to guard my soul from the temptations that I don't even see as temptation. Truly You know what is best for me, and You know me far better than I know myself. Hallelujah! Amen.

# AUGUST 2

Dear Friend, Child of God,

Come to Me, all *you* who labor and are heavy laden, and I will give you rest. Take My yoke upon you and learn from Me, for I am gentle and lowly in heart, and you will find rest for your souls. For My yoke *is* easy and My burden is light.

Matthew 11:28–30

Lord,

I have long labored with my many sins and unholy habits. I have determined to buck up and overcome time and again. I desperately need the beautiful rest that You give. I am weary body, mind, and spirit. I surrender all. Fulfill Your covenant in me. May I learn more of Your meek and lowly heart. Let me humble myself to Your easy yoke. I need to let You take the lead. You have humbled Yourself to far greater depths to bare my burden for me. Let me learn of You—let me continually dwell on Your love for me. I rest wholly in You. Thank You for the beautiful rest You give to my sin-sick soul. Amen.

# AUGUST 3

Dear Friend, Miracle of God,

Then the Pharisees and Sadducees came, and testing Him asked that He would show them a sign from Heaven. He answered and said to them, "When it is evening you say, '*It will be* fair weather, for the sky is red;' And in the morning, '*It will be* foul weather today, for the sky is red and threatening.' Hypocrites! You know how to discern the face of the sky, but you cannot *discern* the signs of the times. A wicked and adulterous generation seeks after a sign, and no sign shall be given to it except the sign of the prophet Jonah." And He left them and departed.

Matthew 16:1–4

Lord,
Forgive me for ever doubting You. Signs of Your holy, creative, and redemptive power are everywhere. Nature cries out with the beauty of Your handiwork. Stems that grow new flowers, plants that regrow fruits and vegetables after picking, worms that regrow another half after being severed—there are innumerable signs in nature. I see You working in my life continuously. You are the Messiah! As Jonah was in the depths of the earth for three days, You, too, were in the depths for three days. And as sure as the great fish spit Jonah out on dry land, You came forth from the grave victorious. I *know* You are working in my life! Thank You so much for what You are doing in me! Amen.

# AUGUST 4

Dear Friend, Loved by the Shepherd,

What do you think? If a man has a hundred sheep, and one of them goes astray, does he not leave the ninety-nine and go to the mountains to seek the one that is straying? And if he should find it, assuredly I say to you, he rejoices more over that *sheep* than over the ninety-nine that did not go astray. Even so it is not the will of your Father who is in heaven that one of these little ones should perish.

Matthew 18:12–14

Lord,
I am Your precious little lamb. You are the Good Shepherd. Of all the universe, of worlds You have created, this earth has gone astray. Yet You left the angels in heaven, the whole universe, and Your perfect communion with the Father and the Spirit. You left Your beautiful throne behind to seek out and save the likes of me. And all heaven rejoices when I let You carry me back to Your loving fold. Thank you for willing that every one of us be saved. I love You, my beautiful and loving omnipotent Shepherd. Hallelujah! Praise Your Name! Amen.

# AUGUST 5

Dear Friend, Daughter/Son of God,

So Jesus answered and said to them, "Assuredly I say to you, if you have faith and do not doubt, you will not only do what was done to the fig tree, but also if you say to this mountain, 'be removed and be cast into the sea,' it will be done. And whatever things you ask in prayer, believing, you will receive."

Matthew 21:21–22

Lord,

I need *true* faith. I need that kind of faith that believes the absolute impossible with no ifs, ands, or buts—the kind of faith that believes that You will do exactly as You say; the kind of faith that fully embraces every single one of Your promises and believes that they *are* accomplished, just as You say, whether I see it or not. I need faith that asks only for the things that You desire, and never my will. Lord, I need a faith that is not a feeling. Forgive me for praying for things that down in my heart I don't believe you will give me. Forgive me for trying to answer my own prayers. Father, I ask for a complete belief and trust in Your power and love. Thank you for answering. In Jesus Name, Amen.

# AUGUST 6

Dear Friend, Loved by the Burden Bearer,

Then He said to them, "My soul is exceedingly sorrowful, even to death. Stay here and watch with Me." He went a little farther and fell on His face, and prayed, saying, "O My Father, if it is possible, let this cup pass from Me; nevertheless, not as I will, but as You *will*." Then He came to the disciples and found them sleeping, and said to Peter, "What? Could you not watch with Me for one hour? Watch and pray, lest you enter into temptation. The spirit is indeed willing, but the flesh *is* weak." Again, a second time, He went away and prayed, saying, "O My Father, if this cup cannot pass away from Me unless I drink it, Your will be done." And He came and found them asleep again, for their eyes were heavy. So He left them, went away again, and prayed the third time, saying the same words.

Matthew 26:38–44

Lord,
Forgive me, my Savior! I am that sleepy disciple who denied You three times. I sleep when I should be watching. O Jesus, forgive me for crushing Your precious heart. What horrible agony You went through, what anguish of heart and soul. You did not want to go to the cross, but You were willing. You confirmed that three times. You were willing to be eternally separated from Your Father, that I might be eternally reunited. Jesus, I don't want to take up my cross. My spirit is willing, but my flesh is terribly weak—I sleep instead of watching. Help me to take up my cross daily. Help me to willingly bear the mental anguish of denying self. Separate my faith from my feelings as You did in Gethsemane. Amen.

# AUGUST 7

Dear Friend, Purchased of God,

Now the chief priests, the elders, and all the council sought false testimony against Jesus to put Him to death, but found none. Even though many false witnesses came forward, they found none. But at last two false witnesses came forward and said, "This *fellow* said, 'I am able to destroy the temple of God and to build it in three days.'" And the high priest arose and said unto Him, "Do You answer nothing? What *is it* that these men testify against You?" But Jesus kept silent. And the High Priest answered and said unto Him, "I put You under oath by the living God: tell us if You are the Christ, the Son of God!"

Matthew 26:59–63

Lord,

Please forgive me for believing the lies the devil has spread about You. From the time of the Garden of Eden, Satan has sold his lies to the inhabitants of this earth. It must be very painful to be so misquoted and misrepresented. Your body was a temple that You allowed me to destroy to purchase my redemption. You were raised on the third day. You did not argue with those who only wanted to condemn You. You have been revealing Your identity and the Father's love for us all along. Why, Lord, am I still not getting it? Please remove my unbelief, and help me to believe that You are the One who can remove sin and death from my life. You are Christ. You most certainly are the Son of God. Amen.

## AUGUST 8

Dear Friend, Loved by the Son,

Jesus said to him, *"It is as* you said. Nevertheless, I say to you, hereafter you will see the Son of Man sitting at the right hand of the Power, and coming on the clouds of heaven." Then the high priest tore his clothes saying, "He has spoken blasphemy! What further need do we have of witnesses? Look, now you have heard His blasphemy! "What do you think?" They answered and said, "He is deserving of death." Then they spat in His face and beat Him; and others struck *Him* with the palms of their hands, saying, "Prophesy to us, Christ! Who is the one who struck You?"

Matthew 26:64–68

Lord,
You are God. You are holy. You are almighty. Yet, You have forever identified Yourself with me because You love me so deeply. You have promised to come again in the clouds with all Your majesty. Please forgive me for not believing that You are the beautiful God You say You are. You loved me, and I deemed You worthy of death. Please forgive me for mocking You. Please forgive me for spitting in Your face by rejecting and ignoring my fellow man. Please forgive me for beating You with my unbelief and striking You with my selfish desires. I love You for what You have done for me. I am nothing. *You are everything*! Amen.

# AUGUST 9

Dear Friend, Freed by the Son,

Now at the feast the governor was accustomed to releasing to the multitude one prisoner whom they wished. And at that time they had a notorious prisoner called Barabbas. Therefore, when they had gathered together, Pilate said to them, "Whom do you want me to release to you? Barabbas or Jesus who is called Christ?" For he knew that they had handed Him over because of envy. While he was sitting on the judgment seat, his wife sent to him, saying, "Have nothing to do with that just Man, for I have suffered many things today in a dream because of Him." But the chief priests and elders persuaded the multitudes that they should ask for Barabbas and destroy Jesus.

Matthew 27:15–20

Lord,

I am Barabbas, son of Papa. I am a condemned criminal. I have sinned against You. I deserve death. I have disbelieved Your promises and snubbed Your care for me. I have handed You over to be crucified because of envy; I prefer myself (my way) over You. Jesus, Your love is a rare and mysterious beauty. I, a guilty sinner, have been set free, while You, an innocent Man, have been put to death. How did Barabbas feel? Did he run away and not look back? Or did he watch You die in amazed awe and stunned wonder? And what about Pilate and his wife? O Lord, I can see that I am all of these. Let me follow You wherever You go, no matter what others do or say. Forgive me, Jesus. Thank You for Your love. Amen.

# AUGUST 10

Dear Friend, Covered by the Lamb,

The governor answered and said to them, "Which of the two do you want me to release to you?" They said, "Barabbas!" Pilate said to them, "What then shall I do with Jesus who is called Christ?" *They* all said to him, "Let Him be crucified!" Then the governor said, "Why, what evil has He done?" But they cried out all the more, saying, "Let Him be crucified!" When Pilate saw that he could not prevail at all, but rather *that* a tumult was rising, he took water and washed *his* hands before the multitude, saying, "I am innocent of the blood of this just Person. You *see to it.*" And all the people answered and said, "His blood *be* on us and on our children." Then he released Barabbas to them; and when he had scourged Jesus, he delivered *Him* to be crucified.

Matthew 27:21–26

Lord,

You have never done anything evil. You have an amazing, unexplainable love that allows you to let Your creatures mock and spit on You, and crucify You. I am not innocent *of* Your blood but *by* it. You have taken the curse of sin for me. You have suffered an eternal death. You could not see through the portals of the tomb when You surrendered Your life on the cross. Only because You are a perfect and holy God could You rise from a death that will be eternal to everyone else who suffers it. I am Barabbas, worthy of death. You, my spotless Savior, died as me, while I looked on in horrified astonishment. I accept the sacrifice You made as me. You are the worthy Lamb slain from the foundation of the world to purchase my redemption. Thank You. Hallelujah! Amen.

# AUGUST 11

Dear Friend, Disciple of Christ,

And Jesus came and spoke to them saying, "All authority has been given to Me in heaven and on earth. Go therefore and make disciples of all the nations, baptizing them in the name of the Father and of the Son and of the Holy Spirit, teaching them to observe all things that I have commanded you; and lo, I am with you always, *even* to the end of the age." Amen.

Matthew 28:18–20

Lord,

Thank you for permission! Thank You for the awesome privilege of sharing Your love with others. I long to be used to clarify and glorify Your perfect character! May the whole earth know that the Father, Son, and Holy Spirit are One in their matchless, eternal faithfulness for us. Thank You for Your promise that You are with us always. Jesus, You are with us through Your own experience as a Man. No one in heaven or earth understands as You do. You understand far better than humanity what it is to fully trust in the Father's love and grace. Thank You for showing the way to a heart free from the deathly clutches of sin. Live out Your life through me. Amen.

# AUGUST 12

Dear Friend, Disciple of Christ,

Then Jesus said to them, "Follow Me, and I will make you to become fishers of men." They immediately left their nets and followed Him.

Mark 1:17–18

Lord,

I want to forsake all, and follow You. Nothing else is really worth following. I want to be a "fisher of men," sharing the gospel with everyone. With Your unfailing love and grace as a lure, no one will fail to notice Your sweet character. Lord, use me to catch hearts for Yourself. Please forgive me for fishing with my own lure; I have deceived many about Your precious character. Spare them, Father. Never let me be the cause of a drowning soul. Use me to save my fellow human beings. Use me to declare Your majesty to the universe. Give me the faith and the grace to follow You in the way that You have asked me to. Amen.

# AUGUST 13

Dear Friend, Disciple of Christ,

Then he said, "To what shall we liken the kingdom of God? Or with what parable shall we picture it? *It* is like a mustard seed which, when it is sown in the ground, is smaller than all the seeds on the earth; but when it is sown, it grows up and becomes greater than all the herbs, and shoots out large branches, so that the birds of the air may nest under its shade."

Mark 4:30–32

Lord,

You have said that the kingdom of God is not just a place but that it is within Your children. Father, I want an open and willing heart that is good soil for planting Your kingdom. Sow the mustard seed of Your precious love and faith in my heart. Let me grow tall and strong in Your ways. May Your gospel of love and peace spring forth in every direction from me. Use me, Holy Spirit, like protective branches that people can come to, to rest and learn more of You. May all who come near me feel relief in the shade of my noncondemning attitude. Fulfill Your covenant in me, Lord. This is my prayer in Jesus' name. Amen.

# AUGUST 14

Dear Friend, Called of God,

When He [Jesus] had called the people to *Himself*, with His disciples also, He said to them, "Whoever desires to come after Me, let him deny himself, and take up his cross, and follow Me. For whoever desires to save his life will lose it; but whoever loses his life for My sake and the gospel's, will save it. For what will it profit a man if he gains the whole world, and loses his own soul? Or what will a man give in exchange for his soul?"

Mark 8:34–37

Lord,
It seems impossible to deny myself. I am wrought through and through with selfish thoughts. I don't want to save this earthly life. It's so full of pain, yet I cling to it as though there's nothing better. Father, please help me to surrender it to You. I choose You. Please take me; my spirit is willing, but my flesh is so terribly weak. I am exchanging my soul for an opportunity to grasp at things that I am not even attaining. Help me to get it through my thick skull that it is not worth it. Don't let me lose my soul while losing in this life, as well, because *nothing* really satisfies me but *You*. O, give me the grace to shine for You! Take my life and let it be used wholly for Your purposes. May the gospel shine on my face and ooze from my lips. I am Yours, Lord. I love You. I love You. I love You. Amen.

# AUGUST 15

Dear Friend, Child of the King,

Then they brought little children to Him, that He might touch them; but the disciples rebuked those who brought *them*. But when Jesus saw *it*, He was greatly displeased and said to them, "Let the little children come to Me, and do not forbid them; for of such is the kingdom of God. Assuredly, I say to you, whoever does not receive the kingdom of God as a little child will by no means enter it." And He took them up in His arms, laid *His* hands on them, and blessed them.

Mark 10:13–16

Lord,

I am often too busy taking care of children's needs to take care of the children. Forgive me for rebuking the trust and faith and interest of children because I feel there are more important things to attend to at the moment. Help me to remember Your words. Help me to have that childlike faith and trust in You that is willing to believe the impossible because it is You who says it. Please cleanse me of my cynical, earth-focused unbelief. Fill my heart with the trust that You had in Your Father as You walked this earth. And Lord, let my arms be always open to the children. As my hands touch them, fill them with Your grace. Bless each and every one. Amen.

# August 16

Dear Friend, Child of God,

And the disciples were astonished at His words. But Jesus answered again and said to them, "Children, how hard is it for those who trust in riches to enter the kingdom of God! It is easier for a camel to go through the eye of a needle than for a rich man to enter the kingdom of God." And they were greatly astonished, saying among themselves, "Who then can be saved?" But Jesus looked at them and said, "With men *it is* impossible, but not with God; for with God all things are possible."

Mark 10:24–27

Lord,
Forgive me for trusting in the riches of this world. Material things cannot fill the soul. Knowledge cannot satisfy the deep heart longings for the peace that Your wisdom and love gives. Activities for humanitarian causes, as wonderful as they are, are not what save the soul. Only You can save, can give peace, can free us from sin. Father, please help me never to even look at or think about the things this world considers gain. May I forsake all, for Your sake. Work the impossible in my heart. Lord I want to be cleansed from all unrighteousness. You *alone* can do this. Fill me with the riches of Your grace. Amen.

# AUGUST 17

Dear Friend, Chosen of God,

So Jesus answered and said to them, "Have faith in God. For assuredly, I say to you, whoever says to this mountain, 'Be removed and cast into the sea,' and does not doubt in his heart, but believes that those things he says will be done, he will have whatever he says. Therefore I say to you, whatever things you ask for when you pray, believe that you receive *them*, and you will have *them*. And whenever you stand praying, if you have anything against anyone, forgive him, that your Father in heaven may also forgive you your trespasses."

Mark 11:22–25

Lord,
How desperately I need the perfect faith and trust of Jesus. I have a weak, unbelieving heart that knows You *can* but doesn't believe You truly *will*. Please forgive me, Lord. I insult You and Your promises with my useless, enabling unbelief. I say I believe, but You see the hidden doubt behind my lofty words. O to have the faith of the centurion, believing beyond the shadow of a doubt that You need to only speak the word, and it is done. Father, my heart is in deep need of forgiveness for so many sins against You, and against Your children, my brethren. Forgiveness in my heart for those who have erred against me seems difficult to find. Please give me the spirit of forgiveness that includes genuine sorrow and abhorrence for sin—not sinners. Lord, I believe. Help Thou mine unbelief. Amen.

# AUGUST 18

Dear Friend, Servant of the Risen Savior,

Now when the Sabbath was past, Mary Magdalene, Mary *the mother* of James, and Salome bought spices, that they might come and anoint Him. Very early in the morning, on the first *day* of the week, they came to the tomb when the sun had risen. And they said among themselves, "Who will roll away the stone from the door of the tomb for us?" But when they had looked up, they saw that the stone had been rolled away—for it was very large. And entering the tomb, they saw a young man clothed in a long white robe, sitting on the right side; and they were alarmed. But he said to them, "Do not be alarmed. You seek Jesus of Nazareth, who was crucified. He is risen! He is not here. See the place where they laid Him. But go, tell His disciples—and Peter—that He is going before you into Galilee; there you will see Him, as He said to you."

Mark 16:1–7

Lord,
You rested in the tomb on Sabbath. It was a complete rest; Your work accomplished. How glorious when Your Father called You forth victorious! The disciples feared needlessly. They did not rest in Your word. The women went to the tomb needlessly. They did not understand Your prophecies. I fail to rest in You, Lord. I am alarmed when I think You are not here. Please forgive my unbelief. Help me to remember that You are victorious in every way. You have conquered death! Thank You for the eternal life You have purchased for me. Jesus, You are going before us, just as You said. Though I may rest in the grave, may I rise victorious when You return and call forth Your own, just as You rose at Your Father's call. Amen.

# AUGUST 19

Dear Friend, Blessed by His Glory,

And there were in the same country shepherds abiding in the field, keeping watch over their flock by night. And, lo, the angel of the Lord came upon them, and the glory of the Lord shone round about them: and they were sore afraid. And the angel said unto them, Fear not: for, behold, I bring you good tidings of great joy, which shall be to all people. For unto you is born this day in the city of David a Saviour, which is Christ the Lord. And this *shall be* a sign unto you; Ye shall find the babe wrapped in swaddling clothes, lying in a manger. And suddenly there was with the angel a multitude of the heavenly host praising God, and saying, "Glory to God in the highest, and on earth peace, good will toward men!"

Luke 2:8–14 KJV

Lord,

Glory to God in the Highest! Indeed, You have given Your peace and goodwill to all. Forgive me for refusing to accept it. How beautiful that You sent Your angel messengers to humble shepherds out in the field. You filled the darkness of the night sky with the brightness of the glory of Your salvation. You fulfilled Your promise to David, to Adam, and to Abraham. You fulfilled Your promise to all. You came, as Abraham's and David's Seed, as a Babe wrapped in swaddling clothes, lying in a manger. Wow! You are indeed God with us. Glory to God in the highest! Amen.

# AUGUST 20

Dear Friend, Called by God,

And it came to pass, as the angels were gone away from them into heaven, the shepherds said one to another, Let us now go even unto Bethlehem, and see this thing which has come to pass, which the Lord hath made known unto us. And they came with haste, and found Mary, and Joseph, and the babe lying in a manger. And when they had seen *it,* they made known abroad the saying which was told them concerning this child. And all they that heard *it* wondered at those things which were told them by the shepherds. But Mary kept all these things, and pondered *them* in her heart. And the shepherd returned, glorifying and praising God for all the things that they had heard and seen, as it was told unto them.

Luke 2:15–20 KJV

Lord,
O to be like the shepherds—to be like the Good Shepherd who faithfully watches His sheep day and night. Lord, when You come in the night of earth's history, may You find me tending Your sheep. May I rejoice to see Your face when You come, just as the shepherds rejoiced to welcome the angels' message of Your coming. The shepherds did not waste any time in coming to You, Jesus. They proclaimed Your name and Your glory all the way. Please forgive me for coming to You so slowly, for sidetracking and faltering. Forgive me for hesitating and choosing not to proclaim Your name because of possible uncomfortable circumstances. Jesus, let me glorify and praise You. Let me proclaim the wonderful works You have done in my life. Hallelujah! Amen.

# AUGUST 21

Dear Friend, Blessed of the Lord,

And the whole multitude sought to touch Him, for power went out from Him and healed *them* all. Then he lifted up His eyes toward the disciples, and said: "Blessed *are you* poor for yours is the kingdom of God. Blessed *are you* who hunger now, for you shall be filled. Blessed *are you* who weep now, for you shall laugh. Blessed are you when men hate you, and when they exclude you, and revile *you*, and cast out your name as evil, for the Son of man's sake. Rejoice in that day and leap for joy! For indeed your reward *is* great in heaven, for in like manner their fathers did to the prophets."

Luke 6:19–23

Lord,

O how I seek for You. How I long for Your beautiful virtue. Heal me body, mind, and spirit. Thank You, Jesus, for Your comforting encouragement. You have truly blessed me. It is because of You, that I have inherited the kingdom of God. Lord, I hunger for You; for Your love, mercy, faithfulness, and righteousness. You do fill me. I weep, Father. My heart is burdened with the sorrows of this sinful world and the sorrows of my sinful life. Let me weep more for the sorrows of my sinfulness. Thank You for filling my with Your Spirit of repentance and restoration. Thank You for Your promise to wipe away all tears. Jesus, thank You for the privilege of being hated for Your sake. You were despised and rejected of men, but You loved me continually. O, I want a continual love for You in my heart. I love You, Father. I love You, Jesus. I love you, Spirit. Amen.

# AUGUST 22

Dear Friend, Eternally Loved,

Now it happened, the day after, that He went into a city called Nain, and many of His disciples went with Him, and a large crowd. And when He came near the gate of the city, behold, a dead man was being carried out, the only son of his mother; and she was a widow. And a large crowd from the city was with her. When the Lord saw her, He had compassion on her and said to her, "Do not weep." Then He came and touched the open coffin, and those who carried him stood still. And He said, "Young man, I say to you arise." So he who was dead sat up and began to speak. And He presented him to his mother.

Luke 7:11–15

Lord,
You are a God of life, not death. You have never wanted death for anyone. You have compassion on those who suffer loss. You suffer loss every time one of Your creatures rejects Your love and grace. You can hardly wait for the day when You will speak, and all the graves of Your resting children will burst open. Thank You for calling the widow of Nain's son back to life to show us that You are the Resurrection and the Life. Jesus, help me to remember how much You love me. Thank You for promising me eternal life. I do not need to cling to this life. I need to cling to You. Amen.

# AUGUST 23

Dear Friend, Called by God,

Saying, "The Son of Man must suffer many things, and be rejected by the elders and chief priests and scribes, and be killed, and be raised the third day." Then He said to *them* all, "If anyone desires to comes after Me, let him deny himself, and take up his cross daily, and follow Me. For whoever desires to save his life will lose it, but whoever losses his life for My sake will save it. For what profit is it to a man if he gains the whole world, and is himself destroyed or lost? For whoever is ashamed of Me and My words, of him the Son of Man will be ashamed when He comes in His *own* glory, and in *His* Father's, and of the holy angels."

Luke 9:22–26

Lord,
Surely You have borne our griefs and carried our sorrows. You know first-hand what it is to be hated and rejected, and to feel alone even in a crowd. You know what it is to be hated by those who claim to be Your brethren. I want to follow You, Lord. I do not want the things of this world any-more; they do not satisfy the longings of my heart. Jesus, I need You and Your strength to help me deny myself. My selfish will seems to cling to me like an infinity of the strongest leeches. Help me to take up my cross daily. I do not want to be found ashamed of Your words. Lord, I do not want You to be ashamed of my words. May my words be but an echo of You. I love You, Lord. Amen.

# August 24

Dear Friend, Fed by the Spirit,

Now it happened as they went that He entered a certain village; and a certain woman named Martha welcomed Him into her house. And she had a sister called Mary, who also sat at Jesus' feet and heard His word. But Martha was distracted with much serving, and she approached Him and said, "Lord, do You not care that my sister has left me to serve alone? Therefore tell her to help me." And Jesus answered and said to her, "Martha, Martha, you are worried and troubled about many things. But one thing is needed, and Mary has chosen that good part, which will not be taken away from her."

Luke 10:38–42

Lord,
You have said to seek first the kingdom of God and all these things shall be added unto me. Please forgive me for doing the opposite of what You have instructed. Like Martha, I am busy trying to serve You. I work hard to give You things that are already Yours. You do not need my physical or material offerings, You want the offering of my heart. I have been too busy telling You what is wrong with others when I should have kept my mouth closed and my ears open. Jesus, when You speak, let me always be at Your feet listening with my whole heart and mind. I do not want to miss the good part. Come into my home, my heart, and dwell with me forever. Let me serve You with faithful obedience to Your Word. Amen.

# AUGUST 25

Dear Friend, Precious to the Father,

And I say to you, My friends, do not be afraid of those who kill the body, and after that have no more that they can do. But I will show you whom you should fear: Fear Him who, after He has killed, has power to cast into hell; yes, I say to you, fear him! Are not five sparrows sold for two copper coins? And not one of them is forgotten before God. But the very hairs of your head are all of more value than many sparrows.

Luke 12:4–7

Lord,

Why do I fear for this life? You have promised to supply all my needs, even though this life is but a moment in time. Please help me to trust You completely. Please take this selfish heart and transform it into something useful for You. Help me to stop trying to preserve my body, except for as it pertains to keeping a clean temple inside so that I can hear and understand You. I do not fear the devil as I should. You are the Conqueror. Keep me behind Your lines. Let me ever live to glorify You. Thank You for keeping me so preciously in Your loving heart. May my heart be for You and Your love. You have died that I may have life and have it more abundantly. Forgive me for serving my salvation, Lord. Let me serve my beautiful Savior. I love You, Jesus. Amen.

## AUGUST 26

Dear Friend, Sustained by the Savior,

Consider the lilies, how they grow: they neither toil nor spin; and yet I say
to you, even Solomon in all his glory was not arrayed like one of these. If
then God so clothes the grass, which today is in the field and tomorrow is
thrown into the oven, how much more *will He clothe* you, O *you* of little
faith? And do not seek what you should eat or what you should drink nor
have an anxious mind. For all these things the nations of the world seek
after, and your Father knows that you need these things. But seek the
kingdom of God, and all these things shall be added to you.

Luke 12:27–31

Lord,
How beautiful are the lilies of the field! They grow and multiply by
Your tender love and mercies. Indeed I toil needlessly to make myself
appear lovely, when I am rotten in my thoughts and the roots of my heart.
Solomon's glory does not compare to the lilies because it was his glory—
not Yours, Lord. Nothing we do can ever compare to the majesty of Your
spoken word. May I ever seek *You*, and You alone. You are my food and
drink; the Bread and Water of life. You clothe me with Your righteousness. You know my needs better than I. Forgive me for usurping Your
role, Father. *You* are God. Amen.

# AUGUST 27

Dear Friend, Child of the King,

And He looked up and saw the rich putting their gifts into the treasury, and He saw also a certain poor widow putting in two mites. So He said, "Truly I say to you that this poor widow has put in more than all; for all these out of their abundance have put in offerings for God, but she out of her poverty put in all the livelihood that she had."

Luke 21:1–4

Lord,
You have blessed every person with gifts. Everything I have, including my every breath, is a gift from You. You have said, "Blessed are the poor in spirit, for theirs is the kingdom of heaven." May I be like the widow. In my spiritual and emotional as well as physical poverty, I give You all that I have, all that I am. Forgive me for only offering You my excess, or the time that I think I can spare and still accomplish what "needs to be done." Jesus, nothing needs to be done more than to fully surrender to and focus on You. Give me the power and victory that comes from You; a power to surrender *all*; a victory from the snares of this world. Amen.

## AUGUST 28

Dear Friend, Cared for by God,

Then, as some spoke of the temple, how it was adorned with beautiful stones and donations, He said, "These which you see—the days will come in which not *one* stone shall be left upon another that shall not be thrown down."

Luke 21:5–6

Lord,

Thank You for the lessons You shared with Your disciples while You were here on earth. Please help me to remember that they are for me, too. You have warned us of the deceptions of Satan. Buildings made by the hands of men will not last, but Your Word will last forever. You knew that the temple building would be destroyed, but that's okay. You have said over and over that You want to dwell in my heart. Father, forgive me for putting my focus on buildings which will pass away. Come and abide in my heart. Rule my every thought, word, and action. I want to be Your holy temple as You have asked. I do not want to be destroyed. I want to be a temple You can dwell in forever. Amen.

# AUGUST 29

Dear Friend, Led by the Truth,

So they asked Him, saying, "Teacher, but when will these things be? And what sign *will there be* when these things are about to take place?" And He said, "Take heed that you are not deceived. For many will come in My name, saying, 'I am *He*,' and, 'The time has drawn near.' Therefore do not go after them. But when you hear of wars and commotions, do not be terrified; for these things must come to pass first, but the end *will not come* immediately."

Luke 21:7–9

Lord,

You have demonstrated Your love for me in so many ways. Thank You for revealing the things that will come to pass on this earth before Your second coming. You do not want Your children to be ignorant. Thank You for coming to earth to reveal the character and the heart of the Father in such a beautiful and personal way. Jesus, please help me to ever look to You to know what is truth and what is not. If anyone varies in any way from You and Your Word, he is not from You. Keep me from following false gospels. Help me to pray without ceasing and to discern Your voice distinctly. Help me to not worry about all the calamities that are happening all around me, but to trust wholly in You. You are in control of this world regardless of how Satan tries to wreak havoc. Thank You. Amen.

# AUGUST 30

Dear Friend, Kept by His Life,

Then he said unto them, Nation shall rise against nation, and kingdom against kingdom: And great earthquakes shall be in diverse places, and famines, and pestilences; and fearful sights and great signs shall there be from heaven. But before all these, they shall lay their hands on you, and persecute *you*, delivering *you* up to the synagogues, and into prisons, being brought before kings and rulers for my name's sake. And it shall turn to you for a testimony.

Luke 21:10–13 KJV

Lord,

When I look around me, it is easy to become disheartened, discouraged, and afraid. But You have told me not to be distressed. You are in control. Help me to remember that You are not causing these disasters. They are caused by the devil and those controlled by him, and by the effects of pollution and abuse of this world and its atmosphere. Please help me to stand firm in my faith in You, no matter what the consequences. Let my life be a beacon of Your merciful love and goodness. Speak Your words through me. Use me for Your honor and glory as a testimony of Your everlasting covenant to all Your children. Amen.

# AUGUST 31

Dear Friend, Child of God,

Settle *it* therefore in your hearts, not to meditate before what ye shall answer. For I will give you a mouth and wisdom, which all your adversaries shall not be able to gainsay or resist. And ye shall be betrayed both by parents, and brethren, and kinsfolk, and friends; and *some* of you shall they cause to be put to death. And ye shall be hated of all *men* for my name's sake. But there shall not an hair of your head perish. In your patience possess ye your souls.

Luke 21:14–19 KJV

Lord,

Please fill my heart and mind with a complete trust in You. Turn my focus heavenward each day, and hold my gaze onto Your character. Fulfill Your covenant in me. I desperately need to be rid of my continual selfishness and pride. I am no match for Satan or those under his powerful control. I need Your faith and Your wisdom. Let me establish the habit now of waiting for Your directions and Your words before I act or speak. Lord, it's not easy being the odd one out, the one who thinks differently from everyone else. But Jesus, this is the life You led—hated by Your own family and Your own people. Yet You had patience in Your soul. My inheritance is not of this world; You are my inheritance. I will wait and trust in You. Amen.

## September 1

Dear Friend, Redeemed by the Blood of the Lamb,

And he said unto them, With desire I have desired to eat this passover with you before I suffer: For I say unto you, I will not any more eat thereof, until it be fulfilled in the kingdom of God. And he took the cup, and gave thanks, and said, Take this, and divide *it* among yourselves: For I say unto you, I will not drink of the fruit of the vine, until the kingdom of God shall come. And he took bread, and gave thanks, and brake *it,* and gave unto them, saying, This is my body which is given for you: this do in remembrance of me. Likewise also the cup after supper, saying, This cup *is* the new testament in my blood, which is shed for you.

Luke 22:15–20 KJV

Lord,
I am in eternal awe at what You have done for me. Your love goes far deeper than words and even actions. It's a small thing that You have given up eating unleavened bread and drinking the pure juice of the vine until You are reunited with all Your children. But what an amazing thing that You forever identified with us, became us, and gave up Your eternal life for us. You allowed Your body to be broken for us. Your heart shattered with the awful weight of my sin and the thought of eternal separation from Your Father. You allowed Your blood to flow freely with the living water of Your heart. May I *always* remember what You have done. May I always remember. Amen.

# SEPTEMBER 2

Dear Friend, Loved of the Father,

And as Moses lifted up the serpent in the wilderness, even so must the Son of man be lifted up: that whosoever believeth in him should not perish, but have eternal life. For God so loved the world, that he gave his only begotten Son, that whosoever believeth in him should not perish, but have everlasting life. For God sent not his Son into the world to condemn the world; but that the world through him might be saved.

John 3:14–17 KJV

Lord,
What a gift! How incredibly awesome! Give me grace to take hold of that gift. Jesus, *I believe* You love me with an everlasting love! Father, thank You for sacrificing Your Son to show me how deep and how wide and how strong is Your love for me! You have said that when You are lifted up, You will draw all to Yourself, Jesus. Let me lift You up in everything I do every moment of my life. Fulfill Your covenant in me. Let the world know when they look at me, that You do not want any to perish, but long for all to have everlasting life. I surrender all. Amen.

# SEPTEMBER 3

Dear Friend, Bride of Christ,

Jesus answered and said to her, "Whoever drinks of this water will thirst again. But whoever drinks of the water that I shall give him will never thirst. But the water that I shall give him will become in him a fountain of water springing up into everlasting life."

John 4:13–14

Lord,
You are indeed the source of my life. I forget to drink water, and my body begins to dry out. It does not function well without water. I consist mostly of water. What a lesson you have given me! How terribly poor and miserable is my life when I am spiritually dehydrated. Without water, my body dies. Without Water, my spirit dies. Every time I stop drinking from You I reap the results of spiritual dehydration. Lord, sometimes I don't realize my need for the Water of Life until I am already sick and in trouble. May I ever drink from You continually. Lord. Fill my cup to overflowing. Quench the dreadful thirst of my heart. May others see You springing forth from my life. *More of You*, and less of me. Amen.

# September 4

Dear Friend, Fed by the Spirit,

"Do not labor for the food which perishes, but for the food which endures to everlasting life, which the Son of Man will give you, because God the Father has set His seal on Him." Then they said to Him, "What shall we do, that we may work the works of God?" Jesus answered and said to them, "This is the work of God, that you believe in Him whom He sent."

John 6:27–29

Lord,

I work so hard to sustain my life and then I realize it is not I that has provided but You. And yet, the things I think sustain me perish away. Lord, give me the food that endures to everlasting life: the Bread of life that renews and sustains my soul. Forgive my pride and unbelief, Lord. Help me to always believe on Jesus, and Him alone, who has purchased my very breath. Father, help me not to labor in vain. Guide my thoughts, my ideas, and my life. You have promised to provide that which perishes as well as that which lasts forever. You alone know my real needs. Father, fill me with Your love and Spirit that I may do Your work. Cleanse me. Change my heart. O how I long to have a full and complete trust in You. Let me empty my selfish heart of all its baggage at Your holy and willing feet. I love You, Lord. I believe in You. I believe in You. Amen.

## SEPTEMBER 5

Dear Friend, Cherished by God,

And Jesus said unto them, I am the bread of life: he that cometh to me shall never hunger; and he that believeth on me shall never thirst. But I said unto you, That ye also have seen me, and believe not. All that the Father giveth me shall come to me; and him that cometh to me I will in no wise cast out.

John 6:35–37 KJV

Lord,
When I eat bread, may I remember that you are not only the Giver of bread, but that *You are the Bread of Life*. Fill the hungering in my soul. You are the Water of Life. May I drink from You. Quench my thirsty soul. Thank You, Father, for Your promise to always take me in when I come to You. I treasure the loving friendship of One who does not reject me no matter what stupid or bad things I've done. O Jesus, please help me to be that kind of friend, too. Fulfill Your covenant in me. I do not want to disappoint or sadden You, my beautiful Friend. Amen.

# SEPTEMBER 6

Dear Friend, Daughter/Son of God,

Then Jesus said to them, "When you lift up the Son of Man, then you will know that I am *He*, and *that* I do nothing Myself; but as My Father taught Me, I speak these things. And He who sent Me is with Me. The Father has not left Me alone, for I always do those things that please Him." As He spoke these words, many believed in Him. Then Jesus said to those Jews who believed Him, "If you abide in My word, you are My disciples indeed. And you shall know the truth and the truth shall make you free."

John 8:28–32

Lord,

How beautiful that You sent Jesus to show how deeply You love us. Jesus, You allowed Yourself to be lifted up in the most damning and despicable way, to show us the beautiful character of the Father. What a beautiful example for us that You depended so closely on Your Father, our Father, for everything. I sit dumbfounded when I contemplate what You have done. O that we would know You, the Father, the Son, and the Spirit! Fill my heart with Your Word, Your truth. How I long to be Your disciple; to sit at Your feet and learn of Your ways. Set me free in Your love. Glory to Your Name! Be lifted up in my life always and forever! Amen.

## SEPTEMBER 7

Dear Friend, Loved by the True Friend,

He that loveth his life shall lose it; and he that hateth his life in this world shall keep it unto eternal life. If any man serve me, let him follow me; and where I am, there shall also my servant be: if any man serve me, him will *my* Father honor. Now is my soul troubled; and what shall I say? Father, save me from this hour: but for this cause came I unto this hour. Father, glorify thy name.

John 12:25–28 KJV

Lord,
Please help me to remember that You gave Your life for me. You identified Yourself with me forever, Jesus. Forgive me for getting so wrapped up in the cares of this world that I forget You have given me a better, eternal future. I want to serve *You*, not me. It touches my heart deeply to contemplate the agony of soul You experienced to show me how deep the Father's love is for me. Help me to be willing to agonize for You. When I'm troubled, I sometimes try to ignore it until it goes away, or I try to rationalize it away. Help me to agonize until my soul is truly surrendered to the will of the Father. Please use me to lift up Christ to the world. May others see You reflected in my life. May they be drawn to You. Thank You for Your gracious wooing. Amen.

## SEPTEMBER 8

Dear Friend, Child of God,

Let not your heart be troubled; you believe in God, believe also in Me. In My Father's house are many mansions: if *it were* not *so,* I would have told you. I go to prepare a place for you. And if I go and prepare a place for you, I will come again and receive you to Myself; that where I am, *there* you may be also. And where I go you know, and the way you know.

John 14:1–4

Lord,
I surrender the trouble in my heart to You—and there is a lot of it. Please remove it. I believe in Christ the Son and God the Father. I believe in the Comforter, the Spirit. Thank You, Lord, for preparing a place for me. I so much want to be with You. Jesus, I know You have entered the Most Holy Place to intercede for me. And I know that *You are the Way.* It is through You that I can boldly come to the throne of grace. You are in the Most Holy Place, interceding for me and preparing an eternal place for me. You are preparing a new heart, a heart that will surrender all and let You reign forevermore. Thank You for fulfilling Your covenant in me. Praise be to You alone. Amen.

## SEPTEMBER 9

Dear Friend, Taught by the Spirit,

But the Helper, the Holy Spirit, whom the Father will send in My name, He will teach you all things, and bring to your remembrance all things that I said to you. Peace I leave with you, My peace I give to you; not as the world gives do I give to you. Let not your heart be troubled, neither let it be afraid.

John 14:26–27

Lord,
Please help me to get rid of everything that prevents me from becoming intimately close with Your very awesome and omnipotent Self. Thank You for never leaving me comfortless. Thank You for the wisdom and guidance of the Holy Spirit. Teach me, Lord. Let me be immersed in Your Word. Fill my heart and mind with thoughts of You; thoughts that the Holy Spirit can help me recall in times of need. I know the only way to have true peace is to not just listen to, but to surrender to the teachings of the Holy Spirit. Help me to truly surrender all, and to stay continuously surrendered. Thank You for Your true peace, a peace that has no fear. Amen.

## SEPTEMBER 10

Dear Friend, Beloved of God,

This is My commandment, that you love one another as I have loved you, and *that* your joy may be full. Greater love has no one than this, than to lay down one's life for his friends. You are My friends if you do whatever I command you.

John 15:12–14

Lord,
What a beautiful commandment! And as all Your commandments, this is a promise that you will fulfill in us if we only allow. What a beautiful treasure—Your agape love! Fulfill Your covenant in me. How desperate is my heart for Your kind of love that did not lay down just Your physical life, but laid down all Your personal dreams and desires to live selflessly for me. Help me to lay down my life for You, Jesus; not just my physical life in this world, but my whole heart and mind, and my selfish will. I surrender all. Please make me a true friend. Amen.

## SEPTEMBER 11

Dear Friend, Bride of Christ,

And in that day you will ask Me nothing. Most assuredly, I say to you, whatever you ask the Father in My name He will give you. Until now you have asked nothing in My name. Ask, and you will receive, that your joy may be full.

John 16:23–24

Lord,
Forgive me for using Your Name so flippantly. Your Name is Your character. You are love—agape. Jesus, I want to pray in Your character, Your likeness, like You do. I believe Your Word is power. Your Word accomplishes what it says, as You say it. I need the power of Your Word in my life. Fill me with Your Spirit. Thank You for loving me and for hearing my pitiful cries. Forgive me for praying for what I want, in the way that I see best, and then saying that it is in Your name. What blasphemy are so many of my prayers! How can I pray in Jesus' name unless I know what You want for me? I want my joy—the joy that You have for me—to be full. I want to know You and be used by You. In Jesus Name, Amen.

## September 12

Dear Friend, Loved by the Three in One,

Jesus spoke these words, lifted up His eyes to heaven, and said: "Father, the hour has come. Glorify Your Son, that Your Son also may glorify You, as You have given Him authority over all flesh, that He should give eternal life to as many as You have given Him. And this is eternal life, that they may know You, the only true God, and Jesus Christ whom You have sent. I have glorified You on the earth. I have finished the work which You have given Me to do. And now, O Father, glorify Me together with Yourself, with the glory which I had with You before the world was."

John 17:1–5

Lord,
That dreadful hour had come when Christ knew that He must empty every last drop of Himself without fail to prove what magnificent love You have had for Your children since before time began. You gave Jesus, the Man, authority over all flesh. Jesus, You have conquered sin *in* the flesh! To have eternal life is to know You and to know the Man who took authority of my sinful flesh and resisted sin and the Man who has completed the gift of victory over sin in my flesh, which is eternal life at the right hand of the Father. Behold the Man! O what an incredibly beautiful God! What an incredibly beautiful Savior! Holy Spirit, fill me to overflowing with that most precious faith of Jesus Christ, even the faith that overcomes the world! Jesus, You have finished Your work. Let it shine through me. Amen.

## September 13

Dear Friend, Disciple of Christ,

I have manifested Your name to the men whom You have given Me out of the world. They were Yours, You gave them to Me, and they have kept Your word. Now they have known that all things which You have given Me are from You. For I have given to them the words which You have given Me; and they have received them, and have known surely that I came forth from You; and they have believed that You sent Me.

John 17:6–8

Lord,
What an awesome prayer of faith Jesus prayed for me. Knowing that His disciples, and I, would soon forsake Him, He said that we believed on Him. How beautiful! Father, You gave Your Son to me, and gave me to Your Son—put me in Him—as a gift for forever! Amazing love! How can it be? Jesus, You have done, and are continuing to do, an overwhelmingly outstanding job of revealing the heart of the Father toward me. Fulfill Your covenant in me, Lord. Let me magnify the heart of the Father as did Jesus. Everything I have, body, mind, and spirit, is a gift from You. Jesus, thank You for Your faith! Amen.

# SEPTEMBER 14

Dear Friend, Joint Heir with Jesus,

I pray for them. I do not pray for the world but for those whom You have given Me, for they are Yours. And all Mine are Yours, and Yours are Mine, and I am glorified in them. Now I am no longer in the world, but these are in the world, and I come to You. Holy Father, keep through Your name those whom You have given Me, that they may be one as We *are*. While I was with them in the world, I kept them in Your name. Those whom You gave Me I have kept; and none of them is lost except the son of perdition, that the Scripture might be fulfilled.

John 17:9–12

Lord,

How sweet and endearing is Your conversation among Yourself. The Father, Son, and Spirit are truly One. How precious is Your love and care toward me. Please be glorified in me. I long to be a beautiful reflection of You. Jesus, You care so tenderly that I will not be left alone. Use me to show such care for the millions around me who feel desperately alone. Thank You for walking in this world with me, yea, as me. You have ever kept me in You heart of agape and faith. You have never forced me to love You, and You tearfully allow Your omnipotent grace to be rejected. Yet You have gone to unthinkable, eternal lengths to woo and caress the heart of every one of Your created beings. Thank You eternally for the precious treasure of Yourself. I love You, Lord. Amen.

# SEPTEMBER 15

Dear Friend, Witness of God's Love,

But now I come to You, and these things I speak in the world, that they may have My joy fulfilled in themselves. I have given them Your word; and the world has hated them because they are not of the world, just as I am not of the world. I do not pray that You should take them out of the world, but that You should keep them from the evil one. They are not of the world, just as I am not of the world. Sanctify them by Your truth. Your word is truth. As You sent Me into the world, I also have sent them into the world. And for their sakes I sanctify Myself, that they also may be sanctified by the truth.
John 17:13–19

Lord,
Fulfill Your joy in me. Fill me with Your Word. Fill me with the faith of Jesus that can magnify Your marvelous love, though the world hate me for such a contrast. Keep my heart from the evil one who surrounds me with tempting lures. Let this mind be in me which was in Christ Jesus, a mind that refused to yield to temptation. Remind me that this evil world is not my inheritance, but a new kingdom is even now growing within my heart. Sanctify me by Your truth. May my heart and mind become a pure fountain of Your word. Use me to preach the gospel of Jesus Christ by every thought, word, and action. Let me die that You may live in me supreme, forever. Amen.

# September 16

Dear Friend, One with Christ,

I do not pray for these alone, but also for those who will believe in Me through their word; That they all may be one, as You, Father, *are* in Me, and I in You; that they also may be one in Us, that the world may believe that You sent Me. And the glory which You gave Me I have given them, that they may be one just as We are one; I in them, and You in Me; that they may be made perfect in one, and that the world may know that You have sent Me, and have loved them as You have loved Me.

John 17:20–23

Lord,
Thank You so much for Your prayer for me. Thank You Jesus for Your pure example of what it means to be one with the Father. To be one with Your Father, You surrendered Your will totally, completely, and continually. There is no other way for us to be one in You on this earth. Only a complete surrender to You will put me in total harmony with You and with others who are completely surrendered to You. Jesus, I am still steeped in selfishness, pride, and unbelief. Fulfill Your covenant in me. As I surrender to You, fill my mind with Your mind. Give me Your thoughts. Give me pure desires that shun evil. Fill me with Your faith. The world needs a clear united picture of You. Unite me with Your clear picture of Yourself. Amen.

# SEPTEMBER 17

Dear Friend, Brother/Sister of Christ,

Father, I desire that they also whom You gave Me may be with me where I am, that they may behold My glory which You have given Me; for You loved Me before the foundation of the world. O righteous Father! The world has not known You, but I have known You; and these have known that You sent Me. And I have declared to them Your name, and will declare *it,* that the love with which You loved Me may be in them, and I in them.

John 17:24–26

Lord,

The tender care that Christ showed in His prayer for me two-thousand years ago fills my heart with a sweet, beautiful peace. Jesus, after thirty-three years of being used and abused by Your ungrateful creatures, just before You laid down Your life for me, You told Your Father that You desired to have me with You for eternity. This is precious! What a deep and sincere love for me that extends back to before the foundation of this world! Your faith is incredible, Jesus! You declared that I would know You, because You knew that Your unmatchable love would draw and hold me to Yourself. Thank You for declaring Your name to me. Fill me with Your love. Fill me with Yourself. Live in me, and I in You. Amen.

# September 18

Dear Friend, Held by the Savior,

Then Jesus came out, wearing the crown of thorns and the purple robe. And *Pilate* said to them, "Behold the Man!" Therefore when the chief priests and officers saw Him, they cried out, saying, "Crucify *Him*, crucify *Him!*" Pilate said to them, "You take Him and crucify *Him*, for I find no fault in Him." The Jews answered him, "We have a law, and according to our law He ought to die, because He made Himself the Son of God." Therefore, when Pilate heard that saying, He was the more afraid.

John 19:5–8

Lord,

Pilate, a Roman, saw something holy and pure in You to cause him to cry out, "Behold the Man!" Please forgive me for calling out, "Crucify Him," each time I prefer my own way instead of Yours. You gave instructions to Moses to stone anyone who blasphemed. The priests and rulers tried to stone You more than once, but You had not blasphemed and it was not Your time yet. Finally, they managed to have You crucified; hung on a tree. This was me, Lord. I have determined to have my own way so that I deem myself worthy of following those who crucified You. O Jesus, how horribly I have treated Your eternal love for me. Forgive me, Jesus. Cleanse me of the selfishness that crucified You. Let me behold the Man! Amen.

## SEPTEMBER 19

Dear Friend, Spared by the Son of God,

Therefore, when Pilate heard that saying, he was the more afraid, and went again into the Praetorium, and said to Jesus, "Where are You from?" But Jesus gave him no answer. Then Pilate said to Him, "Are You not speaking to me? Do You not know that I have the power to crucify You, and the power to release You?" Jesus answered, "You could have no power at all against Me unless it had been given You from above. Therefore the one who delivered Me to you has the greater sin." From then on Pilate sought to release Him, but the Jews cried out, saying, "If you let this Man go, you are not Caesar's friend. Whoever makes himself a king speaks against Caesar."

John 19:8–12

Lord,
You have an eternal amount of patience. You remained silent and calm while Your accusers used lies and threats to secure Your death. Jesus, You have patiently waited for me to stop condemning You and start listening to Your humble wooing of my heart. You have remained calm and loving while I rant and rave as if I am wiser or more powerful than You. Please forgive me for delivering You to the cross. You have an unmatchable love to take my deserved death upon Your holy Self. You have given me the power of choice; the power to choose condemnation or life. You have purchased my pardon and freedom from sin. Help me to choose You, Jesus. I want the freedom from sin that You alone can give. Fulfill Your covenant in me. Amen.

# SEPTEMBER 20

Dear Friend, Called of God,

Then the high priest said, "Are these things so?" And he [Stephen] said, "Brethren and fathers, listen: The God of glory appeared to our father Abraham when he was in Mesopotamia, before he dwelt in Haran, and said to him, 'Get out of your country and from your relatives, and come to a land that I will show you.' Then he came out of the land of the Chaldeans and dwelt in Haran. And from there, when his father was dead, He moved him to this land in which you now dwell."

Acts 7:1–4

Lord,

Stephen was willing to proclaim Your promises before those whom he knew only wanted to condemn him. He had studied Your words, and the history of Your holy promises. He, like Abraham, believed in Your Word. Father, fill me with the faith and trust in You that causes a complete surrender to Your ways. I want to follow You in complete faith. I want to go where You send me and speak only Your words. You know full well that I am incapable of this, Lord. But You are very capable. Your beautiful desire for me is that I will become a pure reflection of You. This is what I long for. Fulfill Your covenant in me. Scour the waste matter of selfishness, pride, and unbelief from my heart. Cleanse me with Your merciful loving-kindness. Amen.

## SEPTEMBER 21

Dear Friend, Child of the Everlasting Covenant,

And *God* gave him no inheritance in it, not even *enough* to set his foot on. But even when *Abraham* had no child, He promised to give it to him for a possession, and to his descendants after him. But God spoke in this way: that his descendants would dwell in a foreign land, and that they would bring them into bondage and oppress *them* four hundred years. 'And the nation to whom they will be in bondage I will judge,' said God, 'And after that they shall come out and serve Me in this place.' Then He gave him the covenant of circumcision; and so *Abraham* begot Isaac and circumcised him on the eighth day; and Isaac *begot* Jacob, and Jacob *begot* the twelve patriarchs.

Acts 7:5–8

Lord,
I often forget that my real inheritance is not of this world. I am so used to using my brain to figure things out. If only I would use my brain to figure out that Your promises are sure and that it is nothing for You to do the "impossible" to accomplish them. Now I am steeped in the bondage of sin, but it will not always be so. Even before the foundation of the world, You released my bondage by the promise of salvation through Jesus Christ. You are even now loosening the chains of selfishness and unbelief from me. You are bringing me out for Your service. You have given me baptism to proclaim and remind me that I am dead in to the bondage of the flesh and alive in You. Thank You for being such an intimate and deeply caring God. I love You. Amen.

# September 22

Dear Friend, Guarded by the Father,

And the patriarchs, becoming envious, sold Joseph into Egypt. But God was with him and delivered him out of all his troubles, and gave him favor and wisdom in the presence of Pharaoh, king of Egypt; and he made him governor over Egypt and all his house. Now a famine and great trouble came over all the land of Egypt and Canaan, and our fathers found no sustenance. But when Jacob heard that there was grain in Egypt, he sent out our fathers first.
Acts 7:9–12

Lord,
I am no different than Joseph's brothers who sold him into Egypt. I'm afraid that I actually have no idea how many times I have sold my brothers and sisters on this earth into bondage and despair and onto a path away from You. Not only my words and actions have turned people away, but the mere look on my face and my posture have sent the most degrading messages to others. Forgive me, Lord, for making spiritual and emotional slaves of those around me by my attitudes. Father, I want to be like Joseph, faithful to You under every circumstance. When I feel that I am being enslaved by others, help me to remember that I am free in Jesus Christ. When there is a spiritual famine in the land, use me to open countless granaries of Your love and truth. Amen.

# SEPTEMBER 23

Dear Friend, Forgiven by the Author of Forgiveness,

And the second *time* Joseph was made know to his brothers, and Joseph's family became known to the Pharaoh. Then Joseph sent and called his father Jacob and all his relatives to *him*, seventy-five people. Then Jacob went down to Egypt; and he died, he and our fathers. And they were carried back to Shechem and laid in the tomb that Abraham bought for a sum of money from the sons of Hamor, *the father* of Shechem.

Acts 7:13–16

Lord,
Joseph, who was sold as a slave by his brothers, willingly forgave them and gave them an abundance of food at no cost to feed their families. Jesus, You, who were sold as a slave to our sin while You were sinless, willingly forgave us and have supplied us with an abundance of spiritual food and blessings at no cost to feed us and our families. Though I have wandered away from You and indulged myself in my own personalized, selfish misery, You have called me back to Yourself. I am buried in You. You have provided my redemption. Thank You for feeding me and my family with Your Living Water and Bread of Life. I am nothing. You are everything. Amen.

# SEPTEMBER 24

Dear Friend, Loved by the Everlasting,

But when the time of the promise drew near which God had sworn to Abraham, the people grew and multiplied in Egypt till another king arose who did not know Joseph. This man dealt treacherously with our people, and oppressed our forefathers, making them expose their babies, so that they might not live.

Acts 7:17–19

Lord,

You had prophesied to Abraham and told him that his descendants would be slaves in Egypt for four hundred years. This was not the first time that those who do not know You have persecuted those who do know You. This was not the last time for persecution, either. The saddest part of this story is that the descendants of Abraham, Isaac, and Jacob slowly forgot that they were Your children and that, through You, they were over-comers. Help me to remember that I wrestle not with flesh and blood, but with principalities and powers of darkness. When I am tempted to feel persecuted and sorry for myself, save me from being so distracted and put my focus back on You. No one has ever been dealt with so treacher-ously as You were, Jesus, but You endured to the end. Please give me Your faith—a faith that endures to the end. Thank You, in Jesus' name. Amen.

# SEPTEMBER 25

Dear Friend, Kept by the Father's Plan,

At this time Moses was born, and was well pleasing to God; and he was brought up in his father's house for three months. But when he was set out, Pharaoh's daughter took him away and brought him up as her own son. And Moses was learned in all the wisdom of the Egyptians, and he was mighty in word and in deeds. Now when he was forty years old, it came into his heart to visit his brethren, the children of Israel.

Acts 7:20–23

Lord,
You chose Moses before the foundation of the world to represent You. The king tried to destroy him as a baby, and so King Herod tried to destroy You when You were a baby. You did not abandon Moses while he was been trained in the Egyptian ways. You had already revealed Yourself to him when he was but a lad. He knew he was really an Israelite. He knew he belonged to You. Lord, help me to never forget that I am Your child. I am a spiritual Israelite. No matter what I am being taught by the powers and teachers that be in this world, help me to always turn to the Holy Spirit for instruction in every matter. Amen.

## SEPTEMBER 26

Dear Friend, Child of God,

And seeing one of *them* suffer wrong, he defended and avenged him who was oppressed, and struck down the Egyptian. For he supposed that his brethren would have understood that God would deliver them by his hand, but they did not understand. And the next day he appeared to two of them as they were fighting, and *tried to* reconcile them, saying, "Men, *you* are brethren; why do you wrong one another?" But he who did his neighbor wrong pushed him away, saying, "Who made you a ruler and a judge over us? Do you want to kill me as you killed the Egyptian yesterday?" Then, at this saying, Moses fled and became a dweller in the land of Midian, where he had two sons.

Acts 7:24–29

Lord,

Moses knew that You were a God who cared about the injustices that happen in this world. But, like me, he did not fully understand or believe that You had, and have, everything under control. Moses took the matter into his own hands and made a mess for himself and others. This is the story of my life, Lord. Please forgive me for trying to do Your job. Please forgive me for not trusting You. Help me to be usable for Your almighty plan. I do not want others to fear me as they feared Moses. I do not want to kill others with my words, gestures, or attitudes. Too often I make a mess and have to flee the scene. Thank You for Your ability to continue drawing all to Yourself regardless of the messes I make. Amen.

## SEPTEMBER 27

Dear Friend, Chosen by God,

And when forty years had passed, an Angel of the Lord appeared to him in a flame of fire in a bush, in the wilderness of Mt. Sinai. When Moses saw *it*, he marveled at the sight; and as he drew near to observe, the voice of the Lord came to him, saying, "I am the God of your fathers—the God of Abraham, the God of Isaac, and the God of Jacob." And Moses trembled and dared not look. Then the Lord said to him, "Take your sandals off your feet, for the place where you stand is holy ground."

Acts 7:30–33

Lord,

Through history I have seen this pattern: when we trust You, we long to be in Your presence and see Your face, but when we are fearful and unbelieving of Your love, we tremble and hide from You. Adam and Eve loved Your company until they believed the serpent's lie; then they hid from You. Moses hid from You until You drew him closer and closer to Yourself, to the point that he begged to see Your face. Father, You are not only the God of Abraham, Isaac, and Jacob, You are my God, my Friend. You long to speak to me. I am longing more and more to listen to You. Thank You for coming to my wilderness and finding me. I love the way You woo me. You are a holy God. Amen.

# September 28

Dear Friend, Loved by the Mighty Deliverer,

"I have surely seen the oppression of My people who are in Egypt; I have heard their groaning and have come down to deliver them. And now come, I will send you to Egypt." This Moses whom they rejected, saying, "Who made you a ruler and a judge?" is the one God sent *to be* a ruler and a deliverer by the hand of the Angel who appeared to him in a bush. He brought them out, after he had shown wonders in the land of Egypt, and in the Red Sea, and in the wilderness forty years.

Acts 7:34–36

Lord,

You are a God who hears when I cry. You already know my need. You want to free me from the slavery of sin. You have already accomplished my deliverance. I need to claim it. I claim the victory You have won for me. You have shown many mighty wonders to prove Your love for me. I am nothing; You are everything. Please help me to remember that You are the One who accomplishes things. I need only to be willing. Help me to stop trying to accomplish things and become totally willing to let You do the accomplishing. I want to be used to show others Your matchless power and love. Mold me and fashion me into a holy vessel for Your omnipotent purpose. You are my Deliverer. Amen.

# SEPTEMBER 29

Dear Friend, Rescued Before Birth,

This is that Moses who said to the children of Israel, "The Lord your God will raise up for you a Prophet like me from your brethren. Him you shall hear." This is he who was in the congregation in the wilderness with the Angel who spoke to him on Mount Sinai, and *with* our fathers, the one who received the living oracles to give us, whom our fathers would not obey, but rejected. And in their hearts they turned back to Egypt, saying to Aaron, "Make us gods to go before us; as for this Moses who brought us out of the land of Egypt, we do not know what has become of him."

Acts 7:37–40

Lord,
Thank You for being such a caring, thoughtful Creator, Sustainer, and Redeemer. You foresaw the future, and You were well prepared with a plan. You have always done everything You possibly can to communicate Your love and watch-care for me. Please forgive me for ignoring You and Your prophets and turning to my own devices. Forgive me for becoming impatient with Your plan and turning to unbelief as a solution. Thank You so much for taking the time to speak with Moses, giving him clarity of concepts and information so that he could write of Your goodness for me to read and know You better. You are an awesome God. You never give up on me. This is what draws me so close to You. I love You. Amen.

## SEPTEMBER 30

Dear Friend, Loved in Rebellion,

And they made a calf in those days, offered sacrifices to the idol, and rejoiced in the works of their own hands. Then God turned and gave them up to worship the host of heaven, as it is written in the book of the Prophets: "Did you offer Me slaughtered animals and sacrifices during forty years in the wilderness, O house of Israel? You also took up the tabernacle of Moloch, and the star of your god Remphan, images which you made to worship; and I will carry you away beyond Babylon."

Acts 7:41–43

Lord,
The things the Israelites did in rebellion sound so heinous and offensive. I want to feel glad that I would not do such backstabbing things to You, but this is not true. Please forgive me for serving the idol of myself—my appetite, my wallet, my time and priorities, my convenience, my preferences, and my culture—I have rejoiced in the works of my own hands. You have had no choice but to let me wander in the wilderness of my own selfish pride and unbelief. You cannot accept my insincere gifts of appeasement. In agony, you let me be carried away into sinful depths. Thank You for ever wooing me. Thank You for always being at hand to pull me out of my misery at my slightest willingness to be rescued. Forgive me and cleanse my rebellious heart, O God. Let me serve You in Spirit and in truth. Amen.

# OCTOBER 1

Dear Friend, Ever in His Presence,

Our fathers had the tabernacle of witness in the wilderness, as He appointed, instructing Moses to make it according to the pattern that he had seen, which our fathers, having received it in turn, also brought with Joshua into the land possessed by the Gentiles, whom God drove out before the face of our fathers until the days of David, who found favor before God and asked to find a dwelling for the God of Jacob.

Acts 7:44–46

Lord,
Thank You so much for the tabernacle. Thank You for always giving me a visual object lesson of Your love. You set up the tabernacle to point to and explain Your beautiful plan of salvation. You have not failed to fulfill Your covenant with sinful man. From before the foundation of the world You have been drawing me to Yourself. You will move heaven and earth to bless those who trust in You. You want to dwell with me. This is so touching. Father, I want to dwell with You. I want You to be with me and in me all the days of my life. I want to dwell with You for eternity. Thank You for wanting me in Your presence. Thank You for the fulfilling of Your covenant as You completely cleanse my character so that I can stand before You and not perish. Evict my unbelief and reign supreme in me. Amen.

## OCTOBER 2

Dear Friend, Temple of the Lord,

But Solomon built Him a house. However, the Most High does not dwell in temples made with hands, as the prophet says: "Heaven is My throne, and earth is My footstool. What house will You build for Me?" says the Lord, "Or what is the place of My rest? Has My hand not made all these things?"

Acts 7:47–50

Lord,

You are Almighty God and Ruler of the universe. What can I possibly build that would be something You need? You do not wish to dwell in man-made buildings. You want to dwell in my heart. You do not wish for me to try to serve You of my own accord. You long for me to surrender my heart to You so that You can build a beautiful temple for Yourself out of my life. I want to be a monument and a beacon of Your eternal long-suffering and faithfulness toward mankind. I want to be a compassionate resting place for weary souls. Fulfill Your covenant in me, Lord. Build for Yourself a spotless temple. Make my life Your delightful place of habitation. My heart echoes the prayer of King David: "Create in me a clean heart, O God; and renew a right spirit within me." Thank You for choosing me as Your precious child. I am eternally grateful that You are my Father. Amen.

# OCTOBER 3

Dear Friend, Eternally Loved,

*You* stiff-necked and uncircumcised in heart and ears! You always resist the Holy Spirit; as your fathers *did,* so *do* you. Which of the prophets did your fathers not persecute? And they killed those who foretold of the Just One, of whom you now have become the betrayers and murderers, who have received the law by the direction of angels and have not kept *it*.

Acts 7:51–53

Lord,
You have loved and protected me from before my birth. You bless me with every blessing. And yet I am still focused on myself and on outward appearances and behavior. Please forgive me for a heart that avoids true surrender and ears with selfish, selective hearing. Please forgive me for resisting the patient wooing of the Spirit. I would much rather blame others for Your betrayal and murder than to let You reveal my own evil, disloyal, and murderous heart. You have revealed Your holy law of love and life, and I have not cherished it but hold it up as a banner of condemnation for others. I do not want to continue this pattern. Lord, I need You. Change my heart. Give me ears that select Your words only. Be not far from me. Amen.

# OCTOBER 4

Dear Friend, Witness for Jesus,

When they heard these things they were cut to the heart, and they gnashed at him with *their* teeth. But he, being full of the Holy Spirit, gazed into heaven and saw the glory of God, and Jesus standing at the right hand of the God, and said, "Look! I see the heavens opened and the Son of Man standing at the right hand of God!"

Acts 7:54–56

Lord,

Please forgive me for being angry with those who speak the truth about You. I do not enjoy hearing that I am guilty of crucifying You, but I need to face the reality of my selfish, sinful sickness in order to be healed. Thank You, Lord, for Stephen, the first martyr. Thank You for allowing him to magnify the history of Your faithfulness in contrast with man's unfaithfulness. I need a clear picture of how things stand. Thank You for the glorious glimpse of Your majestic second coming that You shared with Stephen. You are always sharing with and blessing Your faithful children. May I be so filled with the Holy Spirit that I do not value my own life at all but cherish every opportunity to share the beauty of Your character with others. May I see the heavens opened and the Son of Man at the right hand of the Father welcoming me home! Amen.

# OCTOBER 5

Dear Friend, Freely Forgiven,

Then they cried with a loud voice, stopped their ears, and ran at him with one accord; and they cast *him* out of the city and stoned *him*. And the witnesses laid down their clothes at the feet of a young man named Saul. And they stoned Stephen as he was calling on *God* and saying, "Lord Jesus, receive my spirit." Then he knelt down and cried out with a loud voice, "Lord, do not charge them with this sin." And when he had said this, he fell asleep.

Acts 7:57–60

Lord,

Stephen reflected Your character so beautifully. He indeed had Your Spirit of unselfish, redemptive forgiveness. He was willing to give up his life for Your sake. He knew that the inheritance is not of this world. He knew that he would sleep peacefully until You come again and raise him up to spend eternity with You—You graciously showed him a glimpse of Your second coming. O Jesus, I have to say, I will be so excited to watch Saul, who became Paul, meet with Stephen and thank him for his witness. O how Stephen will rejoice to hear what happened to Saul/Paul! You have shown what awesome things a heart of forgiveness can do! When everyone is rushing at me with devilish anger, Jesus, fill me to overflowing with Your Spirit and let me shine as Stephen did, as You did, beaming forth with powerful rays of the light of the gospel. Amen.

# OCTOBER 6

Dear Friend, Saved by Grace,

And he [the jailor] brought them out and said, "Sirs, what must I do to be saved?" So they said, "Believe on the Lord Jesus Christ, and you will be saved, you and your household." Then they spoke the word of the Lord to him and all who were in his house. And he took them the same hour of the night and washed *their* stripes. And immediately he and all his family were baptized. Now when he had brought them into his house, he set food before them; and he rejoiced, having believed in God with all his household.

Acts 16:30–34

Lord,

How wonderful that a man guarding the physically captive but spiritually free realized his own spiritual captivity. How wonderful that You have freed me from ever feeling captive, though my body may be in bonds. I need only to believe on the Lord Jesus Christ. Lord, I believe that Jesus has sacrificed His all as me, to redeem me from the awful bonds of sin. Fulfill Your covenant in me. Jesus, I want not only Your forgiveness but freedom from repetitive sin that holds my heart in bondage. Work Your work in my life. I believe in Your cleansing power. Amen.

## OCTOBER 7

Dear Friend, Protected by the Almighty,

Now when they had escaped, they then found out that the island was called Malta. And the natives showed us unusual kindness; for they kindled a fire and made us all welcome . . . But when Paul had gathered a bundle of sticks and laid *them* on the fire, a viper came out because of the heat, and fastened on his hand. So when the natives saw the creature hanging from his hand, they said to one another, "No doubt this man is a murderer, whom, though he has escaped the sea, yet justice does not allow to live." But he shook off the creature into the fire and suffered no harm. However, they were expecting that he would swell up or suddenly fall dead. But after they had looked a long time and saw no harm come to him, they changed their minds and said he was a god.

Acts 28:1–6

Lord,

How quickly I judge other people by what I see at the moment. Just as the natives judged Paul a murderer, so I condemn others in my mind. Lord, please forgive my critical spirit. Help me to see others through Your eyes. I don't want to think badly or be judgmental of anyone; neither do I want to idolize anyone. The natives of Malta went from condemning Paul to thinking he was a god. Forgive me for looking to people with admiration that belongs to You. Keep my focus on You, Jesus. Strengthen my faith. Help me to remember that You are my Fortress and my Deliverer. Just as the viper could not harm Paul, so nothing can harm me while I remain in Your care. Protect me from the venom of sin, Lord. Amen.

# OCTOBER 8

Dear Friend, Redeemed by the Lamb,

For I am not ashamed of the gospel of Christ: for it is the power of God unto salvation to everyone that believeth; to the Jew first, and also to the Greek. For therein is the righteousness of God is revealed from faith to faith: as it is written, The just shall live by faith.

Romans 1:16–17 KJV

Lord,
Without the gospel of Christ, I have no hope. Jesus, You are not ashamed to identify Yourself with me. You came to my pathetic human level to redeem me. Let me shout Your praises from the housetop forever! Let me not fear the pride and unbelief of self. Let me count it a privilege to suffer with You for the gospel's sake. Use me to declare You righteousness and love. Thank You for supplying me with Your faith that I may stand firm in the gospel. I believe that You, and *You alone*, are my salvation. May I always reveal Your gospel, Your faith, and Your love to those around me. Let the heavens fall, and let the earth be removed; I will stand in You. Amen.

# OCTOBER 9

Dear Friend, Redeemed by the Lamb,

Therefore you are inexcusable, O man, whoever you are who judge, for in whatever you judge another you condemn yourself; for you who judge practice the same things. But we know that the judgment of God is according to truth against those who practice such things. And do you think this, O man, you who judge those practicing such things, and doing the same, that you will escape the judgment of God? . . . For there is no partiality with God.

Romans 2:1–3, 11

Lord,

I am inexcusable, yet I beg for Your mercy and forgiveness. Judging others seems as natural for me as breathing. Truly it is a result of my own evil deficiencies. Father, please cleanse my heart. Remove the ready condemnation and renew a right spirit within me. When I encounter what appears to me to be evil, let me close my mouth and walk away. Let me leave it to You. Thank You for being no respecter of persons. You love each of us with every fiber of Your being. Lord, when You judge me, may You find Your love in my heart. May You find a love that blesses everyone I meet. Thank You for being the Judge. Amen.

# October 10

Dear Friend, Bride of Christ,

Or do you not know, brethren (for I speak to those who know the law), that the law has dominion over a man as long as he lives? For the woman who has a husband is bound by the law to *her* husband as long as he lives. But if the husband dies, she is released from the law of her husband. So then if, while *her* husband lives, she marries another man, she will be called an adulteress; but if her husband dies, she is free from that law, so that she is no adulteress, though she has married another man.

Romans 7:1–3

Lord,

Your Law, which I am bound to, condemns me to death because I am a helpless sinner. I can in no way obey it. You are my Husband. Your perfect and holy Law is Your character; it is who You are. Therefore, Your Law, a reflection of Yourself, is my Husband. Were it not for the perfect plan You established before the foundation of the world, I would forever be condemned by my Husband, the Law, because I have sold myself to sin. Father, Your beautiful Law can never die, it is as eternal as You Yourself. Only I can die. And eternal death is all I deserve. How incredibly precious that You were willing to become me, to take my eternal death; to end the hopeless marriage of my helpless flesh and Your holy Law. Thank You for letting me die condemned by the Law in You. Praise and glory and honor belong to You forevermore for raising me up in You! Fulfill Your covenant in me; reign in my heart forever, Jesus, my perfect Law of love. Amen.

# OCTOBER 11

Dear Friend, Bride of Christ,

Therefore, my brethren, you also have become dead to the law through the body of Christ, that you may be married to another—to Him who was raised from the dead, that we should bear fruit to God. For when we were in the flesh, the sinful passions which were aroused by the law were at work in our members to bear fruit to death. But now we have been delivered from the law, having died to what we were held by, so that we should serve in the newness of the Spirit and not *in* the oldness of the letter.

Romans 7:4–6

Lord,

Thank You for Your eternal solution to my helpless estate. You knew that the Law cannot die. It is a reflection of Your character of love, and You are eternal. You knew that my flesh can only bear fruit to death; therefore, You instituted Your precious plan of perfect love. You became me, assuming my sinful nature. You fulfilled the Law; you treasured every morsel the Father wrote on Your heart so completely that You obeyed it in word and in deed. You were a committed vessel to reflect the Father's love. And You died my eternal death—the wages of my sin. Now You have made me alive through Your perfect victory. I am dead; I died in You on Calvary, but You have made me alive through Your glorious resurrection. Let it never be me who lives, but Christ who lives in me. Fulfill Your covenant in me. Fulfill Your Law in my heart and my life. Thank You for forever identifying with me. Thank You for being my Husband. I am nothing. *You are everything!* Amen.

# OCTOBER 12

Dear Friend, Alive in Christ,

What shall we say then? *Is* the law sin? Certainly not! On the contrary, I would not have known sin except through the law. For I would not have known covetousness unless the law had said, "You shall not covet." But sin, taking opportunity by the commandment, produced in me all *manner of evil* desire. For apart from the law sin *was* dead. I was alive once without the law, but when the commandment came, sin revived and I died. And the commandment, which *was to bring* life, I found to *bring* death. For sin, taking occasion by the commandment, deceived me, and by it killed *me*. Therefore the law is holy, and the commandment holy and just and good.

Romans 7:7–12

Lord,
Your beautiful law is a reflection of Your perfect character of love. When I look at it, I see something that is beyond my reach but very necessary for my survival. Without looking at Your law, I really do not seem like such a bad person. I do my best. However, when I compare myself to Your holy law, I see that I am severely lacking in every detail. The law makes me look like a pathetic, rotten sinner, which is indeed what I am. Your law condemns me to eternal death. Where my flesh would tell me I'm okay, Your law reveals that I am deceived and on the path to certain death. Thank You, Lord for Your holy and just and good commands. Thank You that You will write Your law on my heart. Amen.

# OCTOBER 13

Dear Friend, Child of God,

For as many as are led by the Spirit of God, these are the sons of God. For you did not receive the spirit of bondage again to fear, but you received the spirit of adoption by whom we cry out, "Abba, Father." The Spirit Himself bears witness with our spirit that we are children of God, and if children, then heirs—heirs of God and joint heirs with Christ, if indeed we suffer with *Him*, that we may also be glorified together.

Romans 8:14–17

Lord,

Thank You for adopting me as Your child. *You alone* are our redemption. You would not allow Your Seed to come from Abraham and Hagar's son because Hagar was a slave. Jesus, You did not come from slavery but from freedom. As surely as You are an eternal God, You bring me out of the bondage of sin with Your perfect life on this earth—a life that You freely give to me. You are my true Father. Jesus, You have kept every promise of Your everlasting covenant. I am thrilled to be bonded with You. Thank You for the privilege of suffering with You. May Your Name be forever glorified. Amen.

# OCTOBER 14

Dear Friend, Comforted by the Spirit,

Likewise the Spirit also helps in our weaknesses. For we do not know what we should pray for as we ought, but the Spirit Himself makes intercession for us with groanings which cannot be uttered. Now He who searches the hearts knows what the mind of the Spirit is, because He makes intercession for the saints according to *the will of* God. And we know that all things work together for good to those who love God, to those who are the called according to *His* purpose.

Romans 8:26–28

Lord,
Thank You for Your wise, loving, and gracious Spirit who knows my infirmities better than I. I come humbly to You in my pathetic condition. Is it my selfish prayers that make the Spirit groan or is it that the Spirit is pleading for me with every ounce of His being? Lord, I feel it is both. In my heart, I crave the good things that are for Your purpose, yet I do not seem to know those what those good things are. Thank You for interceding for me. It is an incredible comfort to my feeble heart to know that the Spirit Himself is searching my heart and reconciling me. You have called me. Let my heart of weaknesses answer with surrender. Let me love You, Father, and You will work out all things for good, just as You have said. Amen.

# OCTOBER 15

Dear Friend, Known from Everlasting,

For whom He foreknew, He also predestined *to be* conformed to the image of His Son, that He might be the firstborn among many brethren. Moreover, whom He predestined, these He also called; whom He called, these He also justified; and whom He justified, these He also glorified.

Romans 8:29–30

Lord,
You knew me from before the foundation of the world, and You predestined for me to be conformed to the image of Your Son. You created man in Your image, knowing that You would recreate us through Jesus Christ. You have never wanted anyone to be lost. You long for each and every one of Your children to be with You. I want to be with You. I want to be restored to Your image. Thank You for predestining me to this end. Thank You for calling me to Yourself. Thank You for justifying me with Your holy Life and precious blood. You are fulfilling Your covenant in me. I believe it, though I can't see or feel it, I know it. I know that You keep Your promises. Thank You. Amen.

# OCTOBER 16

Dear Friend, Eternally Loved,

What shall we say to these things? If God *is* for us, who *can be* against us? He who did not spare His own Son, but delivered Him up for us all, how shall He not with Him also freely give us all things? Who shall bring a charge against God's elect? *It is* God who justifies. Who *is* he who condemns? *It is* Christ who died, and furthermore is also risen, who is even at the right hand of God, who also makes intercession for us. Who shall separate us from the love of Christ? *Shall* tribulation, or distress, or persecution, or famine, or nakedness, or peril, or sword? As it is written: "For Your sake we are killed all day long; we are accounted as sheep for the slaughter." Yet in all these things we are more than conquerors through Him who loved us.

Romans 8:31–37

Lord,
Why do I worry? If You are for me, You, the eternal, all-wise, all-knowing, loving God, who cares if anyone is against me? The concern is not for me; it is for whoever may be against me because they are against You. Satan condemns me, but I need not fear. You, Jesus, make intercession for me. You love me with an everlasting and inseparable love. I do not ever need to fear tribulation, distress, persecution, famine, nakedness, peril, or sword. It does not matter if I am killed. It is but a sleep, a rest in the grave until You come again to raise me to life eternal. I am more than a conqueror in You. Praise Your name forever! What an awesome God! Amen.

# OCTOBER 17

Dear Friend, Loved by the Trinity,

For I am persuaded that neither death nor life, nor angels, nor principalities nor powers, nor things present nor things to come, nor height nor depth, nor any other created thing, shall be able to separate us from the love of God which is in Christ Jesus our Lord.

Romans 8:38–39

Lord,

How awesome and amazing and beyond my comprehension it is that You were willing to be separated from Your Father for eternity so that I would know and believe that I can *never* be separated from the Father's eternal love for me. You have loved me while I was yet Your enemy. Only a horrible choice to fully separate myself from You forever can separate me from You. But even then You would still love me. I choose You, no matter what. When I fear death, and when I fear that life is too distracting or overwhelming, remind me that it is not too much to separate me from Your love. When I feel like the powers of darkness are pressing me beyond what I can bear, remind me that Your love is here and able to hold me up against the evil one. Forgive me for acting as if some things are just too much to deal with. Forgive me for making decisions based on the negative feelings the devil puts in my head. Please help me to remember, Lord, that Your love is not just a feeling, but it *is who You are*. You *are* love. Please strengthen my belief in Your omnipotent love for me. Amen.

# OCTOBER 18

Dear Friend, Daughter/Son of God,

I beseech you therefore, brethren, by the mercies of God, that you present your bodies a living sacrifice, holy, acceptable to God, *which is* your reasonable service. And do not be conformed to this world, but be transformed by the renewing of your mind, that you may prove what *is* that good and acceptable and perfect will of God. For I say, through the grace given to me, to everyone who is among you, not to think *of himself* more highly than he ought to think, but to think soberly, as God has dealt to each one a measure of faith.

Romans 12:1–3

Lord,
I give myself to You. I want to serve You with my life. Help me to present my heart to You in a sacrificial manner. I struggle to stay surrendered. I do not know how to represent You rightly. Please renew my mind with the mind of Christ. Transform my thinking from the things of this world to Your perfect will. Father, forgive me for thinking that I am in any way any better than any other person. I am nothing. You are everything. Thank You for the measure of faith that You have given me. May my faith grow stronger and deeper in my heart until I am utterly consumed with a complete and perfect trust in You forever, my beautiful Savior. Amen.

# OCTOBER 19

Dear Friend, Loved by the Father,

Let love *be* without hypocrisy. Abhor what is evil. Cling to what is good. *Be* kindly affectionate to one another with brotherly love, in honor giving preference to one another; not lagging in diligence, fervent in spirit, serving the Lord; rejoicing in hope, patient in tribulation, continuing steadfastly in prayer; distributing to the needs of the saints, given to hospitality. Bless those who persecute you; bless and do not curse. Rejoice with those who rejoice, and weep with those who weep. Be of the same mind toward one another. Do not set your mind on high things, but associate with the humble. Do not be wise in your own opinion.

Romans 12:9–12

Lord,

Please fill me with the mind of Christ; the Mind that abhors evil and clings to good. Help me to think of others instead of myself. May all my activities be according to Your will. I rejoice in the blessings You have showered on me. Give me opportunity to share with others and a heart that thrives on the joy of giving. Father, pour Your love out on my enemies; shower them with Your mercy and goodness. Help me to see them as You see them. Thank You for those who rejoice. My heart grieves with Yours for those who weep. I am nothing, Lord. You are everything. Who is lower than me? Who is greater than You? "Fill me with the mind of Christ" is my prayer. Amen.

# October 20

Dear Friend, Redeemed by the Lamb,

No temptation has overtaken you except such as is common to man; but God *is* faithful, who will not allow you to be tempted beyond what you are able, but with the temptation will also make the way of escape, that you may be able to bear *it*.

I Corinthians 10:13

Lord,

Thank You for Your promise that You will never allow Satan to put more on me than what You can give me the faith to bear. Please help me to remember that Christ has already conquered every temptation that comes my way. Every temptation is indeed a temptation to disbelieve Your love for me and to gratify my selfish desires, feeding my pride and my love of self. Forgive me for my mis-focus, Lord. Help me to remember that *You are faithful*. Thank You for Your promise to never allow me to be overwhelmed by temptation. Remind me, when I feel overwhelmed, that it is a self-inflicted result of unbelief—a pity party for my selfish feelings. Let each temptation be a mere reminder of Your matchless power and grace. Amen.

# OCTOBER 21

Dear Friend, Loved by the Father,

Though I speak with the tongues of men and of angels, but have not love, I have become sounding brass or a clanging cymbal. And though I have the *gift of* prophecy, and understand all mysteries and all knowledge, and though I have all faith, so that I could remove mountains, but have not love, I am nothing. And though I bestow all my goods to feed *the* poor, and though I give my body to be burned, but have not love, it profits me nothing.

I Corinthians 13:1–3

Lord,
How fooled I am sometimes to think that I'm getting it together or doing okay. I judge myself by what I'm doing and how I'm feeling about it. I compromise with my conscience to make myself feel okay. Forgive me, as I am still merely focused on myself and not Your love. When I speak, Lord, sometimes I can hear the gong sounding and the cymbals clanging. Words I speak without You are empty. They come out of my mouth without being considered first. It's easy to clean out the house and give to the poor, but not so convenient to sit and listen to their heart needs or to treat them exactly how I demand to be treated. I need Your holy, agape love. Fill me with Your Spirit of love, I pray. Amen.

# OCTOBER 22

Dear Friend, Loved by the Son,

Love suffers long *and* is kind; love does not envy; love does not parade itself, is not puffed up; does not behave rudely, does not seek its own, is not provoked, thinks no evil; does not rejoice in iniquity, but rejoices in the truth; bears all things, believes all things, hopes all things, endures all things. Love never fails. But whether *there are* prophecies, they will fail; whether *there are* tongues, they will cease; whether *there is* knowledge, it will vanish away.

I Corinthians 13:4–8

Lord,
You know full well I am not always kind. I envy, I gloat, I'm rude, I want my own way, I allow myself to be provoked, I think evil, and I sometimes like to see other people mess up. Essentially I do not have love, at least not Your love. Only You can fill me with Your precious agape love. You have suffered long for me; Your kindness is admirable, but there is nothing to envy in me. Rather than puffing Yourself up to Your exalted position, You humbled Yourself to my miserable existence. Help me, Father, to not be easily provoked, to think no evil, to weep for others iniquities, and to rejoice in truth. I long to be like You, bearing and enduring all things. Help me to believe the best. Give me Your love that never fails. I crave it in my soul. Amen.

# OCTOBER 23

Dear Friend, Loved by the Spirit,

For we know in part and we prophesy in part. But when that which is perfect has come, then that which is in part will be done away. When I was a child, I spoke as a child, I understood as a child, I thought as a child; but when I became a man, I put away childish things. For now we see in a mirror, dimly, but then face to face. Now I know in part, but then I shall know just as I also am known. And now abide faith, hope, love, these three; but the greatest of these *is* love.

I Corinthians 13:9–13

Lord,
Perfect Your character in me, and do away with my partial surrender. I am but a child. I know so little. I see through a glass, darkly. Give me Your eye salve that I may see You clearly. Help me to put away my spiritually childish things and to grow in Your grace. Replace my temperamental, human love with Your complete, perfect agape love. Fill me with the faith of Jesus, the Spirit of hope, and the love of the Father. I long to see You face to face. I crave Your perfect love. Fill me, I beseech You in Jesus' Name. Amen.

# OCTOBER 24

Dear Friend, Redeemed by the Lamb,

Now this I say, brethren, that flesh and blood cannot inherit the kingdom of God; nor does corruption put on incorruption. Behold, I tell you a mystery: we shall not all sleep, but we shall be changed—in a moment, in the twinkling of an eye, at the last trumpet. For the trumpet will sound, and the dead will be raised incorruptible, and we shall be changed. For this corruption must put on incorruption, and this mortal must put on immortality.

I Corinthians 15:50–53

Lord,

I am sinful by nature. You have redeemed me. Your Spirit is convicting my heart of sin. As I confess and repent, You cleanse me—not just in my sin but from my sin. I believe You will completely cleanse and renew my heart, though I am still corrupt—a sinner by nature. I long for the day when the trumpet will sound, when You will victoriously call forth Your children who have been long sleeping in the grave. I long for that day when this old corruptible body shall be changed. Jesus, You gave of Yourself eternally, suffering a miserable, disgraceful life on this earth, and the horrors of Calvary, so that, in the twinkling of an eye, I could be transformed from this sick, mortal body into a beautiful, immortal creation—purchased at the infinite cost of Your precious blood. Jesus, whether I sleep, or I am yet alive when You return, I long for that magnificent day! Amen.

# OCTOBER 25

Dear Friend, Raised by the Risen Savior,

So when this corruptible has put on incorruption, and this mortal has put on immortality, then shall be brought to pass the saying that is written: "Death is swallowed up in victory." "O Death, where is your sting? O Hades, where is your victory?" The sting of death *is* sin, and the strength of sin *is* the law. But thanks *be* to God, who gives us the victory through our Lord Jesus Christ. Therefore, my beloved brethren, be steadfast, immovable, always abounding in the work of the Lord, knowing that your labor is not in vain in the Lord.

I Corinthians 15:54–58

Lord,

You have purchased with Your own blood an incredibly awesome, eternal gift—eternal life for all Your precious children. You took my eternal death for me, which is the wages of my sin. Sin is death. Your law makes my sin stand out bold and clear. Thank You Father, for sending Jesus to rescue me, not just in my sin but from my sin. And what's more, You have given me life eternal! Jesus, *You will* come again! You will change my corruptible, disintegrating body into a new body that will live for eternity. You have prepared a fire for the devil and his angels, but never have You ever intended for any of Your children to experience it. How horrifying that this is what some would choose instead of You. Holy Spirit, make me steadfast, immovable, and abounding in the work of the Lord. Use me to reflect Your character of infinite, selfless love to a world that is sick with the disease of sin that leads to real death. Amen.

# OCTOBER 26

Dear Friend, Comforted by the Comforter,

Blessed *be* the God and Father of our Lord Jesus Christ, the Father of mercies and the God of all comfort, who comforts us in all our tribulation, that we may be able to comfort those that are in any trouble, with the comfort with which we ourselves are comforted by God. For as the sufferings of Christ abound in us, so our consolation also abounds through Christ. Now if we are afflicted, *it is* for your consolation and salvation, which is effective for enduring the same sufferings which we also suffer. Or if we are comforted, *it is* for your consolation and salvation. And our hope for you *is* steadfast, because we know that as you are partakers of the sufferings, so also *you will partake* of the consolation.

II Corinthians 1:3–7

Lord,
You are a merciful and comforting God. Nothing can possibly be more comforting than to know that You have already experienced everything I will ever experience, and You have conquered all of it. You are with me, walking through every tribulation, carrying me. Let me count it joy to suffer as Jesus suffered. Thank You for making me worthy to have fellowship with You. Father, help me to be a comfort to others who are suffering, as You are indeed a comfort to me. Thank You for the fellowship and encouragement of other believers. May many more be drawn close to You to experience the consolation and salvation that only You can give. Let no one suffer in vain, but let all be drawn to You—to Your beautiful and loving heart—to be redeemed by Your love and grace. This is my prayer, in Jesus' worthy name. Amen.

# OCTOBER 27

Dear Friend, Reconciled by God,

Therefore, if anyone *is* in Christ, *he is* a new creation; old things have passed away; behold, all things have become new. Now all things *are* of God, who has reconciled us to Himself through Jesus Christ, and has given us the ministry of reconciliation, that is, that God was in Christ reconciling the world to Himself, not imputing their trespasses to them, and has committed to us the word of reconciliation.

II Corinthians 5:17–19

Lord,

Thank You for reconciling me to Yourself. I could never hope to reconcile myself. What awesome love! Let me die to the old things—all my self-ishness, pride, and unbelief—and make me new in Christ. Create in my a new heart. Renew a right spirit within me. O Lord, shine through me, empty me of my sinful self, and let me be a beacon from which Your glory shines forth like the sun. Give me Your Spirit of reconciliation that I may touch those around me. Thank You for Jesus. Thank You, Jesus! Amen.

## OCTOBER 28

Dear Friend, Bride of Christ,

And He said to me, "My grace is sufficient for you, for My strength is made perfect in weakness." Therefore most gladly I will rather boast in my infirmities, that the power of Christ may rest upon me. Therefore I take pleasure in infirmities, in reproaches, in needs, in persecutions, in distresses, for Christ's sake. For when I am weak, then I am strong.

II Corinthians 12:9–10

Lord,
O what a beautiful promise! No matter what my problem or perplexity, Your grace is sufficient to see me through. And not just sufficient to see me through, it strengthens me as I wait helplessly in weakness. Help me to give You my weaknesses instead of trying to hide or ignore them. Jesus, no one has suffered infirmities, reproaches, necessities, persecutions, or distress like You. Remind me that these things are for Your honor and glory. Only then can I take pleasure in them. Fill me with Your power that is victory. Give me victory that is Your faith. Thank You. Amen.

# OCTOBER 29

Dear Friend, Joint Heir with Christ,

I am crucified with Christ: nevertheless I live; yet not I, but Christ liveth in me: and the life which I now live in the flesh I live by faith in the Son of God, who loved me, and gave himself for me.

Galatians 2:20 KJV

Lord,

I am nothing. *You are everything.* Please help me to remember each breath is a gift purchased with Your blood and matchless love for me. You were crucified, yet I was crucified in You. I died eternally in You; the wages of sin is eternal death. You died the eternal death of a sinner. Only because of Your perfect life could Your Father call You forth. And it is because of Your perfect life, I live! You have purchased my eternal life. Even more exciting, You have provided a way of escape from sin! I do not have to continue this ugly pattern. Cleanse me inside and out. Fulfill Your covenant in me. Give me Your faith. May I love others with the same selfless love with which You love me. Amen.

# OCTOBER 30

Dear Friend, Daughter/Son of God,

For you are all sons of God through faith in Christ Jesus. For as many of you as were baptized into Christ, have put on Christ. There is neither Jew nor Greek, there is neither slave nor free, there is neither male nor female; for you are all one in Christ Jesus. And if you *are* Christ's, then you are Abraham's seed, and heirs according to the promise.

Galatians 3:26–29

Lord,

When You promised to make a great nation out of Abraham, You were not just thinking of an earthly nation, but a spiritual nation—a nation made up of all those who believe in You as did Abraham. Jesus, You have made it possible for me to legally be Your child again. I am forever grateful for this gift. You look at me so differently than others do and differently than the way I look at others. I notice gender, nationality, appearance, class, and all the outward things. I am trained to see a difference, and I automatically make a distinction. Please forgive me, Father, for esteeming myself higher than others; forgive me for believing that I am not as accepted by You as others are. Thank You for Your equal and consistent love and promise keeping. Amen.

# OCTOBER 31

Dear Friend, Taught by the Spirit,

But the fruit of the Spirit is love, joy, peace, longsuffering, kindness, goodness, faithfulness, gentleness, self-control. Against such there is no law. And those *who are* Christ's have crucified the flesh with its passions and desires. If we live in the Spirit, let us also walk in the Spirit.

Galatians 5:22–25

Lord,
I need Your Spirit. My flesh is weak and I often think only of myself. Crucify this flesh and its worldly affections. Replace my selfishness with Your *self-less-ness*. Fill me with Your love that works hand in hand with Your joy, peace, patience, and faith. Your longsuffering kindness and goodness are foreign to my impatient, judgmental thinking. I need You to plant the seeds of Your fruit in me as You uproot my rotten ways. Give me a gentle and meek spirit to care for the hearts of others as You do. Only by Your gracious Spirit will I exhibit self-control. To God be the glory. Amen.

# NOVEMBER 1

Dear Friend, Blessed by the Lord,

Grace to you and peace from God our Father and the Lord Jesus Christ. Blessed *be* the God and Father of our Lord Jesus Christ, who has blessed us with every spiritual blessing in the heavenly *places* in Christ, just as He chose us in Him before the foundation of the world, that we should be holy and without blame before Him in love, having predestined us to adoption as sons by Jesus Christ to Himself, according to the good pleasure of His will, to the praise of the glory of His grace, by which He made us accepted in the Beloved.

Ephesians 1:2–6

Lord,

May I know Your grace and peace. You bless me with every spiritual blessing, yet I ignore many of those blessings and they pass me by. Help me stay at attention spiritually so that I do not miss anything. Let me believe that I have been chosen by You long before the world was created to be Your precious child. You chose to love and save all, Lord. May we never reject You in our hearts. Empty us of ourselves, and fill us with Christ—His character of love, His grace, mercy, and peace, and His thoughts. Thank You, Jesus, for making us acceptable again. Amen.

## NOVEMBER 2

Dear Friend, Saved by Grace,

But God, who is rich in mercy, for his great love wherewith he loved us, even when we were dead in sins, hath quickened us together with Christ, (by grace ye are saved;) and hath raised *us* up together, and made *us* sit together in the heavenly *places* in Christ Jesus: that in the ages to come he might shew the exceeding riches of his grace in *his* kindness toward us through Christ Jesus. For by grace are ye saved through faith; and that not of yourselves: *it is* the gift of God: not of works, lest any man should boast. For we are his workmanship, created in Christ Jesus unto good works, which God hath before ordained that we should walk in them.

Ephesians 2:4–10 KJV

Lord,

Thank You so much for Your rich mercy and unfailing love for us. How grateful I am that while I am dead in my sins, you have purchased my life. Help me to cast away my selfish desires and to accept the full measure of Your beautiful, saving grace. Raise me from my death in sin to the Christlike child You intend for me to be. Please help me to fully realize that You alone can work any good in me. I can do nothing of myself. You knew, before the foundation of the world, what is best for me and the wonderful plans You have for my life. I long to be used by You to the end that others would know You and bask in Your sweet love. Amen.

# NOVEMBER 3

Dear Friend, Student of the Spirit,

For this cause I bow my knees unto the Father of our Lord Jesus Christ, of whom the whole family in heaven and earth is named, that he would grant you, according to the riches of his glory, to be strengthened with might by his Spirit in the inner man, that Christ may dwell in your hearts by faith; that ye, being rooted and grounded in love, may be able to comprehend with all the saints what *is* the breadth, and length, and depth, and height; and to know the love of Christ, which passeth knowledge, that ye might be filled with all the fullness of God. Now unto him that is able to do exceedingly abundantly above all that we ask or think, according to the power that worketh in us, unto him *be* glory in the church by Christ Jesus throughout all ages, world without end. Amen.

Ephesians 3:14–21 KJV

Lord,
What a privilege to be a part of Your family. O to be truly rooted and grounded in Your love. Jesus, I beseech You to fill me with Your faith and fill me with Your Spirit. I crave to go wider, longer, deeper, and higher into Your love. You indeed do far more for me then I could ever ask or think. You take far better care of me that I could ever take myself. Jesus, when I sit and contemplate what it must have been like for You in the closing hours of Your life, I cannot comprehend it. The mental and emotional agony in Gethsemane, the betrayal and denial of Your friends, the pain of nails piercing You through, and the inability to breathe, each by itself seems to be more than I could bear. Yet the worst for You was allowing my sin to drive an impassable wedge between You and Your—our—Father. Your love passes knowledge, yet this is what You want to fill mc with. Glory be to You, Lord, in heaven and on earth. May Your Name be glorified forever. Amen.

# NOVEMBER 4

Dear Friend, Protected by the Almighty,

Finally, my brethren, be strong in the Lord and the power of His might. Put on the whole armor of God, that you may be able to stand against the wiles of the devil. For we do not wrestle with flesh and blood, but against principalities, against powers, against the rulers of the darkness of this age, against spiritual *hosts* of wickedness in the heavenly *places*. Therefore take up the whole armor of God, that you may be able to withstand in the evil day, and having done all, to stand.

Ephesians 6:10–13

Lord,
This battle is not mine, but Yours. Why do I think that a quick prayer for strength is all I need to ward off one who has had thousands of years' experience in deceiving people like me? I am not warring against poor diet or bad habits. This battle is against Your heart, which includes my heart, because You have placed me in Your heart. Then enemy hates Your agape love. The enemy hates me, an undeserving object of Your unfailing love. I love You with my feeble human love. I can in no way ever win this battle. It belongs to You. Please cover me with Your armor. Protect my mind and heart from the ruler of darkness. Let me stand as a beacon of Your agape love and Your peace and rest, faith and victory. Amen.

# NOVEMBER 5

Dear Friend, Covered by the Blood,

Stand therefore, having girded your waist with truth, having put on the breastplate of righteousness, and having shod your feet with the preparation of the gospel of peace; above all, taking the shield of faith with which you will be able to quench all the fiery darts of the wicked one. And take the helmet of salvation, and the sword of the Spirit, which is the word of God; praying always with all prayer and supplication in the Spirit, being watchful to this end with all perseverance and supplication for all the saints—and for me, that utterance may be given to me, that I may open my mouth boldly to make known the mystery of the gospel, for which I am an ambassador in chains; that I may speak boldly, as I ought to speak.

Ephesians 6:14–20

Lord,
You have given to each of us a measure of faith. Multiply Your faith in me into a strong shield against the selfish and prideful temptations of my sinful heart. Consume my thinking with Your salvation instead of my own imaginations. Let me combat all evil with Your holy Word, just as Christ relied on scripture to defend His heart in the wilderness. Father, thank You for the Spirit who interprets my pleas and supplications. May I pray not for myself only, but let me plead for mercy for those who assail me. Thank You, Lord Jesus, for being my Armor. Fill me Your gospel of peace. May I speak boldly of Your gracious mercies. Praise be to You for evermore, in Jesus' name. Amen.

# NOVEMBER 6

Dear Friend, Chosen of God,

Grace to you and peace from God our Father and the Lord Jesus Christ. I thank my God upon every remembrance of you, always in every prayer of mine making request for you all with joy, for your fellowship in the gospel from the first day until now, being confident of this very thing, that He who has begun a good work in you will complete *it* until the day of Jesus Christ;

Philippians 1:2–6

Lord,
Thank You for Your grace and peace. It warms my heart and thrills my soul. Thank You for the prayers and fellowship of those who love to call upon Your name. It gives me courage and strength when the battle seems too strong. Thank You for Your promise that You will finish in me that which You have begun. Please help me to remember that it is Your work and that I need to allow You to do it. Remove my selfish desires that hamper Your work. Sometimes I feel as though I have gone further backward than forward. Thank You for reminding me that You intend to complete this work in me, and are therefore *not* giving up on me. Fill me with a faith that trusts You to completely fulfill Your covenant in me. May I never give up the fight. My confidence is in You, Lord. Amen.

# NOVEMBER 7

Dear Friend, Loved by the Humble Servant,

Let this mind be in you, which was also in Christ Jesus: Who, being in the form of God, thought it not robbery to be equal with God: but made himself of no reputation, and took upon him the form of a servant, and was made in the likeness of men. And being found in fashion as a man, he humbled himself, and became obedient unto death, even the death of the cross. Wherefore God also hath highly exalted him, and given him a name which is above every name: that at the name of Jesus every knee should bow, of *things* in heaven, and *things* in earth, and *things* under the earth; and *that* every tongue should confess that Jesus Christ *is* Lord, to the glory of God the Father.

Philippians 2:5–11 KJV

Lord,
You are awesome. O to have the mind of Christ! I cannot comprehend how Jesus, my Creator, allowed Himself to take on my ugly, sinful nature; to serve the likes of me—this is a beautiful mystery! Yank the self-absorbed ideas out of my heart and mind, and fill me with Your selfless humility. I want to do my own thing and then turn to You to eradicate the consequences. You want better for me. You want my obedience to Your love. You were obedient to the wages of my sin. You have conquered my foes—sin and eternal death. You have given a new and radically different meaning to the words *leader* and *servant*. You, alone, are to be exalted. Angels will never understand the gratitude my redeemed heart feels. I confess, Jesus Christ is Lord! Glory be to *Him* forever more! Amen.

## NOVEMBER 8

Dear Friend, Redeemed by the Lamb,

Rejoice in the Lord always. Again I will say, rejoice! Let your gentleness be known to all men. The Lord *is* at hand. Be anxious for nothing,
but in everything by prayer and supplication, with thanksgiving, let your
requests be made known to God; and the peace of God, which passes all
understanding, will guard your hearts and minds through Christ Jesus.

Philippians 4:4–7

Lord,
I rejoice in You! You are my Creator, Sustainer, Redeemer, my Hope, and
my life; You are my All! May those who look at me, not see me, but may
they see You reflected in my countenance. I need not worry for anything
for You provide all my needs just as You have promised. Countless times
I have been abundantly blessed with beautiful blessings beyond measure.
Forgive me for failing to say thank you. Forgive me for the times I have
doubted Your faithfulness. You have never abandoned Your children. I lay
my heart before You with thanksgiving. You are an awesome God! Amen.

# November 9

Dear Friend, Taught by the Spirit,

Finally, brethren, whatever things are true, whatever things *are* noble, whatever things *are* just, whatever things *are* pure, whatever things *are* lovely, whatever things *are* of a good report, if *there is* any virtue and if there is anything praiseworthy—meditate on these things. The things which you learned and received and heard and saw in me, these do, and the God of peace will be with you.

Philippians 4:8–9

Lord,
Thank You for the Holy Spirit who speaks to my heart and mind, and continually, lovingly, turns my focus back to you. Please help me to use Your principles to test every thought, word, and action. Help me to never utter a word of untruth, but help me to always speak the truth as it is in You. Keep me from dishonorable deeds and activities, and let me ever reflect Your honorable character of love. Forgive me for treating others however I feel like treating them; help me to act justly. My senses are bombarded continually with the filth of this world, Lord; please fill me with pure thoughts of the gospel of peace. The ugliness of my own heart depresses me, so I need to continually behold You. Most reports are not good, Father, so please help me not to waste my time listening. Jesus, may I continually meditate on Your virtue and praiseworthiness. Thank You, God of peace, for ever being near me. Amen.

# NOVEMBER 10

Dear Friend, Strengthened by Christ,

But I rejoice in the Lord greatly that now at last your care for me has flourished again; though you surely did care, but you lacked opportunity. Not that I speak in regard for need, for I have learned in whatever state I am, to be content: I know how to be abased, and I know how to abound. Everywhere and in all things I have learned both to be full and to be hungry, both to abound and to suffer need. I can do all things through Christ who strengthens me.

Philippians 4:10–13

Lord,
Please be the Ruler of my heart so that You, through me, may care for the needs of all those You place in my path. Give me a heart that is content with Your matchless love and mercy. I want to glorify You in all things, in plenty and in hunger, no matter my circumstances. You feed the birds and clothe the lilies. Your loving kindness is endless. Jesus, be my continual and sustaining strength. Let everything I do be for You. Let everything I say be from Your lips. I want to serve You with every fiber of my being! Use me, Father. Use me, Jesus. Use me, Spirit. Amen.

# NOVEMBER 11

Dear Friend, Reconciled in Christ,

For it pleased *the Father that* in Him all the fullness should dwell, and by Him to reconcile all things to Himself, by Him, whether things on earth or things in heaven, having made peace through the blood of His cross. And you, who were once alienated and enemies in your mind by wicked works, yet now He has reconciled in the body of His flesh through death, to present you holy, and blameless, and above reproach in His sight—If indeed you continue in the faith, grounded and steadfast, and are not moved away from the hope of the gospel which you heard, which was preached to every creature under heaven, of which I, Paul, became a minister.

Colossians 1:19–23

Lord,
How can I ever give You enough praise for the glorious things You have done for me, for the glorious things You are doing in my life, and for the glorious things You have prepared for my future? You have become flesh to rescue me from my sinful condition. Keep me grounded and steadfast in Your faith. Never let me move from the knowledge and belief in the hope I have in You. I alienated myself from You by my detestable faithlessness and selfish pride, but You have reconciled me to Yourself through Jesus Christ. You alone can cleanse my character, can present me holy and blameless, and can remove all reproach. Work Your beautiful work in me, Jesus. I believe. Amen.

# NOVEMBER 12

Dear Friend, Raised with Christ,

If then you were raised with Christ, seek those things which are above, where Christ is, sitting at the right hand of God. Set your mind on things above, not on things on the earth. For you died, and your life is hidden with Christ in God. When Christ *who is* our life appears, then you also will appear with Him in glory.

Colossians 3:1–4

Lord,
Please accept my humble gratitude for Jesus' love for me. You have loved me from eternity past. You have laid down Your high position and become me. You have sacrificed Your very eternity to offer eternity to me. Lord, I seek You. Please forgive me for being concerned with the foolish vanities that will perish with this earth. Forgive me for focusing on improving myself, hoping to become more worthy by trying to rid myself of evil, one ugly spot at a time. My inward focus is indeed killing me—body, mind, and spirit. Lift my face up to You, Jesus. Let my feeble self perish in You. Hide me in Your merciful self. May *all* my focus and affections be for You Jesus, my Creator; my Redeemer, my Husband. I am nothing. *You are everything*! Amen.

# NOVEMBER 13

Dear Friend, Chosen by God,

Continue earnestly in prayer, being vigilant in it with thanksgiving; meanwhile praying also for us, that God would open to us a door for the word, to speak the mystery of Christ, for which I am also in chains, that I may make it manifest, as I ought to speak. Walk in wisdom toward those *who are* outside, redeeming the time. *Let* your speech always *be* with grace, seasoned with salt, that you may know how you ought to answer each one.

Colossians 4:2–6

Lord,
I lift up my family and my friends, and I lift up all of Your faithful servants, too. Thank You for the privilege of sharing Your love. Please show me each day the way You would have me to walk. Put Your faith in my heart, Your gracious expressions on my face, and Your words of reconciliation on my lips. Let no bonds of any kind keep me from declaring Your character to others. Give me Your wisdom and Your grace. Help me to use every moment for Your honor and glory. Help me to rely wholly on You for every moment of my life. Amen.

# NOVEMBER 14

Dear Friend, Eternally Loved,

But I do not want you to be ignorant, brethren, concerning those who have fallen asleep, lest you sorrow as others who have no hope. For if we believe that Jesus died and rose again, even so God will bring with Him those who sleep in Jesus. For this we say to you by the word of the Lord, that we who are alive and remain until the coming of the Lord will by no means precede those who are asleep.

I Thessalonians 4:13–15

Lord,
Thank You so much for giving me a hope. Jesus, You are beautiful. You have truly conquered death. You died the eternal death of a sinner such as I. You felt, on the cross, an eternal separation from Your Father, but You took our eternal death to its death. Satan could not hold You in the grave. No one needs to die unless they choose to reject Your precious gift of life. *You* are the *only One* who has paid the wages of sin—death. Now I know that my loved ones are but asleep. I know that You will wake them when You come again. Fulfill Your covenant in me, Lord. I want to be pure gold tried in the fire, ready and waiting for Your glorious return. I do not want to be among those who scorn Your free gift of eternal life. I do not want to die an eternal death that You have already died for me. I do not want Your grace to be in vain. Thank You Jesus for Your beautiful, matchless, agape love for me. Shine through me, Jesus. Shine Your perfect love! Amen.

# November 15

Dear Friend, Resting in Jesus,

For this we say to you by the word of the Lord, that we who are alive and remain until the coming of the Lord will by no means precede those who are asleep. For the Lord Himself will descend from heaven with a shout, with the trumpet of God. And the dead in Christ will rise first. Then we which are alive and remain shall be caught up together with them in the clouds to meet the Lord in the air. And thus we shall always be with the Lord. Therefore comfort one another with these words.

I Thessalonians 4:15–18

Lord,

You are spotless. You are perfect. You are God, and so You arose victorious! Thank You, Jesus. You will call forth all those who have gone to sleep in the grave trusting Your beautiful covenant. I long to be alive, remaining as part of Your remnant, to witness Your awesome appearing in the clouds, as You have said that every eye will see. How precious it will be to hear You command Your sleeping children to arise; how breathtaking it will be to watch them burst forth from their resting places and fly to You. You have conquered the grave indeed! Jesus, please cover me, cleanse me, and fill me with Your Spirit. Make me worthy of the honor of beholding You face to face. Thank You for Your beautiful promise that I will always be with You. Thank You for the comfort Your precious promises bring to my feeble heart. Thank You. Hallelujah! Amen.

## NOVEMBER 16

Dear Friend, Disciple of Christ,

Rejoice always, pray without ceasing, in everything give thanks; for this is the will of God in Christ Jesus for you. Do not quench the Spirit. Do not despise prophecies. Test all things; hold fast what is good. Abstain from every form of evil.

I Thessalonians 5:16–22

Lord,

Hallelujah! Praise the name of Jesus, now and forever more! Jesus, I am eternally grateful for Your love and mercy. May I always be connected with You, just as Christ received every thought, word, and action from You. Open my ears to Your teaching. Help me to stop trying to figure things out myself and then asking You if that's right. I need to do more listening and less talking. I need to listen more and imagine less. Cause me to be obedient to Your ways and Your prophecies. Thank You for revealing the future to dispel all fear. Sanctify me wholly, Lord. Remove all evil and any appearance of evil. Fulfill Your covenant in me. I humbly submit my body, mind, and spirit to Your amazing, cleansing power. Amen.

# NOVEMBER 17

Dear Friend, Sanctified by God,

Now may the God of peace Himself sanctify you completely; and may your whole spirit, soul, and body be preserved blameless at the coming of our Lord Jesus Christ. He who calls you is faithful, who also will do it. Brethren, pray for us. Greet all the brethren with a holy kiss. I charge you by the Lord that this epistle be read to all the holy brethren. The grace of our Lord Jesus Christ *be* with you. Amen.

I Thessalonians 5:23–28

Lord,
The work of sanctification, the purifying of the heart, is the work of a lifetime. It is a work that only You can complete. Please work this work to its completion in my life. Fulfill Your covenant in me. You alone can cleanse my heart. You alone can rid me of my selfish desires. Jesus, You were tempted by Your arch enemy, tempted from every possible angle, and You clung to Your Father every moment. Through the grace of the Father, You denied Your feelings and stood firm in Your decision to at all costs remain loyal to Your mission. Please fill me with Your grace. Fill me with Your faith that is the victory over the world. Amen.

## NOVEMBER 18

Dear Friend, Loved by the Faithful One,

Finally, brethren, pray for us, that the word of the Lord may run swiftly and be glorified, just as it is with you, and that we may be delivered from unreasonable and wicked men; for not all have faith. But the Lord is faithful, who will establish you and guard you from the evil one. And we have confidence in the Lord concerning you, both that you do and will do the things we command you. Now may the Lord direct your hearts into the love of God and into the patience of Christ.

II Thessalonians 3:1–5

Lord,

Are others praying for me? When I long for the prayers of others, I am reminded of how often I utter the quick words, "I'll pray for you," and how quickly I forget them. Holy Spirit, please read the list in my heart of family and friends, of acquaintances and those that I have seen in passing and now cannot fully recall. You know their needs better than I. Father, may Your Name be glorified in each life. Deliver me and deliver my precious brothers and sisters in You from the unreasonableness and wickedness that surrounds us and from unfaithfulness. Keep our focus on You, the Faithful One. Guard us from evil. Establish Your faith in us, Lord, that we will allow You to direct our hearts into Your love and Your patience. Cause us to fulfill Your holy commands. Father, I ask this not only for those on my prayer list, but for every person in this world who has no one to pray for them, I ask for a double portion. This is my prayer, in Jesus' name. Amen.

# NOVEMBER 19

Dear Friend, Disciple of Christ,

And I thank Christ Jesus our Lord who has enabled me, because He counted *me* into the ministry, although I was formerly a blasphemer, a persecutor, and an insolent man; but I obtained mercy because I did it ignorantly in unbelief. And the grace of our Lord was exceedingly abundant, with faith and love which are in Christ Jesus. This *is* a faithful saying and worthy of all acceptance, that Christ Jesus came into the world to save sinners, of whom I am chief.

I Timothy 1:12–15

Lord,
Thank You for giving me life, not only on this earth but by taking my death as me, and giving me eternal life in You. Thank You for renewing my heart and counting me worthy to be used in Your ministry of drawing hearts to Yourself for complete healing. I have taken Your name in vain. I have bad-mouthed and harassed You by persecuting with my tongue and my attitude Your chosen shepherds. I proclaimed to be an example of You when I knew You not. Please forgive me, Lord, for such dreadful and damaging hypocrisy. Thank You for Your exceedingly abundant grace and love and for Your marvelous faith. Indeed, and without any doubt, You came to this world with a determination to save sinners, of whom I am the worst. Thank You! Hallelujah! Amen.

# NOVEMBER 20

Dear Friend, Disciple of Jesus Christ,

But you, O man of God, flee these things and pursue righteousness, god-liness, faith, love, patience, gentleness. Fight the good fight of faith, lay hold on eternal life, to which you were also called and have confessed the good confession in the presence of many witnesses. I urge you in the sight of God who gives life to all things, and *before* Christ Jesus who witnessed the good confession before Pontius Pilate, that you keep *this* command-ment without spot, blameless until our Lord Jesus Christ's appearing, which He will manifest in His own time, *He who is* the blessed and only Potentate, the King of kings and Lord of lords, who alone has immortality, dwelling in unapproachable light, whom no man has seen or can see, to whom *be* honor and everlasting power. Amen.

I Timothy 6:11–16

Lord,
You are Almighty. I cannot stand before You except in Christ, and Christ Jesus alone. You are my Life. I feel like I am a magnet for unrighteous-ness. I gravitate toward thoughts and things that draw me away from You. The magnetic pull seems absolutely overwhelming sometimes. Please help me to flee from even a tiny thought of anything that is not of You. By Your grace and faith, let me pursue righteousness, godliness, faith, love, patience and gentleness. By Your faith alone I can lay hold of eternal life. Let my life be a perfect witness of the blameless King of kings and Lord of lords, Jesus Christ, my honorable and everlasting Savior. Amen.

## NOVEMBER 21

Dear Friend, Banner of the Gospel,

Therefore do not be ashamed of the testimony of our Lord, nor of me his prisoner, but share with me in the sufferings for the gospel according to the power of God, who has saved us and called *us* with a holy calling, not according to our works, but according to His own purpose and grace which was given to us in Christ Jesus before time began, but has now been revealed by the appearing of our Savior Jesus Christ, *who* has abolished death and brought life and immortality to light through the gospel, to which I was appointed a preacher, an apostle, and a teacher of the Gentiles. For this reason I also suffer these things; nevertheless I am not ashamed, for I know whom I have believed and am persuaded that He is able to keep what I have committed to Him until that Day.

II Timothy 1:8–12

Lord,
Thank You for allowing me to testify of Your love and grace. It is a privilege to suffer with Jesus in order to reveal the heart of the Father. Let me never be ashamed to be led by the power of God. Thank You for giving me such a holy and awesome calling. Please use me for Your purpose. Help me to refrain from "going with the flow" when I am trying to avoid conflict. Help me to preserve Your holy character instead of trying to preserve myself from an uncomfortable position. Remove the selfish purposes from my heart. You have abolished death. Let me never cherish the death of selfishness and pride in my heart. I want to stand firm for You come what may. I know whom I have believed and am persuaded that He is able to keep what I have committed to Him until that Day. Amen.

## NOVEMBER 22

Dear Friend, Taught by the Spirit,

All Scripture *is* given by inspiration of God, and *is* profitable for doctrine, for reproof, for correction, for instruction in righteousness: That the man of God may be perfect, throughly furnished unto all good works.

II Timothy 3:16–17 KJV

Lord,

Thank You so much for this beautiful assurance. Man is very fallible, this You well know, and so You have made sure that You inspired the writers of scripture. I can believe that it is Your word. I can believe the doctrines in Scripture. I can believe that the words of discipline and correction are serious, and are for me personally. I can gain essential instruction for righteousness from Your holy Word. Send Your Spirit to continually teach me until I am complete and thoroughly equipped for every good work. I want to be filled with Your Word and Your character. Thank You for speaking to me so personally. Thank You for Your Word. Amen.

## NOVEMBER 23

Dear Friend, Saved by Grace,

But after that the kindness and the love of God our Savior toward man appeared, Not by works of righteousness which we have done, but according to his mercy he saved us, by the washing of regeneration, and renewing of the Holy Ghost; which he shed on us abundantly through Jesus Christ our Saviour; that being justified by his grace, we should be made heirs according to the hope of eternal life. *this is* a faithful saying, and these things I will that thou affirm constantly, that they which have believed in God might be careful to maintain good works. These things are good and profitable unto men.

Titus 3:4–8 KJV

Lord,

I fail and I fall again and again, and You lovingly pick me up, forgive me, and renew Your persistent efforts to cleanse my heart from all unrighteousness. It is because of Your mercies that I am not consumed. I thrive on Your kindness, faithfulness, and righteousness. Please wash me with Your regenerating and renewing Spirit of holiness. Help me to stop diving right back into the pits that You pull me from. I cannot be a proper witness for You while wallowing in my own mire. I surrender my life, my heart, and my will to You. You are my hope, my life, and my *All*. I am nothing. *You are everything*. I believe in You. Work Your works in me. I love You, Lord. Amen.

# NOVEMBER 24

Dear Friend, Bride of Christ,

For verily he took not on *him the nature of* angels; but he took on *him* the seed of Abraham. Wherefore in all things it behooved him to be made like unto *his* brethren, that he might be a merciful and faithful high priest in all things *pertaining* to God, to make reconciliation for the sins of the people. For in that he himself hath suffered being tempted, he is able to succour them that are tempted.

Hebrews 2:16–18 KJV

Lord,

To think that You, Creator of the universe, would take on the sinful nature of ungrateful man is beyond my comprehension. And yet, You did this without hesitation so that You could sympathize first-hand with me and draw me to Yourself. You have suffered everything that I have or ever will suffer and more. You have overcome every temptation that will ever come to me. Who else could possibly be such a loving Mediator for me? You have mediated by becoming me, taking all the punishment for all my wickedness, and unceasingly wooing me to stop shunning Your marvelous gift. You want to reign in me and give me the same victory that You have won. Wow! Fulfill Your covenant in me, Jesus. I surrender every fiber of my being to You in gratitude. Hallelujah! Amen.

# NOVEMBER 25

Dear Friend, Loved by our High Priest Brother,

Seeing then we have a great High Priest who has passed through the heavens, Jesus the Son of God, let us hold fast *our* confession. For we do not have a High Priest who cannot sympathize with our weaknesses, but was in all *points* tempted as *we are, yet* without sin. Let us therefore come boldly to the throne of grace, that we may obtain mercy and find grace in time of need.

Hebrews 4:14–16

Lord,
I can't think of anything more wonderful than having Jesus Christ Himself as my High Priest. Jesus, You do indeed sympathize with my weaknesses. You became Man, taking on my sinful flesh, though You were still my Creator God. You were tempted in every way that I am tempted; tempted to live for self, tempted to give in to pride, tempted to doubt who You were and the promises of Your Father, tempted to doubt that You could make it through to the end of Your mission, and yet, You never sinned. This is what You accomplished for me. I can come boldly to Your throne of grace. You do have mercy and grace for me—mercy, grace, and a way of escape from sin. Rid me of my selfishness, pride, and unbelief, which are the roots of all my sin. Fulfill Your covenant in me, my High Priest, my Elder Brother. How beautiful. Amen.

# NOVEMBER 26

Dear Friend, Purchased of God,

Therefore, when He came into the world, He said: "Sacrifice and offering You did not desire, but a body You have prepared for Me, In burnt offerings and sacrifices for sin You had no pleasure. Then I said, 'Behold, I have come—in the volume of the book it is written of Me—'To do Your will, O God.'" Previously saying, "Sacrifice and offerings, burnt offerings, and offerings for sin You did not desire, nor had pleasure in them" (which are offered according to the law), then He said, "Behold, I have come to do Your will, O God." He takes away the first that He may establish the second. By that will we have been sanctified through the offering of the body of Jesus Christ once for all.

Hebrews 10:5–10

Lord,

You have never wanted or needed our offerings of burnt sacrifice. It was for our benefit that You established the sacrificial system to point to You, the perfect Sacrifice. You, a fully surrendered Heart, are the Sacrifice that is pleasant and accepted by God. Thank You for Your offering that sanctifies me. You want the offering of my heart, my will, my all. Through the blood of Jesus Christ, I surrender all to You. Please forgive me for offering You worthless, rote, selfish, heartless sacrifices, such as money, stuff I don't need anymore, quick prayer on the run, extra Christmas gifts for the needy that make me feel good and don't take too much time, and consenting to take on responsibility at church even though I don't want to. Take my heart, my life. I want to do Your will, O God. I want to be a living sacrifice. I want to accomplish *Your* will in my heart, O God. Amen.

## NOVEMBER 27

Dear Friend, Loved by the Faithful One,

Now faith is the substance of things hoped for, the evidence of things not seen. For by it the elders obtained a good report. Through faith we understand that the worlds were framed by the word of God, so that things which are seen were not made of things which do appear. By faith Abel offered unto God a more excellent sacrifice than Cain, by which he obtained witness that he was righteous, God testifying of his gifts: and by it he being dead yet speaketh. By faith Enoch was translated that he should not see death; and was not found, because God had translated him: for before his translation he had this testimony, that he pleased God. But without faith *it is* impossible to please *him:* for he that cometh to God must believe that he is, and *that* he is a rewarder of them that diligently seek him.

Hebrews 11:1–6 KJV

Lord,

My prayer is for the faith and confidence to believe Your precious promises before I see them, just as Jesus held firm to His eternal plan to save lost humanity though it crushed him on the cross. My heart soaks in the warm beauty of the knowledge of You. You, who spoke and worlds appeared, were willing to be the sacrifice that Abel offered up by faith. You who makes things appear out of nothing, lovingly translated Enoch because of his faith in what You would do to purchase the right for Enoch, and I, to be with You forever. Lord, I believe You. I put all my hope and trust in You. You have heard my cries. Help me to trust You even when it is in direct contradiction to everything I feel inside. The more I seek You, the more of Yourself You reveal to me. How beautiful. How beautiful. Thank You. Amen.

# NOVEMBER 28

Dear Friend, Child of God,

By faith Noah, being warned of God of things not seen as yet, moved with fear, prepared an ark to the saving of his house; by the which he condemned the world, and became heir of the righteousness which is by faith. By faith Abraham, when he was called to go out into a place which he should after receive for an inheritance, obeyed; and he went out, not knowing whither he went. By faith he sojourned in the land of promise, as *in* a strange country, dwelling in tabernacles with Isaac and Jacob, the heirs with him of the same promise: for he looked for a city which hath foundations, whose builder and maker *is* God.

Hebrews 11:7–10 KJV

Lord,

How desperately we need men filled with godly fear as Noah was. How desperately we need men filled with godly fear for the eternal saving of their households from the perils of sin. How desperately we need a faith that would not hesitate to build an ark, though rain was yet unheard of—a faith that takes God at His holy Word. How pitiful, Lord, that I thrive on plans and budgets and paths that seem to me to be clearly and conveniently laid out. I tend to only do things that make perfect sense to me. Please help me to trust completely in You. I want to go when You say go. I want to let You lead me through Your paths of righteousness. I am a stranger in this world. I long for, and wait for, a city with foundations: a place where You are the *only* Ruler. Thank You for paving the way for me, Jesus. I do not travel new road but follow in Your footsteps on Your path. Amen.

# NOVEMBER 29

Dear Friend, Loved by the Almighty,

Through faith also Sara herself received strength to conceive seed, and was delivered of a child when she was past age, because she judged him faithful who had promised. Therefore sprang there even of one, and him as good as dead, *so many* as the stars of the sky in multitude, and as the sand which is by the seashore innumerable. These all died in faith, not having received the promises, but having seen them afar off, and were persuaded of *them,* and embraced them, and confessed that they were strangers and pilgrims on the earth. For they that say such things declare plainly that they seek a country. And truly, if they had been mindful of that *country* from whence they came out, they might have had opportunity to have return. [16] But now they desire a better *country,* that is, an heavenly: wherefore God is not ashamed to be called their God: for he hath prepared for them a city.

Hebrews 11:11–16 KJV

Lord,
Through faith Sarah conceived a child at the age of ninety—an impossible thing—and this child became the father of many. I see, Lord, that if I would but trust *wholly* in You, You would bless me with blessings that multiply as the stars in the sky, though I may not see all things in this life. I want to follow You. I desire a better country, a heavenly country, a heart where You have complete reign. I do not want to keep turning around and heading back to my selfish slavery to sin. I desperately need Your freeing power and leadership in my life. Help me to take You at Your Word and follow through, even though everyone is telling me different. Help me to stop using man's wisdom to decide if something is from You. Father, forgive me for falsely claiming You as God, when I am only serving myself. May You never be ashamed to call me Your child. Amen.

# NOVEMBER 30

Dear Friend, Precious Treasure of God,

By faith Abraham, when he was tried, offered up Isaac: and he that had received the promises offered up his only begotten *son*, Of whom it was said, That in Isaac shall thy seed be called: Accounting that God *was* able to raise *him* up, even from the dead; from whence also he received him in a figure. By faith Isaac blessed Jacob and Esau concerning things to come. By faith Jacob, when he was dying, blessed both the sons of Joseph; and worshipped, *leaning* upon the top of his staff. By faith Joseph, when he died, made mention of the departing of the children of Israel; and gave commandment concerning his bones.

Hebrews 11:17–22 KJV

Lord,
Grant me the faith that caused Abraham to willingly offer up his only son; the faith that caused Isaac to be willing; the faith that at least some would believe and receive Your love when You offered up Your only Son; and the faith of Jesus, who willingly laid down His life for the likes of me. Abraham, Isaac, Jacob, and Joseph listened to Your promises and believed though they could not see into the future. They did not have the beautiful story of the miraculous birth, the baptism, the ministry, the death, and the resurrection of Jesus. They saw it all by faith. Lord, this same faith is available to me. You have made that possible. Lord, I believe; help me overcome my unbelief. Thank You for Your holy Word, a book filled with precious promises of love from beginning to end. Amen.

## December 1

Dear Friend, Standing Firmly in the Truth,

My brethren, count it all joy when you fall into various trials, knowing that the testing of your faith brings patience. But let patience have *its* perfect work, that you may be perfect and complete, lacking nothing. If any of you lacks wisdom, let him ask of God, who gives to all liberally and without reproach, and it will be given to him. But let him ask in faith, with no doubting, for he who doubts is like a wave of the sea driven and tossed by the wind. For let not that man suppose that he will receive anything from the Lord; *he is* a double-minded man, unstable in all his ways.

James 1:2–8

Lord,
I do not remember to count it all joy when I fall into trials. No doubt this is because I have a doubting heart that causes me to waiver and be unstable. Please give me the faith to trust Your wisdom and use each trial to learn more of You. Fill me with Your faith that brings a patience to my heart that will allow You to do Your perfect work in me. I ask You for Your wisdom, knowing that I am nothing, and You are everything. I believe that You long to pour Your wisdom on me liberally. Lord, I believe, help Thou mine unbelief. With You, there is no lack. Thank You for holding me upright with Your grace and truth. Amen.

## DECEMBER 2

Dear Friend, Redeemed by the Lamb,

Blessed *is* the man who endures temptation; for when he has been approved, he will receive the crown of life which the Lord has promised to those who love Him. Let no one say when he is tempted, "I am tempted by God;" for God cannot be tempted by evil, nor does He Himself tempt anyone. But each one is tempted when he is drawn away by his own desires and enticed. Then, when desire has conceived, it gives birth to sin; and sin, when it is full-grown, brings forth death. Do not be deceived, my beloved brethren.

James 1:12–16

Lord,

How can I ever hope to endure temptation, except I cling to You? Jesus, You clung to Your Father every step of the way. Help me to never trust myself. Forgive me for accusing You of evil. Your adversary would have me to believe that You are the one who makes my life difficult; yet, You have said, "My yoke is easy, and My burden is light." Jesus, please send Your Spirit to guard my eyes, my ears, my thoughts, and my heart against the lusts of the flesh. Help me to ever bear You and Your love for me in mind. Cause me to be repulsed at, and eager to banish, every evil thought. Work Your perfect work in my heart and life, Lord. I am Yours. Amen.

## DECEMBER 3

Dear Friend, Blessed of God,

Every good gift and every perfect gift is from above, and comes down from the Father of lights, with whom there is no variation or shadow of turning. Of His own will He brought us forth by the word of truth, that we might be a kind of firstfruits of His creatures. So then, my beloved brethren, let every man be swift to hear, slow to speak, slow to wrath; for the wrath of man does not produce the righteousness of God.

James 1:17–20

Lord,
You want only good for me. You have said, "For I know the thoughts that I think toward you, thoughts of good, and not of evil." You bestow every good thing upon me. Each breath I take is a precious gift from You. Your love and Your mercies change not. You created me in Your own image, then identified with me in my fallen state. You redeemed me, and You have provided victory over sin for my heart. O, the mystery of Your beautiful salvation! Replace my swift and deadly tongue with ears that are quick to listen to You and You alone. Remove my self-centered wrath and fill me with Your agape love. Fill me with Your righteousness. In Jesus' name I praise You for Your everlasting mercy and goodness! Amen.

# DECEMBER 4

Dear Friend, Child of God,

Is anyone among you suffering? Let him pray. Is anyone cheerful? Let him sing psalms. Is anyone among you sick? Let him call for the elders of the church, and let them pray over him, anointing him with oil in the name of the Lord. And the prayer of faith will save the sick, and the Lord will raise him up. And if he has committed sins, he will be forgiven. Confess *your* trespasses to one another, and pray for one another, that you may be healed. The effective, fervent prayer of a righteous man avails much.

James 5:13–16

Lord,
O how I feel afflicted—afflicted with physical and emotional problems that drag down my spirit, afflicted with the insidious disease of sin that drags down my mind, body, and spirit. Lord, let me pray. Let me be cheerful and sing songs of praise. Let me gather with my brothers and sisters and pray for one another. Empty my heart of its selfish desires. Scrape off the façade I wear to make others think I am in better shape than I am. This does not glorify You. Help me to openly confess my faults, to forgive, and to be forgiven. Please heal my heart. Then, Father, I can have the faith to know and claim Your love and healing power over my body and over all Your precious children. Anoint me with Your Spirit, Lord. Heal me. Fulfill Your covenant in me. Make me a useful, healing balm for others. Amen.

# DECEMBER 5

Dear Friend, Child of God,

Likewise you younger people, submit yourselves to *your* elders. Yes, all of *you* be submissive to one another, and be clothed with humility, for "God resists the proud, but gives grace to the humble." Therefore humble yourselves under the mighty hand of God, that He may exalt you in due time, casting all your care upon Him, for He cares for you.

I Peter 5:6–7

Lord,

I do not know how to submit, especially to those who seem to me to be exacting or outright wrong in their view of things. Help me to remember that You are my true Shepherd and that You, Jesus, submitted Yourself to the leaders of the time, though they were so wrong as to put You, the Creator and King of kings, to death. Humble me, please, for I cannot humble myself. My heart is overrun with pride. Give me the will and the strength to admit, not that I can't handle it all but that I cannot handle it at all. Remind me continually, Father, that I am nothing and that You are everything. Cause me to submit to You, the Authority. I want You to be exalted in me and through me. I want to cast my *every* care on You: to cast my *all* and *all of me* on Your beautiful redemptive Self. Your care for me is a precious beacon of relief and peace. Thank You, Father. Thank You, Jesus. Thank You, Spirit. Amen.

# DECEMBER 6

Dear Friend, Taught by the Spirit,

Beloved, I now write to you this second epistle (in *both of* which I stir up your pure minds by way of reminder), that you may be mindful of the words which were spoken before by the holy prophets, and of the commandment of us, the apostles of the Lord and Savior, knowing this first: that scoffers will come in the last days, walking according to their own lusts, and saying, "Where is the promise of His coming? For since the fathers fell asleep, all things continue as *they were* from the beginning of creation."

II Peter 3:1–4

Lord,
Thank You for reminding me, through Your prophets and apostles, of Your beautiful promises to me. Help me to ever treasure Your words and Your commandments in my heart. Keep me pure from scoffers who reek of unbelief. Guard my heart and my tongue; cleanse me from the great pull of my own lusts. Keep my thoughts and my tongue in check, lest I speak as a scoffer or reek as one in by attitude. Only You can keep me faithful to Your Word while all around me are those who mold scripture into their own liking and convenience. All things are continuing as they were as a result of worldwide unbelief and selfishness. Lord, squelch my pride and let things take a powerful, beautiful, different turn—a turn toward Your return to this sick old world. I believe in Your literal second coming! Amen.

## December 7

Dear Friend, Created by His Word,

For this they willfully forget: that by the word of God the heavens were of old, and the earth standing out of water and in the water, by which the world *that* then existed perished, being flooded with water. But the heavens and the earth *which* are now preserved by the same word, are reserved for fire until the day of judgment and perdition of ungodly men. But, beloved, do not forget this one thing, that with the Lord one day *is* as a thousand years, and a thousand years as one day. The Lord is not slack concerning *His* promise, as some count slackness, but is longsuffering toward us, not willing that any should perish but that all should come to repentance.

II Peter 3:5–9

Lord,

You have already shown that You have created the world and can recreate the world. The flood was a work of Your mercy—sparing the human race from an unthinkable depravity. You have promised to never destroy the whole earth with water again, but You have promised that the earth will be cleansed with fire and prepared for a beautiful re-creation. Those who refuse Your free grace and mercy will perish with the earth in fire. I know You do not want any to perish. This is why You are allowing time to go on, in spite of all the disasters that assail us. You are not slack, but I am. You are not willing that any should perish. Help me to also be unwilling that any should perish. Use me to draw all I meet to You. Amen.

# DECEMBER 8

Dear Friend, Child of God,

But the day of the Lord will come as a thief in the night, in which the heavens will pass away with a great noise, and the elements will melt with fervent heat; both the earth and the works that are in it will be burned up. Therefore, since all these things will be dissolved, what manner *of persons* ought you to be in holy conduct and godliness, looking for and hastening the coming of the day of the God, because of which the heavens will be dissolved, being on fire, and the elements will melt with fervent heat? Nevertheless we, according to His promise, look for new heavens and a new earth in which righteousness dwells.

II Peter 3:10–13

Lord,
You told Your disciples when You were here on earth that no one knows the day or hour of Your return except the Father. You also said that Your coming would be heralded by a trumpet and a shout and that every eye will see You. Those that await Your coming clothed in Your righteousness will meet You in the air. You have also said that the earth, and all that remains in it, will be dissolved by fire. This is awesome and exciting! Jesus, please fill me with Your Spirit. Make me holy. Be the author of my conduct. Let me hasten Your coming by allowing You to fulfill Your covenant in me. I want to be used to draw all to You. Amen.

# DECEMBER 9

Dear Friend, Anticipating His Coming,

Therefore, beloved, looking forward to these things, be diligent to be found by Him in peace, without spot and blameless; and consider *that* the longsuffering of our Lord *is* salvation—as also our beloved brother Paul, according to the wisdom given him, has written to you, as also in all his epistles, speaking in them of these things, in which are some things hard to understand, which untaught and unstable *people* twist to their own destruction, as *they do* also the rest of the Scriptures. You therefore, beloved, since you know *this* beforehand, beware lest you also fall from your own steadfastness, being led away with the error of the wicked: but grow in the grace and knowledge of our Lord and Savior Jesus Christ. To Him *be* the glory both now and forever. Amen.

II Peter 3:14–18

Lord,
Only You can cause me to be without spot and blameless. Grant me the peace that comes with a total and complete surrender to Your will and plan for my every breath. My salvation is Your longsuffering, kindness, and perseverance toward me. Let Your Spirit be my Teacher, walking me through the Scriptures in a journey that leads me ever closer to You. Forgive me for clinging to error and dashing headlong toward my own destruction. This is not what You want for me, so let me grow in the grace and the knowledge of my Lord and Savior Jesus Christ. To Him be the glory both now and forever. Amen.

# DECEMBER 10

Dear Friend, Redeemed by the Lamb,

But if we walk in the light as He is in the light, we have fellowship with one another, and the blood of Jesus Christ His Son cleanses us from all sin. If we say that we have no sin, we deceive ourselves, and the truth is not in us. If we confess our sins, He is faithful and just to forgive us *our* sins and to cleanse us from all unrighteousness. If we say that we have not sinned, we make Him a liar, and His word is not in us.

I John 1:7–10

Lord,
Please forgive me for thinking that I am improving and not in such bad shape as I had been, or at least not as bad as most. I do not begin to know the true condition of my heart. Father, please bless me with true heart confession. I don't want just the forgiveness that You give—cleanse me! May Christ's sacrifice for me not be in vain. Cleanse my heart. Fulfill Your covenant in me; remove the very desire for sin from my being. Cause me to hate it, to loathe the depths it plunges me to. Fill me with Your righteousness. Let me walk in Your Light. Let Your Light shine through me. May I ever fellowship with You and with all those who walk in Your paths of righteousness. How I love You! Alleluia! Amen.

# December 11

Dear Friend, Child of the Everlasting God,

Little children, it is the last hour; and as you have heard that the Antichrist is coming, even now many antichrists have come, by which we know that it is the last hour. They went out from us, but they were not of us; for if they had been of us, they would have continued with us; but *they went out* that they might be made manifest, that none of them were us. But you have an anointing from the Holy One, and you know all things. I have not written to you because you do not know the truth, but because you know it, and that no lie is of the truth. Who is a liar but he who denies that Jesus is the Christ? He is antichrist who denies the Father and the Son. Whoever denies the Son does not have the Father either; he who acknowledges the Son has the Father also.

I John 2:18–23

Lord,
I have always needed to be totally immersed in You, and now it seems even more essential than ever before. The world I live in is literally steeping in a pool of utter wickedness and blatant rejection of Your sovereign wisdom and love. People, who claim to be Christians and soldiers for Jesus, are spreading falsehoods about You and Your perfect and holy character. Forgive me, Lord, for claiming to be Your chosen child while acting like the devil. I acknowledge Jesus as my Creator, Redeemer, Brother, Husband, Mediator, and King. Lord God, to You, and *You alone* do I give my confession and allegiance. In You, and You alone, do I put my trust. Protect my heart from all other invaders. Amen.

# DECEMBER 12

Dear Friend, Kept in the Father's Heart,

By this we know love, because He laid down His life for us. And we also ought to lay down *our* lives for the brethren. But whoever has this world's goods, and sees his brother in need, and shuts up his heart from him, how does the love of God abide in him? My little children, let us not love in word or in tongue, but in deed and in truth. And by this we know that we are of the truth, and shall assure our hearts before Him. For if our heart condemn us, God is greater than our heart, and knows all things. Beloved, if our heart does not condemn us, we have confidence toward God.

I John 3:16–21

Lord,
Thank You for laying down You holy life for me. Please fill my heart with Your amazing agape love, a love that gives one hundred percent of itself to receive one hundred percent insult in return. I cannot even imagine this love. My heart condemns me continually. It drags me to great depths of depression and despair. How thankful I am that You are greater than my heart. Cleanse my heart and fill it with Your truth and Your deeds. Father, cleanse me so completely that there is nothing left in my heart to bring condemnation. Give me the loving confidence of Your heart. I love You, Father. I love You, Jesus. I love You, Spirit. Thank You for Your ever-lasting covenant of love. Amen.

# DECEMBER 13

Dear Friend, Loved by the Father,

Beloved, let us love one another, for love is of God; and everyone that loves is born of God and knows God. He who does not love does not know God, for God is love. In this the love of God was manifested toward us, that God has sent His only begotten Son into the world, that we might live through Him. In this is love, not that we loved God, but that He loved us and sent His Son *to be* the propitiation for our sins. Beloved, if God so loved us, we also ought to love one another.

I John 4:7–11

Lord,
I can only love others as I let You love me, and let Your love shine through me. Please forgive me for resisting the outpouring of Your love upon me. You have loved me from the very beginning, before the foundation of the world. You have loved me while I am yet Your enemy. O Father, how desperately I need this kind of love. Fill me with Your compassionate love for those who hurt and abuse me, for those who hurt and abuse anyone. Fill me with Your drawing love for those who openly war against me and against You. Fill me with Your all-consuming love that cleanses my heart from every unclean desire, that fills me with a complete faithful reliance on You, and You alone. Amen.

# DECEMBER 14

Dear Friend, Loved of the Father,

And we have known and believed the love that God has for us. God is love, and he who abides in love, abides in God, and God in him. Love has been perfected among us in this: that we may have boldness in the day of judgment; because as He is, so are we in this world. There is no fear in love; but perfect love casts out fear, because fear involves torment. But he who fears has not been made perfect in love. We love Him because He first loved us.

I John 4:16–19

Lord,
You loved me first because *You are love*. I believe You love me. Please let me dwell in Your love forever. There is no other way to have peace in this world. I dwell unnecessarily in the torment of unbelieving fear. Forgive me for shunning Your beautiful, loving gift of eternal peace. I fear judgment because I fear my own critical misunderstanding of Your love and mercies and of the beautiful plan of redemption and reconciliation that You have performed for me. I fear a complete surrender because it means that I can no longer have my own way. Let Your love cast out *all* my fears. I long for Your faith and Your love. Let me rest in You. Thank You. Amen.

# DECEMBER 15

Dear Friend, Loved by the Faithful One,

For whatsoever is born of God overcometh the world: and this is the victory that overcometh the world, *even* our faith. Who is he that overcometh the world, but he that believeth that Jesus is the Son of God? This is he who came by water and blood, *even* Jesus Christ; not by water only, but by water and blood. And it is the Spirit that beareth witness, because the Spirit is truth.

I John 5:4–6 KJV

Lord,
Hallelujah! Hallelujah! Hallelujah! Thank You, Jesus, for Your faithful victory! Thank You for the measure of faith that You give to multiply and grow and overcome the world! Jesus You have accomplished an awesome victory! It is by and through You that I live and have a most beautiful hope. Baptize me with Your Spirit. Fill my heart with Your faith. Banish all thoughts from my mind that are not born of You. Fill me with Your strength that I may take up my cross and follow You to Calvary, the grave, the resurrection, and an eternal life that forever glorifies Your holy name. Faith is the victory! Faith is the victory! O glorious victory, that overcomes the world! Hallelujah! Amen.

# DECEMBER 16

Dear Friend, Receiver of Blessings,

Now this is the confidence that we have in Him, that if we ask anything according to His will, He hears us. And if we know that He hears us, whatever we ask, we know that we have the petitions that we have asked of Him. If anyone sees his brother sinning a sin *which does* not *lead* to death, he will ask, and He will give him life for those who commit sin not *leading* to death. There is sin *leading* to death. I do not say that he should pray about that. All unrighteousness is sin, and there is sin not *leading* to death.

I John 5:14–17

Lord,
I need Your faith and Your confidence. Lord, I do believe; please help my unbelief. So often my prayers claim Your promises, but You know that my heart rather doubts it. Not that I don't believe You can, but that I doubt that You will. Please forgive me, my Savior, for doubting that You, who gave up everything You could possibly give to show me the height, and depth, and length, and width of the Father's love for me, would *ever* want anything less for me or for anyone, than the most precious blessings. Jesus, help me to pray according to Your will, for the salvation and blessing of all my fellow men. You long to heal and sustain us with Your Word. Keep my heart from praying for things that only bring eternal death. Fill me with Your Spirit and Your confidence to pray for the healing of mind, body, and spirit, in Jesus' name, Amen.

# DECEMBER 17

Dear Friend, Chosen by God,

I rejoiced greatly that I found *some* of your children walking in truth, as we received commandment from the Father. And now I plead with you, lady, not as though I wrote a new commandment to you, but that which we have heard from the beginning; that we love one another. This is love, that we walk according to His commandments. This is the commandment, that as you have heard from the beginning, you should walk in it.

II John 4–6

Lord,
I know that You rejoice greatly when Your children walk in truth. Please continue to dwell in me and renew me with Your everlasting love. Father, write Your commandments on my heart; engrave them into my very being. Take hold of the war within me: that great and terrible battle between the flesh and the spirit. I long to reflect Your love in every direction. I cannot do it, but You can. Let me walk in You, Jesus. Let my steps be Your steps. Let my thoughts and words and actions flow forth from me as from You. Purify my selfish human love until it becomes Your unselfish agape love. I rejoice in You, Lord. Rejoice in me. Amen.

## DECEMBER 18

Dear Friend, One with Christ,

For many deceivers have gone out into the world who do not confess Jesus Christ *as* coming in the flesh. This is a deceiver and an antichrist. Look to yourselves, that we do not lose those things we worked for, but *that* we may receive a full reward. Whoever transgresses and does not abide in the doctrine of Christ does not have God. He who abides in the doctrine of Christ has both the Father and the Son. If anyone comes to you and does not bring this doctrine, do not receive him into your house nor greet him; for he who greets him shares in his evil deed.

II John 7–11

Lord,
The world is full to the brim of different beliefs. Many terribly contradictory things are proclaimed about You and in Your name. Forgive me, Lord, for listening to the teachings of deceivers. Jesus, You have forever identified Yourself with me. You took on my flesh. You conquered sin in the flesh. Let me not lose the opportunity to be victorious as You were victorious. Jesus, fulfill Your covenant in me. Cleanse me within and without. Make me a perfect reflection of Your perfect and holy character. Holy Spirit, guard my ears and my thoughts from any doctrine save Jesus Christ and Him crucified. Amen.

# DECEMBER 19

Dear Friend, Led by the Spirit,

Beloved, I wish above all things that thou mayest prosper and be in health, even as thy soul prospereth. For I rejoiced greatly, when the brethren came and testified of the truth that is in thee, even as thou walkest in the truth. I have no greater joy than to hear that my children walk in truth.

III John 2–4 KJV

Lord,

I appreciate the prayers others pray for me. Please bless all of Your children. Bless my family and friends, both near and far. May they prosper in all things and be in good health. Jesus, prosper our souls with Yourself. Let me walk in the truth and lead others to Your pure, holy character. Empty me of myself and all of my preconceived ideas and fill me with Your Spirit of discernment and truth. Make me an undying, unwavering testimony of Your love, power, and victory over the evil clutches of sin. I love Your ways and long to be like You and with You. Keep my feet on the path of truth. Guard my eyes, my ears, my nose, mouth, and sense of touch from everything that is not truth. I want to meditate solely on You. When I sleep and when I wake, when I walk and when I talk, whatever I am doing, may I always be filled with the truth. Let only Your truth be seen in my life. When others speak of me, let it not be of me, but of You and Your marvelous works that You have brought about in my life. Almighty, loving God, I want You to have the great joy of hearing that this child of Yours walks in truth. Thank You for accomplishing Your work in me. Amen.

# DECEMBER 20

Dear Friend, Led by the Spirit,

To those who are called, sanctified by God the Father, and preserved in Jesus Christ, mercy, peace, and love be multiplied to you. Beloved, while I was very diligent to write to you concerning our common salvation, I found it necessary to write to You exhorting you to contend earnestly for the faith which was once for all delivered to the saints. For certain men have crept in unnoticed, who long ago were marked out for this condemnation, ungodly men, who turn the grace of God into lewdness and deny the only Lord God and our Lord Jesus Christ.

Jude 1–4

Lord,
Please forgive me for looking to others to explain salvation and Your love to me. You have given Your Word to me personally in the Holy Bible. Thank You for the willingness those who truly know You have to share Your love through their daily lives. Please help me to keep my focus on You. Let me rely on Your Holy Spirit to teach and to guide me. Thank You for preserving me for Your holy purpose. Fill me with Your mercy, peace, love, and eternal faith. Thank You for sanctifying my life. Fulfill Your covenant in me. Jesus Christ, You are indeed Lord God. Amen.

# DECEMBER 21

Dear Friend, Saved by His Grace,

But I want to remind you, though you once knew this, that the Lord, having saved the people out of Egypt, afterward destroyed those who did not believe. And the angels who did not keep their proper domain, but left their own abode, He has reserved in everlasting chains under darkness for the judgment of that great day; as Sodom and Gomorrah, and the cities around them in a similar manner to these, having given themselves over to sexual immorality and gone after strange flesh, are set forth as an example, suffering the vengeance of eternal fire. Likewise also these dreamers defile the flesh, reject authority, and speak evil of dignitaries.

Jude 5–8

Lord,

You are a merciful, loving God who does not delight in the destruction of the wicked. You save to the uttermost. Yet, You never force anyone to serve You. You never force Your free gift of salvation on anyone. It seems so easy to follow the crowd, to believe flowery reports of deception. But just as those who rejected You and perished in the wilderness after You delivered them from bondage, those who reject Your free gift of grace will perish. How painful it must have been for You to watch a third of Your angels reject Your infinite love for them and walk out on You. Lord, spare me from the evil clutches of the flesh. Fill me with Your Spirit. Snatch me from the fire with Your redeeming and cleansing power. Amen.

# DECEMBER 22

Dear Friend, Redeemed by the Lamb,

Yet Michael the archangel, in contending with the devil, when he disputed about the body of Moses, dared not bring against him a reviling accusation, but said, "The Lord rebuke you!" But these speak evil of whatever they do not know; and whatever they know naturally, like brute beasts, in these things they corrupt themselves. Woe to them! For they have gone in the way of Cain, have run greedily in the error of Balaam for profit, and perished in the rebellion of Korah.

Jude 9–11

Lord,

Although Adam sold this world into the slavery of sin and death, You bought it back with Your own blood. Before You came as a baby to redeem me, You had already accomplished my redemption by virtue of Your Word before the foundation of the world. Moses was a firstfruit of Your power of resurrection and restoration. He was transfigured with Elijah to show Your power to reclaim the living and the dead. Lord, I believe in the resurrection You will orchestrate at Your second coming. You have purchased resurrection and eternal life for all those who trust in You. Take away my selfishness and fill me with thoughts, words, and actions that profit only You. Amen.

## December 23

Dear Friend, Loved by the Savior,

But you, beloved, building yourselves up on your most holy faith, praying in the Holy Spirit, keep yourselves in the love of God, looking for the mercy of our Lord Jesus Christ unto eternal life. And on some have compassion, making a distinction; but others save with fear, pulling *them* out of the fire, hating even the garment defiled by the flesh. Now to Him who is able to keep you from stumbling, and to present *you* faultless before the presence of His glory with exceeding joy, To God our Savior, who alone is wise, *be* glory and majesty, dominion and power, both now and forever. Amen.

Jude 20–25

Lord,

Please keep Your Spirit ever in me, building a holy faith in me, keeping me in the love of God, and seeking the mercy of Jesus Christ who has redeemed me with His own life. Father, give me the compassion You have for all. Grant me the discernment to distinguish between godly and ungodly. Use me to draw others out of the deadly trap of sin. Fill me with the powerful love You have for sinners that You exercise while hating sin to its very core. Make my life a nugget of Your agape love. Jesus, only You can keep me from stumbling. Only You can present me faultless before the universe—O, this is such an awesome and incredible gift! My heart agrees with Jude. My Savior, my all-wise God, glory and majesty, dominion, and power be to You both now and forever. Amen.

# DECEMBER 24

Dear Friend, Bride of the Eternal God,

John to the seven churches which are in Asia: Grace *be* unto you, and peace, from him which is, and which was, and which is to come; and from the seven Spirits which are before his throne; And from Jesus Christ, *who is* the faithful witness, *and* the first begotten of the dead, and the prince of the kings of the earth. Unto him that loved us, and washed us from our sins in his own blood, And hath made us kings and priests unto God and his Father; to him *be* glory and dominion for ever and ever. Amen. Behold, he cometh with clouds; and every eye shall see him, even they *also* which pierced him: and all kindreds of the earth shall wail because of him. Even so, Amen. I am the Alpha and Omega, the beginning and the ending, saith the Lord, which is, and which was, and who is to come, the Almighty.

Revelation 1:4–8 KJV

Lord,

You have from eternity past been my holy God. Long before You created even angels, You knew the depths of my sinful sickness, and had an escape ready. Jesus Christ, the Faithful Witness, You are so deeply precious to me. You, who conquered eternal death, Your love is victorious and eternal. Your spotless life and innocent blood cleanse my filthy heart. You have made a wretch like me a king and a priest to God. Though I deserve only death, You treat me as a special jewel of rare beauty. I am in speechless awe. How glorious will be the remarkable day when You come in clouds to fulfill Your promise to bring us to live with the Father. Every eye will see You. Though many will try to flee in terror, I believe in You, the Everlasting God who saves to the uttermost. O how You thrill my soul! Amen.

# DECEMBER 25

Dear Friend, Daughter/Son of God,

I counsel you to buy from Me gold refined in the fire, that you may be rich; and white garments, that you may be clothed, *that* the shame of your nakedness may not be revealed; and anoint your eyes with eye salve, that you may see. As many as I love, I rebuke and chasten. Therefore be zealous and repent. Behold, I stand at the door and knock. If anyone hears My voice and opens the door, I will come in to him and dine with him, and he with Me. To him who overcomes I will grant to sit with Me on My throne, as I also overcame and sat down with My Father on His throne. He who has an ear, let him hear what the Spirit says to the churches.

Revelation 3:18–22

Lord,
I want to be like gold tried in the fire. You, the Goldsmith, can purify me through the trials of this world. Let me be rich with Your righteousness. Clothe me with Your love. Anoint my eyes that I may see and discern spiritual truths. Chasten me, Lord. I know I don't like it, but I need Your correction to give me peace, to make me like You. Give me a spirit of true repentance. Jesus, I open the door of my heart to You. Come in. Clean out. Take over. Reign forever. You overcame by faith in the power of Your Father's love. I want to do the same. Give me the faith to trust Your cleansing power, and a love that rebukes all selfishness. May I be like You. Amen.

# DECEMBER 26

Dear Friend, Loved by the Everlasting

And there was war in heaven: Michael and his angels fought against the dragon; and the dragon fought and his angels, and prevailed not; neither was their place found any more in heaven. And the great dragon was cast out, that old serpent, called the Devil, and Satan, which deceiveth the whole world: he was cast out into the earth, and his angels were cast out with him.

Revelation 12:7–9 KJV

Lord,
Satan, the dragon, waged a long and painful war of thoughts, ideas, and words against You. He did everything in his power to convince all that his pride, selfishness, and thoughts of doubt were Your ways and thoughts. He envied Your position as Almighty God. I know that You wooed him with the everlasting patience and love with which You woo me. Satan refused to surrender himself to Your love. You had to cast him out. No one could be happy in his presence. Jesus, though Satan has been cast to this earth and deceived many, You came and made plain the truth about God. You made it plain and clear by sacrificing Yourself for all; for all of us have fallen into his trap of death. Thank You, my Savior, for never changing Your everlasting love for me. Amen.

# DECEMBER 27

Dear Friend, Victorious in Christ,

And I heard a loud voice saying in heaven, Now is come salvation, and strength, and the kingdom of our God, and the power of his Christ: for the accuser of our brethren is cast down, which accused them before our God day and night. And they overcame him by the blood of the Lamb, and by the word of their testimony; and they loved not their lives unto the death. Therefore rejoice, ye heavens, and ye that dwell in them. Woe to the inhabiters of the earth and of the sea! for the devil is come down unto you, having great wrath, because he knoweth that he hath but a short time.

Revelation 12:10–12 KJV

Lord,

Praise the name of Jesus! You have won the victory over sin and death. You have defeated the enemy and laid bare all of his schemes and lies. Jesus Christ, Lamb of God, fulfill Your covenant in me. Give me Your victory, a victory that removes sin from my life; a victory that is not in the least focused on me, or my life, but a victory that is focused on Your beautiful, perfect character of love. When the accuser accuses me of being like him, thank You Jesus, for covering me with Your righteousness. Cleanse my heart and my life. Put Your Spirit within me. The devil is indeed full of wrath because he hates Your love, but Your love is more powerful than all of his great wrath. Hold me in Your everlasting love. Amen.

# DECEMBER 28

Dear Friend, Called by the Redeemer,

And after these things I saw another angel come down from heaven, having great power; and the earth was lightened with his glory. And he cried mightily with a strong voice, saying, Babylon the great is fallen, is fallen, and is become the habitation of devils, and the hold of every foul spirit, and a cage of every unclean and hateful bird. For all nations have drunk of the wine of the wrath of her fornication, and the kings of the earth have committed fornication with her, and the merchants of the earth are waxed rich through the abundance of her delicacies. And I heard another voice from heaven, saying, Come out of her, my people, that ye be not partakers of her sins, and that ye receive not of her plagues. For her sins have reached unto heaven, and God hath remembered her iniquities.

Revelation 18:1–5 KJV

Lord,
You will not abide with Satan's lies about You forever. The devil's defamation of Your holy character will fall, and will reap its final, destructive result. But You have called me out of the confused misrepresentations of You and Your omnipotent love for Your wayward children. You have no other desire but to fill me to overflowing with Your sweet character of holy, agape love—a love that embraces friend and foe to the heart. I know for certain that You do not delight in the destruction of the wicked. You love us all. But because of Your love, You cannot allow sin to continue eternally. Separate me from sin, Lord. Fulfill Your covenant in me. Let me reflect You completely. Thank You for Your warnings and Your promises. Amen.

# DECEMBER 29

Dear Friend, Recreated by the Omnipotent Creator,

Now I saw a new heaven and a new earth, for the first heaven and the first earth had passed away. Also there was no more sea. Then I, John, saw the holy city, New Jerusalem, coming down out of heaven from God, prepared as a bride adorned for husband. And I heard a loud voice from heaven saying, "Behold, the tabernacle of God *is* with men, and He will dwell with them, and they shall be His people, God Himself will be with them *and be* their God. And God will wipe away every tear from their eyes; there shall be no more death, nor sorrow, nor crying. There shall be no more pain, for the former things have passed away." Then He who sat on the throne said, "Behold, I make all things new." And He said to me, "Write, for these words are true and faithful."

Revelation 21:1–5

Lord,

How unworthy I am that You should ever consider me for anything. Yet, You have shown Your great love and concern for me above Yourself. You have forever identified Yourself with humanity. Jesus, You have walked this earth and remained sinless, and clung to the Father's grace to resist evil. You have allowed Your created beings to insult and crucify You while You cried in anguish for my soul. And now You supply us with salvation; not only salvation from the pitiful depths of sin on this earth, but a salvation from this earth. How I long for that day when sin and death are abolished forever. Praise be to You, my faithful God. You will fulfill Your covenant to every beautiful detail, more gloriously than can be imagined. Hallelujah! Amen.

# DECEMBER 30

Dear Friend, Alive by His Blood,

And he said unto me, It is done. I am Alpha and Omega, the beginning and the end. I will give unto him that is athirst of the fountain of the water of life freely. He that overcometh shall inherit all things; and I will be his God, and he shall be my son. But the fearful, and unbelieving, and the abominable, and murderers, and whoremongers, and sorcerers, and idolaters, and all liars, shall have their part in the lake which burneth with fire and brimstone: which is the second death.

Revelation 21:6–8 KJV

Lord,

No one can ever compare to You. You are the Beginning and the End. You are the Fountain of Living Water. You are the Overcomer. It is through You, and *You alone*, that I can overcome. You do not wish that any should ever perish. You have taken the second death for all when You eternally surrendered Yourself on the cross as an atonement for sin. How heartbreakingly tragic that many reject that precious gift and choose an eternal death instead of eternal life with You. I accept Your holy and awesome gift of life, Lord. I accept Your gift of character renewal, Jesus. Cleanse me completely from sin. O I long—I yearn—with all my heart to be eternally removed from this body of death and to be forever restored to what You have always wanted for me. Amen.

# DECEMBER 31

Dear Friend, Bride of Christ,

"And behold, I am coming quickly, and My reward *is* with Me, to give to everyone according to his work. I am the Alpha and Omega, *the* Beginning and *the* End, the First and the Last." Blessed *are* those who do His commandments, that they may have the right to the tree of life, and may enter through the gates of the city. But outside *are* dogs and sorcerers and sexually immoral and murderers and idolaters, and whoever loves and practices a lie. I, Jesus, have sent My angel to testify to you these things in the churches. I am the Root and the Offspring of David, the Bright and Morning Star." And the Spirit and the Bride say, "Come!" And let him who hears say, "Come!" And let him who thirsts come. Whoever desires, let him take the water of life freely.

Revelation 22:12–17

Lord,
You are Almighty God. And one day You will put an end to sin. Father, I want to do Your will. I want You to put an end to sin in my life, now. I want to be Your bride, ready, spotless, joyfully awaiting Your coming. Let me even now spend all my days and my nights saying, "Come," to those around me. I thirst, and I come to You and am filled. Let me proclaim the Living Water to all. You have freely offered Yourself to all. I accept Your gift. I believe in You. Thank You eternally for fulfilling Your covenant in me. I am nothing. You are the Alpha and the Omega, the Beginning and the End, the First and the Last, the Root and the Offspring of David, the Bright and Morning Star. You are everything! Hallelujah! Amen.

CPSIA information can be obtained
at www.ICGtesting.com
Printed in the USA
LVOW03s1540201215

466830LV00008B/10/P

9 781498 457491